Your Foundation in Health and Social Care

SAGE has been part of the global academic community since 1965, supporting high quality research and learning that transforms society and our understanding of individuals, groups and cultures. SAGE is the independent, innovative, natural home for authors, editors and societies who share our commitment and passion for the social sciences.

Find out more at: **www.sagepublications.com**

Your Foundation in Health and Social Care

Second Edition

Edited by **Graham Brotherton** and **Steven Parker**

Los Angeles | London | New Delhi
Singapore | Washington DC

Los Angeles | London | New Delhi
Singapore | Washington DC

SAGE Publications Ltd
1 Oliver's Yard
55 City Road
London EC1Y 1SP

SAGE Publications Inc.
2455 Teller Road
Thousand Oaks, California 91320

SAGE Publications India Pvt Ltd
B 1/I 1 Mohan Cooperative Industrial Area
Mathura Road
New Delhi 110 044

SAGE Publications Asia-Pacific Pte Ltd
3 Church Street
#10-04 Samsung Hub
Singapore 049483

Editor: Alice Oven
Assistant editor: Emma Milman
Production editor: Katie Forsythe
Copyeditor: Elaine Leek
Proofreader: Anna Gilding
Indexer: Judith Lavender
Marketing manager: Tamara Navaratnam
Cover design: Lisa Harper
Typeset by: C&M Digitals (P) Ltd, Chennai, India
Printed and bound by CPI Group (UK) Ltd,
Croydon, CR0 4YY

First edition published 2007. Reprinted once in 2011
This edition first published 2013

Library of Congress Control Number: 2012947156

British Library Cataloguing in Publication data

A catalogue record for this book is available from
the British Library

MIX
Paper from
responsible sources
FSC® C013604
www.fsc.org

ISBN 978-1-4462-0884-7
ISBN 978-1-4462-0885-4 (pbk)

Contents

About the Editors and Contributors

Ruth Beretta is a Staff Tutor with the Open University in the South West of England, with responsibility for modules in Nursing and Health and Social Care programmes. She is a registered nurse with experience in teaching and examining in pre-registration nursing, across foundation degrees, and undergraduate and postgraduate education. Her areas of interest are the experience of students in higher education and the development of transferable skills through education and public policy.

Graham Brotherton is Head of Working with Children Young People and Families at Newman University in Birmingham. Prior to working in further and higher education he spent a number of years in a variety of roles in the Social Care sector. His main research interests are in family policy and social inclusion.

Helen Davies is a Senior Lecturer in Education and Professional Studies at Newman University, Birmingham. Her research interests lie in Early Years Education and student experience in higher education.

Judith Mann has worked as a Lecturer and Programme Manager at Cornwall College Cambourne where she taught on the Foundation Degree in Health and Community Studies and The Social Work Degree. Her first career was in social work with a particular interest in mental health and children and family work.

Dr Gill McGillivray is Programme Leader for Early Childhood Education and Care at Newman University in Birmingham. She has a BSc (Hons) in Human Psychology, an MA in Early Childhood Studies from the University of Sheffield and the focus of her PhD research was professional identity construction in the early years workforce in England. She led on an EU funded international project 'Play and Learning in the Early Years for Inclusion' (PLEYIn) from 2009–2011 with partners in Romania and Poland. Gill has been involved in the delivery and management of Foundation Degrees at Newman University since 2004.

Prof Robert Mears is Dean of School: Science, Society and Management in the School of Society, Enterprise and Environment at Bath Spa University. He has published extensively and his main interests are in the sociology of health and illness and health policy.

Steven Parker works for the Open University as a course tutor in the Faculties of Health and Social Care, and Social Sciences. He has worked as a Lecturer and Curriculum Area Manager working on a range of Foundation Degrees and progression to honours programmes in Health and Social Care, Psychology and Early Childhood Studies. His professional practice background is in social work.

Nadine Pearce has worked as a Lecturer and Programme Manager for the Foundation Degree in health and Community Studies. She has also taught psychology on a range of other Foundation Degrees including Complementary Health Therapies, Healthcare Practice and the CFP for Pre-Registration Nursing. Her professional background is in nursing and nurse education.

Introduction

Welcome to the second edition of *Your Foundation in Health and Social Care*. This book was written to support students taking Foundation Degrees and in revising it we have tried to take account of the comments of students and tutors in response to the first edition. It is hoped that the book will also be useful to students on related higher education courses. It could also support NVQs at Levels 3 and 4. The book is designed to support you in at least three ways:

1 By providing you with advice on different aspects of your programme, e.g. academic study skills or making the most of placement/work-related learning.
2 By providing you with chapters dealing with key areas of study you are likely to encounter on your course.
3 By identifying useful sources of additional information to support you in your studies.

In order to do this the book is divided into two sections together with a final chapter that pulls together the themes of the book. The first section consists of Chapters 1–3 and looks at approaches to studying. Chapter 1 focuses on study skills and how to approach the academic part of your course. Chapter 2 looks at getting the most out of placements and work-related learning and Chapter 3 looks at identifying research and information to support your course and at how to evaluate the usefulness of different sources of information.

In the second section (Chapters 4–9) there is an overview of a range of areas relevant to studying health and social care. Chapter 4 considers the social context, Chapter 5 the issue of personal and professional identity and Chapter 6 the role of values. Chapter 7 deals with the policy and organizational context, Chapter 8 deals with psychology for health and social care, and Chapter 9 interpersonal skills and communication. The final chapter seeks to pull together some of the key themes of the book and look at where health and care services might be going.

Health and social care has undergone a dramatic period of change over the past 25 years and this shows no signs of abating. To give just two examples: in the period since the first edition we have seen the emergence and part disappearance of Every Child Matters and we are about to see yet another reorganization of the NHS. Whether you work in the health sector or adult or children's social care, both the structure of services and ideas about what constitute good practice have changed considerably and it is clear that this process is going to continue. Words like empowerment or advocacy and concepts like consumerism and the mixed economy of care (all of which are explored in this book) are forcing us to look carefully at almost everything we do. You are therefore either entering or developing your career at an interesting and challenging time. The challenges of working in a vital area of work at a time when the population is both ageing and becoming more diverse will create a new range of both opportunities and problems, and will require us all to rethink many areas of policy and practice in ways that will affect the whole workforce – issues such as how we decide who gets access to services, under what circumstances, how much 'say' they have about the services provided for them, and who provides the services in the first place. All are central and at times controversial issues and are discussed throughout the book. They are questions on which there are differing perspectives and about which you need to think carefully from your personal perspective. We hope the book will help you in thinking about these issues as your course progresses.

How to use this book

This book is intended to give you an overview in relation to each of the areas it covers. As the courses it supports are higher education courses, it cannot and should not be the only source you use, and whilst we aim to give a clear overview for each topic you will need to read/research more fully. To help with this each chapter has suggestions for further reading and Chapter 3 contains detailed advice on where you can look for appropriate material to support your studies.

It is hoped that this book will support you throughout the duration of your course and that you will continually 'dip' in and out of the material. Within each chapter there are a range of activities designed to help you to think about key ideas and issues, and it is hoped that you will pause and reflect on these as the opportunity to reflect is an essential element of learning. Some chapters also include some final questions; again these are to help you to reflect upon and apply the chapter's content.

Using the language of health and social care

In coming to terms with completing a course in higher education it is important to learn the professional language of health and social care. While every effort has been made to avoid jargon, there are inevitably terms with which you will not be familiar. These are explained within the text; however, if terms either within the text or in your wider reading are not familiar to you we have included a glossary at the end of the book and there is an excellent and very comprehensive glossary of health and social care terms available at the www.cpa.org.uk website.

In concluding this brief introduction we would like to take the opportunity to wish you every success with your studies and we hope this book contributes to their successful completion.

Section One

Approaches

1

Approaching Learning

Ruth Beretta

Summary Chapter Contents

- Learning in higher education
- Learning how to learn
- Learning styles
- Managing time effectively
- Effective reading and note-taking
- Writing essays and reports
- Using references and bibliographies
- Plagiarism and how to avoid it

Learning objectives

By the end of this chapter, you should be able to:

- Identify some of the challenges in successful study in higher education and how you can work to overcome these.
- Identify your preferred learning style and adapt learning strategies to help you make good use of your time and develop your learning skills.
- Use effective reading and note-taking skills.
- Make good use of reading lists and assignment guidelines to produce constructive essays and reports.
- Reference academic writing with a recognized referencing system and avoid plagiarism.

Introduction – the importance of developing skills for learning for a Foundation Degree

In this chapter we will be focusing on learning for a Foundation Degree (known as a Higher National Diploma in Scotland). Foundation Degrees integrate academic and work-based learning, so are designed to equip you with skills and knowledge relevant to your employment in health and social care. Although it is a qualification in its own right, a Foundation Degree may link with an opportunity to progress to an Honours Degree. Importantly, it develops your ability to exercise personal responsibility and make decisions (QAA 2010); this last point emphasizes the importance of working in your chosen profession in the area of health and social care, being able to use available evidence to support care decisions (see Chapter 5) and also to demonstrate a critical awareness of alternative solutions to problems or issues; in other words, to develop critical practice (see Chapter 4).

Being a critical learner does not mean criticizing and being negative. It means:

- Being constructively critical and evaluative
- Being open to consider all possibilities
- Being reflective
- Being rational and using a reasoned approach
- Being responsible and accountable for your actions. (adapted from Cottrell 2011)

This chapter aims to address the approaches to learning which can assist in your development to become that critical practitioner.

Learning *how* to learn

When working as well as studying on a course, many of us need to make best use of our time and ensure we develop our skills and knowledge base as effectively as possible. For many people, that means learning *how* to learn. It sounds very straightforward, but often we have memories of previous learning experiences, which may have been negative ones. However, we all have the capacity to develop learning skills and skills of reflection that can improve our time management and make for effective academic and evaluative practice.

It may be useful to spend a few moments reflecting on your own motivation for starting the Foundation Degree and considering:

- Why am I doing this course?
- What knowledge and skills do I already have?
- What knowledge and skills do I hope to gain?
- What has previously helped me to make opportunities for study?
- What may get in my way?
- Am I ready to start taking responsibility for decisions I make?

The answers to these questions will be personal and depend upon your own circumstances. But if you can think ahead to find answers to these questions, you will be better prepared to meet the challenges you may face as your course progresses, both in preparing for your work-based learning experiences and in reflecting on what you have learned. This is why learning how to learn is so important.

In thinking about the challenges ahead, you may well see managing your time effectively as a key area, especially as you are likely to be working as well as studying for your course. You also need to be aware that learning in higher education is likely to include some approaches that may be new to you.

- Use of time:

  - You have much more flexibility in how to use your time. If you decide not to attend lectures, you may not be asked to account for where you have been, so it is up to you how you spend that time.
  - You will be given assignments at the beginning of term which should be produced by a given deadline; you may not be given further prompts about the work, so you need to be organized.
  - There is an expectation that you will use time away from college or university to read extensively around your topic area.

- Approaches towards learning:

  - You can expect a wide range of learning and teaching methods to be used, including the use of educational technologies. These may include virtual learning environments (VLE), wikis and blogs, as well as academic jargon you may not be used to (technologies will be discussed in more detail later in the chapter).
  - Learning in higher education is not just remembering facts; it is about using or applying those facts and evaluating them. Reasoning skills and being able to justify your actions will be important, so that you can link theory to practice.
  - You will be given responsibility for your own learning and it may be up to you to seek tutorial support rather than a lecturer asking to see you at regular intervals throughout the course.
  - You will be expected to read your course handbook and be aware of issues such as regulations regarding handing in work, referencing styles and procedures governing your course.

Learning styles

We all learn things in different ways and it is important for you to recognize what works best for you.

How do you learn best?

Think back to an experience when you found it very easy or very enjoyable to learn something. It may have been a household project, something at work or even an experience from school. What was it that made it a good learning experience? Was it the teacher? Was it because you were particularly interested in the topic? Was it the way you were taught?

Now think back to a learning experience that was difficult or unpleasant. What happened that was different to the first experience? Do you think the situation could have been managed differently?

What do these experiences tell you about the way you learn best?

You may have identified that you enjoy learning experiences which actually involve physically doing something. It is much easier to learn how to bake a cake by mixing the ingredients together and watching the mixture satisfactorily rise in the oven than just to read a series of recipes! And having a conversation with a hearing-impaired person teaches you much more about communication skills than any textbook!

You may associate a poor learning experience with an impatient teacher who does not like to be interrupted by questions, or with a period of inactivity. For some topics such as human biology, there is no substitute for learning about body organs and systems to understand how the body works by studying anatomy texts. But it becomes much more interesting when that knowledge is used to inform us about how medications work in the body, or how disease processes attack the body.

On the other hand, you may have associated a good learning experience with a lecture in which you gleaned a great deal by listening to an expert talking about his or her topic area with enthusiasm and then being stimulated to read up on the topic following the lecture. You may have considered a poor experience to be an unstructured session when you were preparing groupwork for a later presentation.

This shows us that there are a number of learning styles and we respond differently to different situations. It has been suggested that we should identify which is our preferred learning style or styles, and aim to use this style as often as possible to maximize our learning. One (of many) ways of looking at this is the VARK model.

VARK categories

These are categories of learning styles which we may use:

Visual (V): This preference means you prefer to use visual information for learning, such as charts, graphs, diagrams.

Aural/Auditory (A): This means you prefer to learn by hearing material such as lectures, group discussions, presentations and tutorials.

Read/write (R): This means you prefer to learn by seeing information displayed as words, so you prefer to read and make notes.

Kinesthetic (K): This means you prefer to learn by movement or by actually doing something, so you would prefer to learn 'on the job' or by role play, or by a mixture of activities in a session.

Access the VARK website at www.vark-learn.com to identify your learning style and find out how to make the best use of it.

ACTIVITY

What is the value of knowing your preferred learning style?

If you are aware of your preferred learning style, it can help you to study more effectively by using techniques to help you understand and process information. Some of the tips below may be useful.

If you are a *visual learner* you prefer visual information and remember things best when you have seen them. So, to help you process information:

- Use pictures, charts and maps when possible.
- Use planners, organizers or goal-setting charts.
- Highlight important points by underlining or using a highlighter pen.
- Use models when they are available.
- Read and recopy notes for revision.

If you are an *auditory learner* you learn best by listening or being involved in discussion. So, to help you process information:

- Talk things through as you learn them, in a tutorial group or with friends.
- Read aloud to yourself when possible.
- You may find it helpful to experiment whether you study best with music in the background or in silence.

If you are a learner who prefers *reading and writing* then higher education should be ideal for you! You should be able to process reading text and writing notes and essays, but you may find it useful to:

- Convert graphs, charts and diagrams to words.

If you are a kinesthetic learner, you learn best by *doing something*. So, to help you process information:

- Take plenty of breaks while studying.
- Move around as you learn and revise.

   Remember that these learning styles identify your *preference* for learning only. That does not mean that they are your strengths or that you should only consider a single learning style for use in all situations. It is important to work on developing a range of strategies to cope with the variety of learning situations you will encounter. You may well find your learning style will differ depending on the topic you are learning about, and most of us use all four styles at certain times.

Making good use of your time

Studying for a Foundation Degree means devoting time to study as well as actually working, so you may find that giving yourself enough time to devote to studies is difficult, particularly if you have family or other commitments.

ACTIVITY

There are many texts that suggest it may be helpful to list all the things you do in a day (including evenings) for the period of a week to help you see where your time is spent. You may want to try this using a table like the one shown in Table 1.1 if you are unsure where study time is going to fit into your life. Make sure you are honest!

Table 1.1   Record of activities

	Mon	Tues	Wed	Thurs	Fri	Sat	Sun
7.00	Ironing	Sleeping					
8.00	Breakfast	Breakfast					
9.00	Children to school	Study day (College)					
10.00	Shopping						
11.00	Coffee with a friend						
12.00	Lunch						
13.00	Reading time						
14.00							
15.00	Collect children						

Completing the table should show you where there is the possibility of making study time and this can then become part of your weekly routine, though of course most of us lead busy lives and sometimes we have to adapt. You also need to think about where you can study and try to find somewhere where you can work quietly with minimum disturbance.

Use any course information provided by your lecturers to help you plan your time. You will need to work out how to meet deadlines for handing work in, as well as keeping a timetable of when you are attending taught sessions and allocating time for private study.

Tips for planning your time

1 **Make plans:** Use a planner that you feel comfortable with, such as a diary, Filofax, wall planner or electronic diary to identify important commitments, such as lectures, tutorials, seminar presentations, examinations, assignment deadlines. It may be useful to identify different activities in differing colours and, if you are a visual learner, you may want to hang your planner on the wall or stick it on the 'fridge.
2 **Organize your study time:** Organize your planner on a weekly basis depending on your deadlines and schedules. Make a note of when you have lectures and work to attend and decide how you will use unscheduled slots for reading, assignment writing, library visits, etc.
3 **Organize your personal and social time:** Make sure you have a balance between work and leisure time. You cannot work if you are too tired and you cannot expect to have no time to relax, so make sure you have time to sleep, exercise, spend some 'quality time' with the family as well as time to study. Completing a table like the one shown in Table 1.1 shows you how much time you spend at work and how much at leisure.
4 **Set priorities:** You need to decide which are the most important things to work on and which can be left for a while. Clearly, if you are preparing a seminar presentation for next week, it is more important to be working on that than revising for an examination in three weeks' time.

So, to make the best use of your time:

- **Getting started:** Set yourself clear, realistic goals. Split a big task into smaller, more manageable ones. If there are study tasks you do not like, try putting them at the start of a study session. Get them finished and reward yourself by doing things you enjoy doing.
- **Keeping going:** Try to have variety when you study, so aim not to do the same thing hour after hour. Break up long study sessions with a walk to review your progress and then come back to work feeling refreshed.
- **Know when to stop:** When you have achieved the goal you set for yourself, stop and reward yourself. Take some time to do something interesting but not

essential. Do not start a new task if you do not think you have time or energy to complete it.

- **Know what gets in your way:** If there are things that get in your way, such as noise, poor concentration, distractions such as the family or housework, be active in overcoming them by choosing where you study and sticking to your schedule.

Making time for reflection

You may have realized that we have already asked you to take time to reflect on some issues, such as your motivation for starting your Foundation Degree and which is your preferred learning style. Reflecting or giving further consideration to something that has happened in our lives is something most of us do quite naturally and quite frequently. This might be talking over a night out with friends the following day and considering whether the nightclub you chose to visit was the right one for a future trip out, or you might be mulling over whether your holiday destination was good value for money. Soap operas on television expect us to reflect between episodes – giving consideration to the actions by the characters involved and what we can expect to see in the next instalment. Some of the activities shown on reality TV cause reflection even amongst the media, as differing views are raised on what is and what is not acceptable viewing. We do not always refer to this way of thinking and understanding as reflection though.

Practitioners on professional programmes in health and social care use reflection as a means of making sense of the world. We also need to use reflection as a means of integrating subject knowledge with the knowledge we need for practice; it is this that enables us to develop competence in our work. For example, a health worker who has been visiting a client in their home over the past month to dress a leg ulcer will observe the rate of healing and make judgments about what is the appropriate treatment. If the health worker then attends a course on tissue viability and is made aware of a new product or means of dressing ulcers, they would probably explore the available evidence about the product and reflect on whether it is suitable to use with their client. If the rate of healing is speeded up or the ulcer becomes less painful, this has been a helpful therapeutic intervention for the client, brought about by the application of subject knowledge and reflection on practice.

However, anyone who has tried to encourage a confused older person that it is beneficial to drink at least two litres of fluid per day will realize how difficult this can be and that there is considerable skill in ensuring the person remains hydrated and avoids complications of dehydration such as a sore mouth, increasing confusion and constipation. The available evidence would agree that the confused person needs fluids, but will not necessarily provide the answers on how to get the person to drink – much of that knowledge comes with the experience of the practitioner and is based on previous, similar encounters. This is why work-based learning is so important in health and social care. It is for these types of situations that Schön in 1983 considered that professionals working in areas such as social work and health care tend to describe what they do in terms of providing care or making decisions about care differently to what they actually do, and he suggested this is because working with people and providing care is 'messy' with no hard and fast rules to be followed. He further suggested such practitioners use 'reflection-in-action' which is 'thinking on our feet' and 'reflection-on-action' which is when we mull over the situation we were dealing with afterwards. You may find that you not only learn from those that you work with on placement, but also from reflections about your experiences after your placement, especially if you share these with your colleagues or supervisor.

Take a few moments to read the difference in the reflection-in-action and reflection-on-action thoughts of Manuel, a health care support worker in a rehabilitation unit:

Reflection-in-action:

Oh goodness, she really is angry – she's going to disturb all the other patients – should I get her a cup of tea? Let's get her into the visitor's room before she screams the place down! Oh no! I think she's going to hit me!

Reflection-on-action:

Poor Mrs Green – she came to visit her husband as she has done every afternoon since he had his stroke, only to be met by the physio who told her he is being discharged later today. She was expecting him home next week once his electric bed has been brought downstairs and a commode delivered for him, so heaven only knows how she will manage him for the rest of this week. I did hear that we need to make some beds ready for acute admissions, but it doesn't seem fair on Mr and Mrs Green ....

ACTIVITY

What is the purpose of reflection-in-action and reflection-on-action?

This example serves the purpose of demonstrating that the health care team may say they prepare for patients' discharge and ensure relatives who are caring for them at home are well supported – but in practice, patients may have to be discharged in an emergency to make a bed available for what is seen as a more urgent need.

In the example, it shows that reflection-in-action occurs quickly as a whole cascade of thoughts comes into our minds and we try to make sense of what we see and hear and try to make a decision about how to act. The health care support worker's immediate concern was to make sure the rehabilitation unit was not disturbed by the visitor, so the action was to usher her away as quickly as possible.

Reflection-on-action can take place when there is time and space for it to happen. It helps to explain why situations develop in the way they do and it gives us a chance to consider whether the best course of action was followed and if not, what could have been done differently. It also gives us an opportunity to explore how we feel about that event. Clearly Mrs Green was upset and she need more than just a cup of tea but also an explanation of the situation and reassurance that she would be helped to cope with her husband's impending discharge.

Can you think of a situation you have been involved in where you perhaps used reflection-in-action and reflection-on-action, even though you may have been unaware of it? Was it useful? Or did it leave you with some uncomfortable thoughts?

Authors such as Pearson and Smith (1985) suggest reflection is particularly relevant to work-based learning (sometimes called experiential learning, or 'learning by doing') as it helps us to make sense of that experience. But knowing what counts as an experience can be difficult, which is why using models of reflection can be useful, and one of the most popular is that of Gibbs (cited in Quinn, 1988), who suggests the experience is a description of what happened.

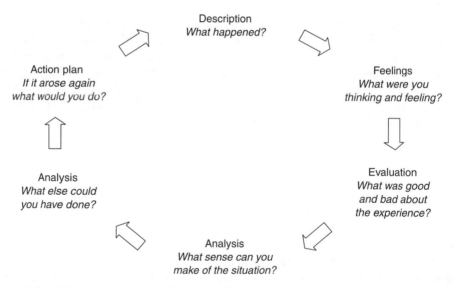

Figure 1.1   Gibbs' model of reflection

- So how would Manuel make use of Gibbs' model in reflecting on that incident with Mrs Green?
- Description: *Apparently, the physio met Mrs Green before she went in to see her husband and told her he was being discharged later that day. Before she had an*

opportunity to say anything, he was bleeped and he went off the ward. Mrs Green was visibly shaking and crying when I saw her – she was very noisy and starting to shout.

- Feelings/thoughts: *I thought this was very odd! Mrs Green is usually such a quiet lady, obviously dedicated to her husband – she has never once missed a day visiting. I wondered what on earth had gone wrong and wondered if she was heading for some sort of breakdown herself. I wanted to move her to somewhere where she would not disturb other people and where we could talk quietly – but I also wondered if she was becoming violent so I didn't try to put my arm round her to comfort her in case she hit me.*
- Evaluation: *I think I did the right thing in trying to get Mrs Green to come into the visitors' room with me – but I should perhaps have made sure someone else knew where we were going in case she collapsed or became aggressive. I didn't like this situation – I always felt I got on well with Mrs Green up until then.*
- Analysis: *It seems the physio had made the decision that Mr Green could be discharged without checking with the discharge liaison team whether his home care package was set up, so Mrs Green was really worried that she would not be able to cope with her husband at home and that she would let him down. I felt really uncertain about how to manage the situation – it all happened so quickly and Mrs Green was behaving so differently to how she usually is. It was my instinct to put an arm around her shoulder, so it was strange not doing this.*
- Conclusion: *I don't think I could have done anything differently – unless if I had known that the physio intended to speak with Mrs Green, I would have made sure they went to the visitor's room and asked if they wanted a qualified staff member with them. I should probably also have thought more about my own personal safety and made sure another staff member was with me – but then again, I didn't want Mrs Green to feel overwhelmed.*
- Action plan: *I will suggest to the charge nurse that all the rehabilitation team should have access to our communications book so they can see the state of readiness of the discharge plans. Although I can see now that Mrs Green did not really pose a threat to me, this is a good reminder that I should take the in-house training on managing difficult situations and de-escalation techniques.*

I hope you can see that the use of a reflective model allows an experience or an event to be described and analysed so that some sense can be made of it. However, even in this situation, there is still an element of uncertainty about the course of action taken, but by rationalizing on the actions, this uncertainty can be managed. This is one of the ways in which a critical practitioner can consider different possible actions and make reasoned judgments about actions. And experiences don't just have to be those that occur in practice – it could be something that occurs as a result of attending a lecture, or reading a journal article that prompts you to consider a new way of working, or a comment made by someone.

Price and Harrington (2010) summarize the value of incorporating reflection into practice as:

- Providing an opportunity to celebrate practice – when we reflect on something that went really well
- Providing an opportunity to correct practice

- Understanding ourselves – why did we act in the way we did? How do we feel about something? Do we need to get some support or further training?
- Understanding others – working in a multidisciplinary team can provide many opportunities for conflict if not dealt with in a confident and professional manner
- Understanding the profession – we do not always understand why, for example, budgetary constraints interfere with the opportunity to provide best quality care or why our instincts may not coincide with professional ethics or codes of conduct
- Providing an opportunity to challenge assumptions – you may have been working in your area of practice for some time before embarking on your Foundation Degree: using reflection should enable you to see a 'bigger picture' of your work setting.

What should you study?

Now you have identified space and time for study, it is important to set about studying the right things. Make the most of materials given out accompanying each module or unit of study, such as course handbooks and module guides. You may also find that your course uses Web-based resources, such as Virtual Learning Environments (VLEs) like Moodle or Blackboard. Some organizations, particularly the Open University, make extensive use of online learning and almost all elements of the module or course can be accessed from the Web.

Module guides and handbooks will contain learning outcomes or objectives, which you can use to identify the depth and breadth of an area you will study. You will notice that these contain descriptive words such as 'describe', 'analyse', 'evaluate', 'list', which should indicate the amount of detail you should give to the topic. (We will cover this area again in looking at essay writing.)

As well as identifying learning outcomes or objectives, the module guide should also provide a list of suggested reading for the module. This will be a list of resources you should aim to be familiar with in order to be able to address the module content and to be prepared for the module assignment. The resources may be a list of books, journals, TV programmes/videos and Web-based materials. Clearly, if a substantial list were provided you could not possibly read all the items, but you should be familiar with the set texts or the recommended texts for the module. You also need to identify which texts you wish to buy to have your own copy, rather than relying on borrowing from the library what are going to be very popular books.

The set or recommended textbook(s)

The set textbook or recommended texts are important and you should make use of them. Don't forget that library staff will know the usual books and journals used by your course, so always make the most of the staff by asking questions and seeking their advice on literature searches. You may find that some set texts are so popular you will only find them in the reference section or short-loan section of the library, so make the most of electronic versions where possible, especially as these are likely to be the most up-to-date versions.

Where to start finding information for your course

Lecturer notes and reading lists are clearly one of the most important sources of identifying the information you need to find in order to address the course content and be prepared for assignments. You will probably also carry out a Web search using an appropriate search engine (this is discussed more fully in Chapter 3), but you need to take care that Internet sources are relevant and you can trust the academic credibility and author of such articles. You must, though, make use of appropriate books and journals, as Web sources alone are unlikely to give your work sufficient academic 'depth'.

Using educational technology and Web-based resources

Virtual Learning Environments (VLEs) such as Moodle and Blackboard are increasingly being used in education. Such VLEs can be used by lecturers and students to download module materials, access reading materials and presentations and many also use forums, which can be described as a public mailbox, where information can be placed and discussions can take place online. This means that you can keep in contact with your lecturer and the rest of your student group, even if you are working remotely. You have the opportunity to keep up with module materials by reading in advance of planned sessions, you can swap ideas with other members of your group on a discussion topic and you can work collaboratively to put together a project or a report.

ACTIVITY

What do you think are the potential disadvantages of relying heavily on forums to support your learning?
    You may have identified:

- the need to work online for considerable periods, which might prove difficult, especially if you struggle to gain access or have a slow broadband connection
- a conflict with time management as you complete other work as well as online commitments
- not many in the group contribute so the discussion is not as rich as it could be
- the group is so enthusiastic about the forum you struggle to keep up with all the postings and are unsure which ones you can safely ignore (hopefully, your lecturer should be managing this aspect of the forum and should be summarizing the postings at regular intervals).

What are the potential advantages?

(Continued)

(Continued)

You may have identified:

- the opportunity for a group discussion or group task which can be contributed to at a time that suits you (forums are identified as *asynchronous*, that is, the conversation is not in real time)
- forums provide evidence that your group is working together, which may be an important learning outcome
- using forums can give a greater depth to discussion about a topic – especially if those posting messages are encouraged to justify their position and reason for making the comment
- it can help you work out a problem through sharing it with colleagues.

Other technologies you may encounter during the course of your Foundation Degree could be:

- **Wiki**: this is a tool for creating and editing documents, as all users can add, delete and edit material. An example that most of us have used is Wikipedia, which is a free online encyclopaedia. You may be asked to contribute to a wiki if your group is preparing a document or report that you all need to contribute to. (One of the reasons Wikipedia is not a respected academic source to use as a reference is that there is no control over who contributes the information, so it cannot be considered to be reliable.)
- **Blog**: a blog is usually a personal webspace that can be used to keep a journal of thoughts and ideas. If it is opened and shared, you can be invited to leave a posting of your thoughts on the topic which can be most valuable in relation to gaining information about people's opinions on a topic.
- **Twitter**: Twitter is a form of social networking where the contributor can write up to 140 characters and reach all those who subscribe to the network.
- **YouTube**: this is a video-sharing webspace which anyone can contribute to. It is a source of a lot of light-hearted entertainment, but the Open University also makes use of YouTube to air some of its materials.

Using texts as supporting evidence for your course

Once you have located a text, you need to evaluate it. Is it worth using your precious library allowance on it?

- Check the introduction and conclusion, which will tell you the purpose and scope of the book and what kind of student it is written for. Is it right for you?
- Is it written at the right academic level? Check for an index, references and bibliography – if any of these is lacking it may not be scholarly enough for your purpose.

- Is the author a known authority on the subject? Is it written from a particular theoretical or ideological perspective? If so, you must be aware of this (check with tutors if you are unsure).
- Was this book recommended by a lecturer? If so, use it – especially if he or she wrote it or edited it.
- What is the date of publication? Is there a more recent edition of the book or is there a journal article with more recent information on the topic? Remember that books contain information that may be two years old before they are even published, but journals may have information that is only six months old.

If you decide to take the book out of the library, you need to make the best use of it you can as quickly as possible. Do not forget that other students on your course may also want to read the book and it can be recalled at any time, reducing the amount of time you can keep it for.

As you read the book, keep the following points in mind, but remember that different strategies work best for different people so try different approaches until you find ones that 'work' for you:

- Set yourself a time limit, per page, per chapter, per book. Keep to the time limit by using your watch and your planner to make sure you do not slip behind your schedule.
- Reading the text for the first time means you should 'skim read' it. This means you need to train your eyes to see more. Usually when we read, we see only two or three words at a time, but with skim reading, you need to start reading from the middle of the page or in a zigzag so that you are taking in more words at once. Once you get used to this, it is easier to get a sense of what each page is about quickly. Key words will become obvious to you so that you can make a note to go back to that passage to read it in more detail later.
- If you find it difficult to skim read, perhaps because you have dyslexia, you may find 'ladder reading' helpful. This is taking the first line of each paragraph to get an understanding of the passage which should then give you a sense of the whole piece.
- Try to avoid going back over a sentence if you are speed reading. Make sure you keep to your time limit.
- Always remember *why* you are reading the book. It is easy to get bogged down in detail and forget the real reason for reading that section. If you come across unfamiliar words, make a note of them and their definitions to help you remember.
- Although it is slower, you may find it helpful to read out loud, particularly if the ideas you are reading about are unfamiliar. Reading out loud helps us to process information more quickly, and as we only tend to remember a tenth of what we read, it is a more active way of absorbing information.
- You may also find it helpful to be asking questions of what you read. What are the main points of this chapter? Is the content believable? Is it of value for my assignment?

Reading skills

Reading is a vitally important activity in working towards your Foundation Degree and it needs to form a part of your daily schedule. Try also to get into the habit of always having reading material with you so that you can dip into a book or article at any time, whether you are making a train journey, waiting at the dentist for your appointment, or sitting in the car waiting to collect the children from school. Your reading may also be online, so if you can make use of a laptop, iPad or iPhone, even better!

We have already outlined the importance of using reading techniques to get the most out of library sources as quickly as possible. Five more ways you can improve your reading are as follows.

Checking your style of reading

Styles of reading can be changed to suit the situation in which we are reading:

- Scanning, for a specific focus: This is the technique we use when we are looking for a name in the telephone directory. We move our eyes quickly up and down the lists of names until we see one that looks familiar and then focus in until we find the name we want. In the same way, scan reading means we are moving our eyes quickly over the page until we find words or phrases that match what we are looking for. It may be particularly useful to scan the introduction or preface of a book, the first or last paragraphs of chapters, and the concluding chapter of the book, to see if they are going to be useful to you. Scan the abstract section of a journal article, to see if it is worth reading the whole article.
- Skimming, for getting the gist of something: This is the technique we use when going quickly through a newspaper or magazine – we tend to pick out the main points but miss out the details. It is useful to skim read a passage before deciding whether to read it in detail, or to refresh your understanding of a passage after you have read it in detail. We suggested earlier that skimming is important when choosing a book in the library or bookshop and deciding if it is the right one for you.
- Detailed reading, for extracting information accurately: This is when you read every word of the text and work to learn from the text. This technique calls for careful reading, so you may find it helpful to skim read it first, identifying if there are any words you are unsure of and may need to use a dictionary for. You can use sticky notes to mark pages you need to concentrate on rereading. Then go back and read it in detail, making sure you understand all the points that are raised.

Become an active reader

Reading for your course is not the same as reading a novel. You need to be actively involved with the text and making notes to help your concentration and understanding. Some tips to help with active reading are:

- Underlining and highlighting: You can do this with your own books or photocopies, but not on borrowed books! Make sure you make a photocopy first and use a highlighter pen or underline parts of the text you consider to be the most important. If you are a visual learner, you may find it helpful to use different colours for different aspects of your work – but take care you do not end up highlighting whole paragraphs as this is a waste of effort. It is useful to read the text first without a pen in hand to avoid this temptation!

- Note key words: To do this you need to record main headings as you read and then add one or two key words for each section of the text. You could do this by writing in the margin of the text or keeping a notebook with you as you read.
- Questioning what you read: You need to have some idea of the questions you want the text to answer before you start reading and note these down. You can then add the answers from the text as you read. This also focuses your reading into key areas.
- Summaries: Pause after you have read a section and make a note of what you have read in your own words. You can then skim through the section again and fill in any gaps left in your notes.

Speed up your active reading

We hope you will have realized how important it is to learn from reading. You can train your mind to be active by using the SQ3R technique, which stands for Survey, Question, Read, Recall and Review.

Survey

Get together the information you need to focus on your work:

- Read the title to help prepare for the subject.
- Read the introduction or summary to see what the author thinks are the key points.
- Notice the bold face headings to see what the structure is.
- Take note of graphs, charts or tables – they are usually helpful.
- Notice the reading aids, italics, bold face, questions and activities in the chapter – they are usually there to help you remember and understand.

Question

Use the headings in the text as questions you think each section should answer. This means your mind will be actively engaged in trying to find answers.

Read

Read the first section looking for answers to your questions. Make up new ones if necessary.

Recall

After each section, check that you can answer your questions, preferably from memory.

Review

Once you have finished the chapter, go back and see if you can answer all the questions. If not, go back and refresh your memory.

Spot signposts for reading

As you get used to a writer's style, you should be able to recognize how the writer sets out work to give you a signpost of what is to follow in the text. A couple of examples are:

- 'Three advantages of ...' or 'A number of methods are available ...' should lead you to expect several points to follow.
- The first sentence of a paragraph may lead you to a sequence 'One important cause of ...' followed by 'Another important factor ...' and so on, until 'The final cause of ...'.

You can take advantage of this style of writing when skimming and scanning and use each point as a question in SQ3R.

Broaden your use of words and vocabulary

You will always come across new words when you are reading and the context in which they are used may not give you enough information to be able to understand them. If you do not find out what they mean, how to use them and how to say them, then you will only ever be able to use words you are familiar with!

You need to be able to use technical words or jargon associated with your subject area. Write the words down, look up their meanings and find out how to pronounce them. To do this, it is worth investing in a dictionary, preferably not a 'concise' or 'compact' one, but one that will not only show you how to spell a word but also give you:

- Alternative definitions
- Derivations (where the word comes from)
- Pronunciation (can be really useful in preparing for a seminar or presentation)
- Synonyms (words that have similar meanings, such as 'shut' and 'close') and confusables (words that seem to be the same but actually are different such as 'affect' and 'effect', 'advice' and 'advise').

You may also find a thesaurus useful as this can help to make the language you use more varied by giving you alternative words with the same meaning. Another way of increasing your vocabulary is by reading a 'quality' newspaper at least twice a week and being sure you treat the reading as you would a piece of text, using the techniques above.

Become a critical reader

We hope that by now you will understand that just reading and making sense of your reading is not enough for the critical learner! The critical learner will be reading and have some questions about the piece of reading:

- What is the overall argument this piece is making?
- Does it conflict or agree with other articles/books you have read?
- What does it use as supporting evidence? Is it reliable?
- Is this actually relevant and useful for my practice? (adapted from Cottrell 2011)

Taking notes and making use of them

In talking about reading skills, the importance of your being an active learner and using questions and notes to engage with your reading to help your concentration, your understanding and remember more of what you read, has already been identified. The same is true of notes made at lectures and seminars, which should be an active process for learning.

Take a few moments to reflect on how you currently make notes at a lecture or seminar. Think about:

- What is achieved by making notes?
- What uses do you have for your notes?
- Where and how do you keep your notes after the session?

ACTIVITY

Making notes is going to be an invaluable part of your day at college or university, because they form a vital part of the information you need to acquire from your course. They create some order to your sessions and you probably label them with the session number, the lecturer's name and the date. They record your progress through lectures and texts, and they provide vital revision notes for assignments and examinations.

You may be a student who does not believe it is necessary to make notes since the lecturer invariably gives a handout for the session and all you have to do is turn up to the session and listen. However, it is rare for a handout to contain all the information imparted during a lecture and it is very difficult to concentrate on what is being said for up to an hour unless you are actively involved in learning.

Making the most of lectures

Lectures are used at college or university for two main purposes:

- to give an overview of a subject, which means you need to fill in the detail; and
- to give detailed information on a topic, which means you will need to fill in the background.

In both instances, you will note that lectures will not give you the full amount of information you need to know about the topic area or to prepare for assignments. You are expected to read around the lectures to supplement the information provided by your lecturer.

Preparing for lectures

Your module guide should identify the order in which your lectures will be delivered to you and any reading associated with each session. Doing some preparatory reading will make it easier for you to follow the lecture and also allow you to judge more easily how detailed your notes need to be.

During the lecture

Obviously the most important role in the lecture is for you to listen to what is said. However, active learning is the most effective, so note-taking is also important and this means you need to be in a place where you can see and hear what is going on and away from distractions. The skill of note-taking in a lecture is to summarize what has been said or written in a clear, concise form and with no facts left out, so you need to consider the best way of making notes.

Be selective

Note-taking does not mean writing down everything you see or hear. Your notes need to be a summary of essential points of a text or a lecture, so you need to be selective about what you write down.

Notes should help you to:

- Remember what was said.
- Fix information in your mind.
- Use information for assignments.
- Revise when necessary.

Find out what the lecture is about

Apart from the date and title, do not try to write anything at the start of the lecture. Listen to find out what the content is going to be and maybe write down key words and ideas, which do not have to be in complete sentences. This way you have an idea of the direction the lecture will be taking and you can supplement the key words with other notes as the lecture progresses.

Find the best way of recording information

Some students always use 'linear notes', but these are best used when there is progression to the topic area, such as the example shown in the box.

Anaemia

Definition: Anaemia is the lack of oxygen-carrying capacity of the blood

A. Types of anaemia
B. Problems caused by anaemia
C. Implications for care for a person with anaemia
A. i) Iron deficiency anaemia. Iron deficiency anaemia is ...

Some students find it more helpful to use diagrammatical notes, such as mind maps or spidergrams, as in the example shown in Figure 1.2. These can be particularly helpful to visual learners.

Make the most of handouts

Many lecturers distribute handouts in lectures, often before they start to speak. Some even make them available on the VLE for the module, so you can access them prior to the session. There may be spaces left on the handout for you to fill in your own notes and supplement the lecture slides or it may be left up to you to 'customize' the

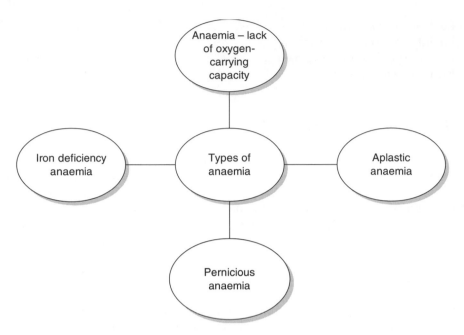

Figure 1.2 Example of diagrammatical notes

notes by using highlighters or pens to pick out key points, to note meanings of words in the margins or to pick out a reference for further reading. This will help you to be an active learner so you will remember you have read the handouts and be able to see the key points of the session straightaway when you come back to them.

After the lecture

Whichever method of note-taking you use, it is important to do something with your notes and make sure they can be used in the future. If you took notes to extend your memory, you need to be sure you can retrieve the information. It is easy to end up with large piles of notes (a piling system rather than a filing system!) if you store all your notes in the same file or use the same notebook for all modules. After the lecture you should try to:

- Go through your notes within 24 hours of making them, while the lecture is still fresh in your mind.
- Tidy up your notes and make them legible if you need to.
- Pick out key points with highlighters or marker pens and make sure key references can be found.
- Summarize your notes if you need to, especially if you will need to revise these notes for an exam.

- Fill in your notes with examples and facts that you would not have had time to note down in the lecture.
- Follow up any key points with reading and check out issues in your textbooks.
- Check out with your friends any points you do not understand, or ask the lecturer before the beginning of the next session.
- Revise your notes before the following week's lecture so you can be reminded of the topic.

Writing essays

Writing essays or assignments is a very common form of assessment in higher education. The topic for an assignment is usually set as soon as a new module is launched, with an identification of the required number of words and the academic style needed.

Essay writing gives you an opportunity to:

- Explore a topic in detail by reading widely around a subject.
- Develop skills for producing an academic argument.
- Demonstrate that you can identify and use evidence to support your arguments.
- Tackle a topic in a new and original way.

Clearly, essay writing is an essential skill for all undergraduate students. Many of the problems students encounter arise from either leaving the writing of the essay until far too late in the module, or not really addressing what is required for the essay. The actual sitting down to write the essay comes quite late in the process: there is a considerable amount of preparatory work to be undertaken first.

Read the question

This seems so basic, but it is really important to appreciate how each word in an essay title makes a difference to the way it is answered. See the examples below:

1 Discuss the use of good interpersonal skills in a care context.
2 Explain the use of good interpersonal skills in a care context.

The first example expects the assignment to contain arguments for and against the use of interpersonal skills, with examples of how they can affect the relationship with a person. The second example would only expect you to state what good interpersonal skills are and account for them.

So, by misreading or misinterpreting just one word, the assignment content could be completely different and at least 50 per cent of the marks would be missed. Some other key words (sometimes called the 'descriptors') used in essay titles are identified in Table 1.2. It is important you have a good understanding of them.

Table 1.2   Key words used in essay titles

Account for	Give an explanation of why something is the way it is
Analyse	Examine the subject in detail, breaking it down into sections to identify how and why
Argue	Make the case for something
Assess	Evaluate something, using evidence to support assessments
Comment on	Write explanatory notes, giving a view on
Compare	Consider the similarities (and sometimes differences) between two things
Contrast	Put two things in opposition to expose the similarities and differences between them
Criticize	Make judgements about the merits of theories, supported by evidence
Define	Give the exact meaning of a word, phrase or concept
Describe	Provide a full and detailed account of something
Discuss	Investigate and explore the arguments for and against something
Evaluate	Make an appraisal of the worth of something, supported by evidence
Explain	Interpret and account for something
Illustrate	Use a figure or diagram to explain or clarify, or make clear by using examples
Justify	Give reasons for decisions and conclusions
Outline	Give the general principles of a subject
Prove	Demonstrate or establish the truth or accuracy of something, using evidence
Summarize	Give a concise account of, omitting details and examples
Trace	Follow the development or history of a topic

Make sense of the question

A major part of preparing to answer an essay question is researching around the topic and reading. Therefore, it makes sense to be sure you understand what the question asks you to do.

Here is an example of a question and how it can be made sense of:

Older adults should be the responsibility of the social care system rather than the health service. Discuss.

1 Firstly, you could put a box around the activity words, by looking at what the question asks you to do. In this case, it is 'discuss'.
2 Then you could underline the key things the question asks you to discuss. In this case it is 'Older adults', 'responsibility', 'social care' and 'health service'.
3 It is important to look at the words that are not underlined to see if it makes a difference if they are not included. In this instance, the word 'should' makes a big difference to the meaning of the essay.
4 Finally, you may find it helpful to make a grid and as items from your reading uncover issues relating to the different arguments you are making, you can add them to the appropriate square.

Read for the essay

The previous section identified some tips for reading texts and making notes. In order to prepare for your essay, make sure you do the following:

- Check your guidelines. What is the word limit? What is the hand-in time? Are there any requirements for writing style, font, references, etc.?
- Select materials. Always keep the question in mind as you start to read. Make sure you use lecture notes, handouts and recommended reading.
- Move to more detailed texts. Go on to look at articles in journals, references in handouts, references in selected texts and an Internet search if required.

Make a plan of the essay

Once you are clear about the essay title and have done some background reading, you are ready to plan the essay. You probably have a number of ideas and planning should help to put these ideas into some sort of logical order before you start to write.

Your ideas may need to be sorted into two sections: argument and evidence.

The *argument* is a summary of your answer to the question. It should develop throughout the essay, with every point building on the one before. The main argument is the core of the essay and will probably only be about five or six sentences. However, each sentence will need to be explained and will need to be supported by evidence. You may also need to introduce arguments that conflict with the sentence, so that you can explain why one view is not as watertight as another.

The *evidence* is the material you use to back up your argument. This is the result of your reading and may consist of facts, material from set texts, other people's ideas, and so on. The evidence to support your essay and your analysis of it will form the bulk of the essay. However, always remember that it is there to support your argument and you will need to explain why you are introducing it as evidence and its role in the argument. This is known as signposting and can be likened to a barrister identifying why he or she is calling a particular witness to the stand to testify in a case.

The plan can be written however you like – so long as it makes sense to you and allows you to add enough detail to be realistic. Some lecturers will ask to see a draft of a plan to give you advice before you set about writing the essay proper, so it needs to be understandable to them as well. You could write your plan as a mind map – particularly helpful if you are a visual learner. Fill a whole sheet of paper with your ideas of how the essay should be structured and use different colours or highlighter pens to link points. Or your plan could be a series of numbered points with an item of argument and supporting evidence attached to each. Or you could identify each point on an index card, which could contain cross-references to other work or important quotations, and then arrange these in various sequences until you feel you have the order that works best. You can then number the cards before you start to write.

Write the essay

Finally you are ready to write the essay – or at least, the first draft of the essay. You may find yourself following the route identified in Figure 1.3 before you are happy with a final submission of your work:

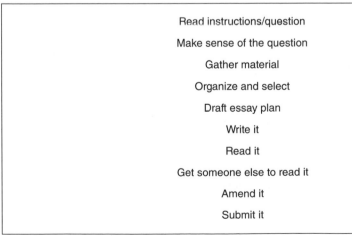

Figure 1.3   Suggested route for an academic essay

Style of writing for the essay

Academic essays usually ask for a formal style of writing which is in the third person: that is, the essay does not use 'I', 'we' or 'you'. It is generally also unacceptable to identify gender. The only exceptions to these rules may be if you are asked to write a personal diary or a piece of reflective writing.

Examples are given in Table 1.3 of unacceptable and acceptable writing styles:

Table 1.3 Academic writing style

Unacceptable style	Preferred academic style
During this essay, I will discuss three factors which can influence health. The factors I have chosen are diet, smoking and exercise.	During this essay, three factors which can influence health are discussed. These factors are diet, smoking and exercise.
During the assessment interview, the carer should ensure she allows time for the patient to ask questions. If the patient is confused it may be necessary to ask one of his relatives to confirm details.	During the admission interview, the carer should allow time for the person to ask questions. If the person is confused it may be necessary to ask a relative to confirm details.

What should be the content of an essay?

Academic essays should be made up of three components: an introduction, a conclusion and a main body or the main content.

The introduction

The introduction has two main functions:

- It focuses the reader's attention on the central themes of the essay and should pick up some of the key words from the essay title.
- It should give the reader some understanding of the order in which you are going to develop your ideas throughout the essay.

This introduction links up with some words from the title of the essay and uses signposting to tell the reader what to expect in the essay.

You may find it preferable to write the introduction at the end, when you have already developed your arguments. To do this, though, you need to be sure you have a good plan to work from.

The conclusion

The conclusion also has two main functions:

- It pulls together and summarizes details of the arguments you have been developing throughout the essay.
- It refers the reader back to the essay title, demonstrating that you have answered what you were asked to answer.

The main rules for the conclusion are:

- Do not be tempted to add new material in the conclusion.
- Do not end your assignment with a quote.
- Do not make the conclusion more than a couple of paragraphs long.

The main content

The main content is the application of the argument and the evidence referred to earlier. Remember that the academic essay is not a narrative: that is, it is not just a series of facts. Your aim is to construct an argument by showing that you can use knowledge, not just have it. This is why it may take some practice and several drafts of an essay before you feel ready to submit it.

The main areas to consider when writing the main content of the essay are:

1 Relevance of the material used: Make sure you read the title of the essay carefully and make sense of it before you start to search for related reading material.

   Check your essay guidelines and look to see if the lecturer has given pointers for how you should address the essay or the amount of breadth and depth you should cover.

2 Using written sources: Writing an academic essay provides written evidence of your ability to research a topic, produce arguments, organize your thoughts in a logical, coherent and critical manner and reach a suitable conclusion. You will not be able to do that unless you carry out wide and critical reading, understanding and evaluating as you read.

   Make sure you use at least the set text for the essay, but depending on the level of the work, use at least another six sources and relevant, up-to-date journal articles.

   Where possible, avoid using direct quotes in your work. Paraphrasing gives you the opportunity to use more than one author's opinion and demonstrates your ability to analyse others' work, not just to copy it.

3 Making a reasoned argument: Your essay needs to be logical and fluent. Sometimes, your guidelines will advise you that you are allowed to use subheadings, but most often your work will be a continuous piece of writing. This means it must:

○ Make connections between points and points of view.
○ Link the discussion to the essay title, the introduction and the main theme of the essay.
○ Not be your point of view; it must be supported by relevant evidence.

This really is the importance of using signposts in the essay. If you are making up furniture from a flat pack and do not follow the written instructions in the correct order, you may end up making a wardrobe instead of a table!

Similarly, in our example essay paragraphs will need to be written to address the issues of: what is considered to be an older adult and how this perception has changed over the past few generations; how older people have traditionally been cared for by the family and how the family structure is changing in today's society; what the medical model is and its view of the older adult; what independence for an older person means and the advantages and disadvantages to the older person of continuing to live in the community; and so on. Each topic area needs to be supported by evidence from reading, reinforced and then the next topic area moved to.

You need to read through and check how the meaning of one point relates to another. Does it: Support it? Contradict it? Lead on from it? You can link one to the other by phrases such as:

Consequently, it may be seen that ...
As a result, it can be concluded that ...

which show how one thing occurs as a result of another.

By contrast ...

expresses a change of direction.

However ...

suggests an alternative viewpoint.

Despite the fact that ...
Although it has been demonstrated that ...

give the opportunity to offer additional evidence or suggest there is another way of seeing the argument.

Another helpful tip is to check the first sentence of every paragraph. Does it relate to the question? If not, is it relevant?

4 Making sure the standard of presentation is good: Having put so much work into preparing your essay, why risk putting the marker in an instantly bad mood because you had not checked the presentation? Take the time to read through your work, making sure that it makes sense, that the ideas flow logically, that it is interesting, that you have used a wide vocabulary and that the spelling and referencing are correct. Make sure you have used the correct size font, left margins and have an extra copy of your work.

It is worthwhile reading your work aloud to check the length of sentences, to make sure you have used a mix of present tense and any other tense and that you have not made any unintentional repetitions or puns. Many of us use a spell-checker on the computer but they are no substitute for proof reading your work or getting a critical friend to do so.

Keeping your eye on the time!

Essay writing is time-consuming and is a skill that requires practice. Make sure you allow plenty of time to go through all the stages identified and, if possible, have some sleep before you look critically at your final draft again, before you submit it. And make sure you can rely on your computer and your printer not to let you down – a technical error like running out of ink will not usually be an acceptable reason for late submission of work.

Making the most of feedback

Having spent so much time and effort in preparing an essay, it is surprising how little attention students tend to pay to the feedback provided by tutors or lecturers. Many students simply note whether they have passed or not and take no note of the (sometimes copious) comments made on the script – which often contains really helpful advice on how to improve future work. Receiving an essay back following marking is a good opportunity for reflection – what worked well and what do you need to improve on? Take the time to read the comments through and match them up with the marking criteria; if you cannot understand how the marker arrived at the mark, make sure you ask them to explain.

Writing a report

Writing a report requires a very different writing style to writing an essay. You may be required to write at least one report during your Foundation Degree, possibly to write up an investigation or an aspect of work-based learning.

A report is different to an essay in three main ways, as shown in Table 1.4.

Table 1.4   Key features of a report

In purpose	A report needs to conclude with clear recommendations about what action is suggested as a result of the findings; an essay, particularly a discussion, may conclude that further investigation is required
In structure	A report has headed and numbered sections, with an index in front, and may contain one or more appendices; most essays are a continuous piece of writing
In style	A report will always be written in the third person, avoiding 'I' or 'we'; some essays may encourage use of personal pronouns

You will probably be given a standard format for your report to follow, which may be contained in the academic guidelines for your college or university. It is most important that you follow the guidelines, as marks are usually awarded for the layout as well as the content of the report and the ease with which relevant information can be found. That means paying particular attention to headings, subheadings, margins and the spacing of sections.

A typical standard report structure is identified in Table 1.5.

Table 1.5 Structure of a report

Title page	This shows the report title, author's name, date, the person or organization for whom the report has been written
Summary	The summary needs to be at the beginning of the report to be easily accessible
	It should be written as an abstract of the whole report (including the conclusion and recommendations) so cannot be written until last
Contents page	This has a particular style – see next section
Introduction	This should be brief – usually only one paragraph. It may include: • Terms of reference • Aims and objectives • Methods of investigation • Background information • Definitions of any key terms
Main body of the text	This is the substance of the report and should be divided into sections to identify how the investigation was carried out and what are the findings
	Organize it logically with headings, but keep to essential information only
	Use figures, graphs, diagrams to explain points
Conclusion	Draw together the findings, avoiding the introduction of new material
Recommendations	Identify the recommendations that appear from the previous chapters and place them in a numbered list. This may be the first section to be read, so it needs to make sense independently
References	List all references used
Appendices	Include any documents or information which add to the reader's understanding of the report

The contents page of the report

The contents page should be placed after the title page and summary. It should list all sections of the report, including introduction, conclusion, recommendations and appendices. Sections within the main body of the text should be given appropriate headings and identified in the contents page.

Any charts, graphs and tables need to be listed and the appendices should also be identified separately.

There are two main ways to number chapters or sections on the contents page:

- Alpha-numeric

	Page
Summary	1
1 Introduction	2
2 First chapter heading	3
a) Section heading	3
i) Subheading	5
ii) Subheading	6
...	
12 References	50

- Decimal

	Page
Summary	1
1 Introduction	2
2 First chapter heading	3
2.1 Section heading	3
2.1.1 Subheading	5
2.1.2 Subheading	6
...	
12 References	50

Using references and bibliographies

Citing sources and referencing them are vitally important in any academic work. This means identifying where the evidence supporting your work comes from to ensure both you and the marker of your work can find it again. Failure to reference your work may result in the academic offence of plagiarism, which is discussed later.

Citing sources

You should be provided with academic guidelines from your college or university for the precise way in which you should use references. However, in general, the following types of sources should be cited if used:

- Direct quotes
- Paraphrases – text that has been rewritten but is still essentially drawn from someone else's work
- Statistics
- Studies
- Theories and ideas
- Interpretations of events that are not one's own
- Facts that are not common knowledge.

You need to cite your sources in two different places: firstly, the point at which a document is referred to in the text of your work; and secondly in a list at the end of the work. The precise way in which you do this will vary between institutions and you need to find and use the specific guidelines that apply to your course.

Plagiarism

Plagiarism is the act of taking and using another person's ideas and presenting them as if they were your own. This is regarded in academic terms as stealing. In order to avoid being found guilty of plagiarism, you must be certain that the reader can distinguish your work from the work of others, so it is essential you reference your work accurately.

Plagiarism is not just about copying an assignment from another student or author. It may also refer to items such as audio-visual work, software programs, Internet articles, an electronic journal, graphics, diagrams or a person's website without acknowledgement of the source.

Therefore, plagiarism includes:

- Submitting work as if it were your own which has been wholly or partially drawn from other sources without citation.
- Work prepared by someone other than yourself, purchased or otherwise.
- Identical or highly similar work submitted by different students; and work originally prepared for submission elsewhere. This means that if you use the same work for an assignment elsewhere on the course, you are plagiarizing your own work!

In each of the examples below, identify:

a   Whether the students are guilty of plagiarism or if there is another reason for their actions.

b   Why you made your decision and what the student(s) should have done.

Identifying examples of plagiarism 1

1   Susie submits her first essay for marking. It uses some large chunks of text from a textbook that the lecturer recommended. There are sections that are copied out word for word without the use of quotation marks. There are no references to the text in the essay but it is listed in the references at the end of the work.

2   John, Jason, Jane and Jamilla have worked together on a project and they have been asked to submit an individual account of the work as an assignment. Jane, Jamilla and John submit work with whole sections which are almost identical.

3   Mustafa, a final-year student, hands in his dissertation which refers to a large number of sources. He has included many in-text references and quotes. There are several sections which come from an Internet site that has not been referenced.

You may have considered the following:

Example 1: Susie has obviously tried to follow the assignment guidelines and has used the text recommended by the lecturer. However, she clearly misunderstands how to cite references, since she has used the material from the book in the text but not used quotation marks or written the name of the author in the text. It is poor academic practice to use lengthy quotations, but if the original author's words are used word for word, they must be acknowledged by a reference.

You may decide that Susie has demonstrated poor academic skills since this is the beginning of her course. She needs to check her academic guidelines on referencing and try to avoid using long quotations in essays.

Example 2: Jane, Jamilla and John have not followed the project guidelines, because they were asked to submit individual pieces of work. They have plagiarized because they have submitted identical copies of work.

You may decide that they need more guidance on how to work in a group but to keep their own notes and avoid working on drafting the essay together, before the work is resubmitted.

Example 3: Mustafa is a final-year student submitting a dissertation and should therefore be very familiar with academic rules for the submission of work. He has referenced correctly in the text but has made omissions in citing his Internet sources.

At such a stage in the course, Mustafa has no excuse for not referencing correctly. He will be penalized and needs to consult his referencing guidelines before resubmission.

Summary

- Studying for a Foundation Degree means you need to organize yourself sufficiently well to manage your work time and your study time. You will find it helpful to follow some tips to improve your learning skills and learn how to learn. It is never too late to improve your study skills.
- Learning how to learn includes managing time, developing effective reading and writing skills, identifying how to prepare and write essays and reports, and demonstrating how to cite sources to ensure your work is referenced and avoids plagiarism.
- It is worthwhile taking time to explore your resources for study in terms of time, space and what your course requirements are.
- It is helpful to identify your preferred learning style and try to make the most of your study time by using the resources that suit you best.
- Always read information supplied by your university or college, to ensure you follow guidelines when preparing and presenting written work for assessment.

Further reading

Burns, T. and Sinfield, S. (2003) *Essential Study Skills: The Complete Guide to Success at University*. London: Sage. An excellent and easily readable book brimming with ideas and activities on how to approach studying.

Cottrell, S. (2003) *Skills for Success*. Basingstoke: Palgrave Macmillan. This book was written primarily to assist students to meet personal development planning requirements. It is full of advice for students in higher education who

(Continued)

(Continued)

want to capitalize on their learning experiences and start to prepare for the world of work.

Arksey, H. and Harris, D. (2007) *How to Succeed in Your Social Science Degree*. London: Sage. A thoughtful and insightful book with a focus on the actual experience of being a student.

Oko, J. and Reid, J. (2012) *Study Skills for Health and Social Care Students*. Exeter: Learning Matters. This book is written to support students on Foundation Degree courses.

Many universities and colleges produce their own study skills guidance and advice for students and these are often available to use whether or not you are enrolled on a course with the university. Some noteworthy sites worth visiting are: Southampton University, The Open University, The University of Plymouth and Bournemouth University which has a specific homepage for Foundation Degree students. There are downloadable documents and links to other sites for study skills.

2

Learning through Work and Placement: Becoming Reflective

Graham Brotherton, Helen Davies, Gill McGillivray and Steven Parker

Summary Chapter Contents

- Work-based learning and placement
- Entering the workplace
- Reflecting on practice
- Developing a framework of reflection
- Reflection and empowering practice: praxis and Paulo Freire

Learning objectives

By the end of this chapter, you should be able to:

- Understand the concept of work-based learning and its role within Foundation Degrees and other courses in health and social care.

(Continued)

(Continued)

- Make use of mentoring or supervision and other support within the workplace.
- Develop a framework to reflect on your practice in work-based learning.
- Recognize the importance of praxis and work-based learning as the practical application of values to develop empowering approaches to practice.

Introduction

Foundation Degrees are intended to provide students with the knowledge, understanding and skills that employers need. The work-based learning element or placement of your foundation degree enables you to demonstrate the knowledge and skills that will increase your employability after you graduate from your course.

Skills for Care has published National Occupational Standards in Health and Social Care, and it is these standards which specify the vocational competences that workers are expected to demonstrate. The standards are regarded as a measure of quality and are seen as an indicator of the skill level and competency of the workforce.

The National Occupational Standards relevant for a Foundation Degree for Health and Social Care are at Level 4. You can view these at the Skills for Care website (www.skillsforcare.org.uk).

The work-based learning on your Foundation Degree will provide you with an opportunity to demonstrate your practice skills. This chapter explores what is meant by work-based learning and provides you with a framework to reflect upon your practice and get the most from your practice experience. To learn from work-based learning you need to be able to learn from the experience by applying your knowledge to your practice and develop your skills through a process of reflection.

What is work-based learning?

On one level the answer to this question is obvious: work-based learning is any form of learning that either takes place within or relates directly to your experience of the workplace. One of the distinguishing characteristics of Foundation Degrees is that they emphasize the role of work-based learning, as do many other health and social care courses, so getting to grips with the practicalities of work-based learning is an important element of your course.

Your work-based learning experience or placement is likely to be an assessed component of your Foundation Degree. You may be asked to keep a learning journal to record and note how you felt about your workplace activities. This will become the basis of your reflective learning, as you will be asked to reflect upon your practice. Other assignments from other modules may require you to relate particular knowledge to your practice experience. And later, perhaps in your second year, you may be set a particular research topic related to your workplace.

In order to make the most of workplace learning you should, if you are not working already, try to find a placement you are genuinely interested in. You also need to consider the following questions: What area of health and social care are you concerned about? Where do you want to make that difference? To make sure you get the placement that is right for you, it is of paramount importance that you discuss placement opportunities with your course tutors. It is also important to discuss your placement with the placement supervisor to make sure that your potential placement will provide you with the practice experiences you need to demonstrate the skills you wish to develop and the knowledge you have gained from your course and make a meaningful difference to a person's life.

While on placement it is important to make the most of your practice opportunities. Use the experience to take responsibility appropriate to your role as a student on placement and take a proactive approach to seeking support from placement supervisors and college tutors so that your placement meets your learning needs. If you are using your own workplace as a placement this can be difficult but it is important to distinguish between your day to-day role and your needs as a student.

In order to help you make sense of the placement element of your programme, this chapter will explore categories and aspects of skills, explain some terminology, provide a policy context for skill development, and offer suggestions for ways in which you can take responsibility for personal and professional skill development through the use of learning journals. You will also be encouraged to reflect on wider aspects of the placement experience too, including relationships, personal qualities and confidence. We hope that the information within the chapter is useful to you if you are already in employment or if you are undertaking a work placement as part of your Foundation Degree, and that it supports you in making it a worthwhile experience for all involved: yourself, the placement provider and the clients served by the workplace.

A typology of skills

Consideration of terminology is a useful starting point. It is important to reflect on what is generally accepted to be a skill, a competence and knowledge, certainly for the purposes of this chapter, so we have some shared understanding. You may have already considered what skills are, and how they might be different from knowledge or competences. A skill can be defined as an ability to undertake a task well, usually as a result of practice. A competence can be considered to be the demonstrable ability to carry out a task, indicative of a skill yet to be accomplished. The Dreyfus brothers (1986) proposed a progressive model of skill acquisition (see Table 2.1 below, adapted from Eraut 1994: 124). This has potential value in allowing us to reflect on whether firstly we can agree with such a model in terms of its categories and progression, and secondly whether we can apply it to our own development and that of others.

Both skills and competences are different, but not separate from the cognitive function of knowledge. For practitioners to become skilful, or expert in Dreyfus' terms
(1986), competences and knowledge will both be acquired and developed through
experiences, tuition and reflection in the workplace. Thus for the purposes of this chapter, the term 'skill' is used in a broad context, not excluding competence and knowledge.

We all have individual and varied prior experiences and learning that have a
bearing on how skilful or competent we feel we are, in a placement context. It
is important to reflect on this, and Table 2.1 may be useful for you to take an
analytical perspective at this point on aspects of the tasks you may be expected to
undertake as you begin your placement.

Table 2.1   Summary of the Dreyfus model of skills acquisition

Level 1	Novice
	• Rigid adherence to taught rules or plans • Little situational perception • No discretionary judgement
Level 2	Advanced beginner
	• Guidelines for action based on attributes or aspects (aspects are global characteristics of situations recognizable only after some prior experience) • Situational perception still limited • All attributes and aspects are treated separately and given equal importance
Level 3	Competent
	• Coping with crowdedness • Now sees actions at least partially in terms of longer-term goals • Conscious deliberate planning • Standardized and routinized procedures
Level 4	Proficient
	• See situations holistically rather than in terms of aspects • See what is most important in a situation • Perceives deviation from the normal pattern • Decision making less laboured • Uses maxims for guidance, whose meaning varies according to the situation
Level 5	Expert
	• No longer relies on rules, guidelines or maxims • Intuitive grasp of situations based on deep tacit understanding • Analytic approaches used only in novel situation or when problems occur • Vision of what is possible

Source: Eraut 1994: 124

Using Table 2.1 as a starting point, consider a range of activities that you undertake in a work-based context, and which levels of skill acquisition you are able to apply, if any, to those situations. Examples could be talking informally to clients, talking to practitioners to arrange placement tasks or making notes from observations. How useful is the table in helping you think about what you need to do to move onto other levels?

Such analysis has potential for discussions with supervisors to identify where you feel you have relevant prior experience and where you feel less confident, and thus contexts in which more support may be necessary. The Dreyfus model (1986) therefore allows some introspective reflection on our possible level of skill acquisition; the following activity takes a more outward-looking view.

What over-arching skills do you consider to be important to be an effective health and social care practitioner?

In your response to the above activity, you may have identified skills that relate to the application of specific knowledge, or interpersonal skills that are required to work effectively with colleagues, clients and other professionals, or possibly skills that are important for academic achievement. The Common Core (Department for Education and Skills 2005) sets out six areas of skill and knowledge for those working with children, young people and families, and provides another reference point for consideration of what you might think is important in terms of skills and knowledge for health and social care. Table 2.2 provides a summary of some of the types of skills you may be expected to demonstrate at some point in your professional and academic development with examples or illustrations selected from the existing National Occupational Standards for example. According to Rodd (2006: 52), a typology is a 'means of, or framework for, classifying selected factors or features', and the typology below is intended to illustrate how different skills can be grouped together.

Skills can be assessed through the assessment of assignments as part of your Foundation Degree (if the skills have been written into the Foundation Degree programme). It is likely that you will be assessed in some way as an outcome of work placement, and you should ensure you know what is expected of you in terms of tasks and research for assignments towards your Foundation Degree. Assignments may ask for reflection and/or demonstration of some of the categories of skills in Table 2.2 and the activity below is designed to initiate consideration of skills you may have utilized, but not necessarily been aware of at the time.

Table 2.2 A typology of skills for Foundation Degree students

Category	Explanation	Example or illustration
Subject specific skills	Skills expected to be demonstrated to be successful in your chosen field of work at an appropriate level	The National Occupational Standards are undergoing review at the time of writing. Skills for Health and Care is the sector skills council with responsibility for development of subject specific skills for health and social care. However, requisite subject specific skills may include creating care plans or supporting independence.
Generic and/ or transferable skills	Skills that can be applied to both different work situations and real life contexts outside work	Personal organization, communication, interpersonal skills, research skills, numeracy, computer literacy. 'Simply put, they are the skills you acquire during any activity in your life – not just your studies – that can be applied in other situations, i.e. they are transferable! You can acquire skills through all sorts of activities: employment, projects, volunteer work, hobbies, sports, virtually anything' (University of Cambridge 2006).
Key or core skills	Skills that are important for effective functioning in the workplace	Communication, information and communication technology, application of number; improving own learning and performance; problem solving; working with others.
Academic and study skills	Skills required to be successful at the appropriate level of study	Students (at Certificate level or Level 4) 'Will have a sound knowledge of the basic concepts of a subject, and will have learned how to take different approaches to solving problems. He or she will be able to communicate accurately, and will have the qualities needed for employment requiring the exercise of some personal responsibility' (QAA 2001).

Sources: University of Cambridge (2006) and QAA (Quality Assurance Agency for Higher Education) (2008)

ACTIVITY

Consider the types of skills outlined in Table 2.2 and select specific incidents involving clients from your own work experiences and/or employment when you have been required to demonstrate one or more types of skill. How important was the skill or skills to contributing to the outcome for the client and/or colleagues?

Reflection on specific incidents in the workplace that utilized one or more of the types of skills illustrated in Table 2.2 may well indicate the complexity and interplay between types of skill. You may want to return to the incidents you have used in this activity for your learning journal. Applying a real life example to a theoretical framework, however, often reveals the difficulty of such frameworks in terms of their usefulness and limitations, but they can offer a starting point for analysis.

You may want to reflect on the usefulness of such categorization of skills in order to develop some criticality. Also, which categories do you consider to be essential for effective work practice, if any?

ACTIVITY

There is also overlap between the types of skills identified in Table 2.2 and this demonstrates the challenges that face skills sector bodies, employers' organizations, government departments and other professional groups in working with categories, typologies and standards in order to inform workforce development. Indeed, there is an extensive range of information available for employers and employees relating to skills development, and some relevant websites are suggested at the end of this chapter that provide further details.

Levels of skill and achievement

A complex interplay of skills, knowledge, experience and expertise are required by employees to be able to undertake their work roles to the satisfaction of their employers, their clients and themselves. In the light of this the current drive to create a range of competences that constitute occupational standards at various levels is open to criticism for being too simplistic and reductionist, and not placing sufficient emphasis on the complexity of skill acquisition and development. Allied to this argument is the role that intuition and other similar cognitive functions have to play in the development of professional expertise, alongside values and beliefs, and these aspects of work practice will be returned to later. You will also be encouraged to reflect on these aspects of your own development in the skills audit later in the chapter.

Before moving onto the next section, take a moment to consider what knowledge you have acquired during lectures and taught sessions as part of your Foundation Degree that you have had the opportunity to apply in the workplace. Making explicit links between theory and practice is important in the development towards expertise and proficiency. Examples might include an understanding of legislative frameworks or research findings into the difficulties of inter-agency working.

ACTIVITY

Employability skills

What do employers want, and what do they look for? Perusal of details of job descriptions including essential and desirable requirements will provide you with such information and is easily available on the Internet. It is important that you develop an awareness of the expectations and requirements of employers, and understand the language used by them to make selections for employment. If you are returning to study after taking time away from being a student, you will have different experiences to offer compared to others and it is important to acknowledge the transferable and key skills that you will have developed. Frequently cited requirements in health and social care are likely to include 'good communication skills', 'effective team-worker' and 'able to prioritize work demands' for example. Research has found that students themselves recognize the importance of such skills. Shah et al. (2004) asked graduates about their perceptions of their employability skills on graduation. They found that 'oral and written communication, team working, personal organization, self-motivation and subject knowledge' (2004: 9) were identified as being most useful.

ACTIVITY

Gather some job details for the type of work you do, or you aspire to do. (You will need to look in relevant journals and publications for job advertisements. Many job details are provided online, so the information is usually freely available.) Make a note of the essential and desirable specifications, and audit what specifications you can meet.

If you have discovered that there are several essential and/or desirable specifications that you have yet to meet, the learning journal and audit suggestions outlined later in this chapter may be useful in finding ways to identify and acquire new skills and knowledge.

Work placement provides unique opportunities for you to enhance and develop such skills as well as gather evidence and reflections from specific episodes or incidents.

It is important, however, not to see aspects of employability, skills and knowledge, as separate or compartmentalized. Workplaces do not permit skills to be acquired in a linear or structured manner. Instead, as students or employees we have to deal with challenges as and when they arise, and reflect on the holistic learning and development opportunities they present.

When learning opportunities arise in the workplace, specific information, such as context, conditions, changes in new episodes compared to previous episodes, for example, enhances outcomes and impact on learning. Diaries, journals or similar records can therefore be instrumental in helping us to reflect on and understand challenges and learning that takes place at work that might otherwise pass as insignificant. Suggestions as to how to begin to use journals or diaries follow later in this chapter.

Coping with work demands and being able to see beyond the immediate demands of the day-to-day challenges in a job are expected in the health and social care sector. Your degree of flexibility, how you cope with transitions and adjustments you have made in your professional practice in response to learning, will strengthen your employability. Supportive workplaces and opportunities for employees and students to have space for honest and open discussion about day-to-day events and incidents, as a team or through individual supervision, are essential in resolving conflict. As a student on placement, it is important that you know what support systems are in place for you to share successes, achievements and potential conflict too.

There are two further and significant areas for reflection and personal development that could be argued as being critical for success in placement learning and potential employment. These are curiosity and confidence.

Curiosity is essential if students on placement are to become skilful and knowledgeable practitioners (and researchers). Practitioners should be curious, and interested in the clients they encounter (but not to the point of intrusion). They should want to listen to their 'stories' and build relationships. You will need to be informed about the policies and practice of workplaces in order to work within the expectations of colleagues and supervisors. The more we have an inquiring mind and thirst to find answers to questions of why, what, who, how, when and where, the more we can make sense of the learning opportunities that arise through placement.

Making the most of your mentor or practice supervisor

If you have experience of mentoring or supervision try to think about good or bad experiences – what made it 'work' or not 'work'?
   Can you use this to improve your experience of mentoring now?

ACTIVITY

While the precise arrangements will vary from programme to programme, access to some form of mentor or supervisor will be very helpful for you to get the most out of work-based learning. Mentoring can take a variety of forms from the provision of a named experienced member of staff within an organization with a formally designated role to informal support form experienced colleagues. Though a formal mentor may be the best solution in most situations, this will not always be possible. You are strongly advised to try to make some form of mentoring or practice supervision arrangement where possible.

In most cases the college or university will also provide you with a tutor to support your work-based learning. The precise allocation of roles between mentor or supervisor will again vary between organizations but should include most of the following:

- Providing you with objective but supportive feedback on practice.
- Support and guidance as to your role in the workplace and how this evolves.

- The opportunity to discuss and develop your reflective practice skills.
- Advice on acceptable standards of both practice and, where relevant, college/ university assessments.
- The opportunity to 'sound out' ideas in a non-judgemental way.
- Advice on finding relevant information inside and outside the workplace.
- An advocate who will ensure your interests and concerns are appropriately addressed.
- A positive but questioning and challenging approach to practice and professional development.

In order to facilitate this there are a number of practical things both you and your mentor or supervisor can do to ensure that the relationship is effective. From a student's point of view this will include:

- Being prepared for mentoring and supervision meetings with a list of key issues you want to discuss.
- Ensuring that your mentor or supervisor is kept fully up to date about your progress and any ongoing concerns.
- Discussing your progress in an open and constructive way.
- Being prepared to accept and reflect upon constructive criticism.
- Sharing your reflective accounts and other aspects of your college/university work.

In return you should be able to expect from your placement supervisor and mentor that they:

- Make appropriate time available to you.
- Provide you with thoughtful and constructive feedback.
- Read any written material that you wish them to (though it is important that you consider how much you can realistically expect them to find time to scrutinize).
- Address any concerns that you may have in a non-judgemental way.

A constructive relationship between a mentor, supervisor and a student requires effort on both sides, a willingness to work through the inevitable difficulties which will occur and the requirement on both sides to accept that things will not always run smoothly.

Learner contracts/agreements

One way in which some people seek to make the mentoring process work is through the use of contracts or agreements that attempt to set out how the arrangements will be organized in terms of frequency of contact, the way supervision will be organized, how confidentiality will be managed and the practice opportunities provided to you. It can be particularly useful if the college or university is included as this provides a framework for negotiation and clarification about the specific roles of the student (and how this might overlap with your role as 'worker' where this is relevant), mentor and work-based learning support tutor. It is likely that your college or university will provide you with a handbook that covers most of these issues.

Using the workplace as a basis for assignments

One of the challenges of work-based learning is 'capturing' the learning that does take place in order to support your college or university assignments. You can obviously utilize your learning journal, diary or any other records you keep, but these are not always easy to 'translate' into the specific requirements of academic writing. In addition there are complications about respecting confidentiality and how far you can use specific examples to support wider ideas about theory, policy or practice. The following guidelines may help you in doing this:

- Ensure that you respect confidentiality. While examples from the workplace are very helpful, they need to be presented in ways that do not allow any individual to be identified. It is likely that your institution will have guidance on how to present placement or workplace-related material – check with your tutor.
- Make sure that you get the balance right in terms of the level of detail for any examples you use; too little detail and it is impossible for the person who will read your assignment to get a full understanding of the situation. Remember that they were not there at the time of any incident and need sufficient information to be able to evaluate your example and any conclusions you draw from it. On the other hand, make sure you do not go into excessive detail: this uses up valuable words where there is a word limit on a piece of work and will make your work too descriptive.
- Always think about why you are using the example and what ideas, concepts, etc., you are trying to relate it to. Take a little time to organize your example in relation to this: what are the aspects of the example that are relevant in terms of the ideas or concepts you are trying to explore? How can you make these links in a clear and appropriate manner?

Using work-based learning to improve practice

As a student you are in many senses in a useful position to act as a conduit between your workplace/placement and the wider professional community. As well as using the experience you gain in the workplace for your own personal and professional development, you have the opportunity to use the knowledge and skills that you are gaining through study as a way to improve practice within the workplace, e.g. by applying an action research approach (see Chapter 3) to problems within the setting or by researching current notions of good practice with your user group in the literature. This can of course be difficult in some cases in terms of maintaining effective relationships either as a student in placement or as a worker who spends time outside the setting, but with careful and diplomatic negotiation it can be perceived as beneficial for all concerned.

Entering the workplace

While on placement you will be entering the workplace as a student and this is a distinction you need to draw in your own mind even if you work there already. For our purposes the workplace can be said to consist of a number of interrelated areas all of which can be important for your learning. The workplace will have its own organizational culture, with its own set of values, philosophy, ethos and policies. The organization is influenced by a range of stakeholders including work colleagues that you may meet for the first time and later work with and the people who use the service. The physical environment of health and social care you enter may be specifically designed to provide a service or it may be in someone's personal living space in their own home or within a residential service.

The workplace environment is made up of a series of spaces some of which are public and others private. Some spaces and places may be for living, others for working and others for visiting. Some spaces may be all three. You may be working with individuals or with groups. You may find yourself in formal or informal situations. These different situations will have different rules and protocols and the different places may have different atmospheres. The time, space and place for social care is multifaceted and complex and as Pearce and Reynolds (2003) remind us, this ambiguity of social care adds to its complexity.

ACTIVITY

Spend some time thinking and reflecting upon your work-based experience or placement:

- Make some notes
- Describe your workplace:

  ○ What kind of service do you provide, e.g. residential or day service?
  ○ Who uses the service?
  ○ Who works there?

How diverse are your staff and service users in terms of:

- Age
- Experience
- Gender
- Ethnicity
- Qualifications?

Identify the working environment in terms of:

- Public space
- Private space
- Formal duties
- Informal duties.

What happens in these areas?

- Who is in these areas?
- Are there staff-only areas?
- Do people who use the service have any private space?
- How do people's roles change between spaces?

The different places and roles that people have within them at different times demonstrate the complexity of space within the health and social care workplace.

Learning in the workplace

There are a number of ways in which we learn in the workplace. To give some examples, we learn by observing, we learn by doing, we learn through conversations with colleagues, we learn through supervision. In order to maximize workplace learning we need to find ways of collecting, reflecting upon and analysing our experiences.

Try to list five things that you have learned in the last six months which relate to work.

- How did you learn them?
- Who from?
- What impact have they had on the way in which you approach your work?

ACTIVITY

Academic versus work-based learning

One of the problems with work-based learning is how to make effective links between the academic content of your course and your vocational experiences. The ability to link 'theory' with 'practice' is an essential skill that you need to develop.

'Academic' learning is traditionally conceived of as relating to theory, the research and evidence base underpinning ideas and concepts, the policy that may come from government and the ideas of values and moral principles, all of which are covered in this book. Vocational learning is thought of as relating to practice and the development of your practice skills. One of the key elements of Foundation

Degrees is the way in which they seek to link the academic and the vocational, an approach shared with most 'professional' training in health, social care and related areas. Academic learning is often caricatured as learning by thinking and vocational learning as learning by doing. The ability to reflect upon your practice by making explicit links between your academic learning and vocational experience becomes an essential method of learning. Reflection attempts to reconcile the academic and vocational and has an emphasis on evaluating practice through theory and knowledge and then using this to refine practice.

A further element within this is that it makes explicit the concept of judgement. Decisions in health and social care are rarely clear cut: most rely on an ability to interpret information which is in itself complex and may be contested (i.e. different people may have different interpretations of what the 'facts' of a situation are and how they could or should be interpreted). Judgements are therefore themselves difficult and contestable and require the ability to reflect upon situations in structured and systematic ways. The framework for reflection provided in this chapter provides a structured approach for your reflection on your work-based learning and enables you to develop the skills to be a reflective practitioner.

Principles and values

Values and personal qualities in addition to skills contribute to the ability and effectiveness of employees in the workplace. A willingness to be introspective is a prerequisite to being able to identify our personal beliefs, aspirations and professional principles, all of which influence our attitudes and behaviours at work. Metacognition 'is being able to reflect on one's own learning through analysis and evaluation of the learning processes of the work undertaken' (Gomersall 2004: 205), and thus has a valuable role to play in the context of personal commitment to learning. The extent to which students, trainees or employees are aware of their own attitudes to the multiplicity of contexts in which their work takes them (with clients, with other professionals, with colleagues, with mentors and trainers for example) will influence their potential to understand such attitudes and make adjustments if needed.

A commitment to professional principles and a desire to become a reflective practitioner in health and social care become apparent in how we deal with clients. Part of reflective practice is considering how others see us, and in the range of workplaces where health and social care practitioners may work there are often vulnerable clients who require practitioners with skills and knowledge that translate into sensitive, empathetic and informed practice. Ideally, practitioners are mindful and motivated to develop such skills too, regarding reflective practice as an aspect of lifelong learning in the workplace.

So far in this chapter we have explored some of the generic and specific skills, competences and knowledge you will be required to demonstrate as a student or in your chosen career. As mentioned earlier, work placement offers you the unique opportunity to develop and enhance these skills; however, experience alone does not automatically lead to the acquisition of new skills and knowledge (Dewey 2007).

Aitchison and Graham (in Criticos 1993: 161) suggest that 'experience has to be arrested, examined, analysed, considered and negated in order to shift it to knowledge'. It is worth considering how you can use the learning opportunities that arise on work placement to improve and enhance skills that not only make you more effective as a practitioner but also help your future employability. A good place to start is by completing a skills audit. However, finding the evidence to support your skills audit can be sometimes difficult and problematic unless you have a way of recording your learning opportunities. A diary or a reflective learning journal is one way of examining your own values and working practices as well as the values and practice of others (Stroobants et al. 2008). In this next section we examine the benefits of keeping a learning journal and provide you with some example formats.

Reflecting on practice

The essential tool for learning in the workplace is the skill of reflecting on practice. Thinking about events with a model that provides us with different perspectives enables us to see things differently. As Mr Morfin in *Dombey and Son* reflects:

> how will many things that are familiar, and quite matter of course to us now, look when we come to see them from that new and distant point of view which we must all take up, one day or another? (Dickens 1896: 598)

The process of thinking over and reflecting on what you have done is an important part of professional development. Eby (2000a) defines reflection as enabling practitioners 'to make sense of their lived experiences through examining such experiences in context'. Reflecting on our practice is part of our 'personal commitment' to seek out answers to the questions that are raised by our practice.

Practice is an important learning experience and this experiential learning is an important aspect of being a health and social care practitioner. As an individual practitioner you are an active learner and your everyday practice experience forms part of that learning.

Kolb's basic concept from his learning cycle (Figure 2.1) is that we constantly learn from our experience. We have an experience and we look back upon it. We reflect on that experience from a range of different perspectives, examining what went on in the experience.

Through the process of reflection we develop a better understanding and link our actions to theoretical ideas. We may even develop our own theoretical ideas of how we need to improve our practice. From our new ideas and generalizations we then move on to new ways of working in which we test out our ideas. Our new ideas are implemented in our practice, which in turn gives us a new experience. The process of learning becomes cyclical and we continue to learn through our experiences. So we continually test our ideas in practice and change them in light of new experiences.

Reflection is about thinking about our actions. Initially it is our conversation with ourselves. So how do you think?

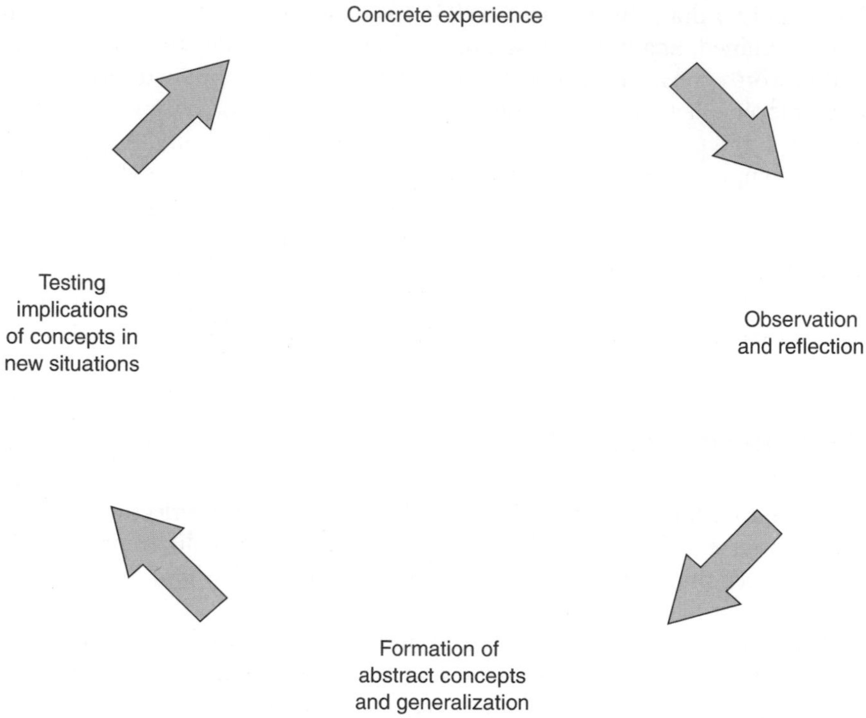

Concrete experience

Testing
implications
of concepts in
new situations

Observation
and reflection

Formation of
abstract concepts
and generalization

Figure 2.1   Kolb's learning cycle (Kolb 1984, cited in Eby 2000a)

How do you think?

Let us take some time out to reflect on how we think.

Take five minutes or so to think about something that has happened today – it could be a conversation with someone at work or college or a piece of work you where involved in.

Did you talk to yourself?

- Silently in your head
- Or out loud?

What language are you using?

- Where does your language come from?
- What perceptions and meanings are in the language you use?
- How does emotion enter into your conversation with yourself?
- Who owns the language you are using?

What form does your conversation with yourself take?

- Are you asking yourself questions?
- Are you answering and replying to yourself?
- Or are you describing the day's events in sequential order in words?

Do you think in pictures?

- Do you visualize any of the events?

Do you think in feeling?

- What emotions did you experience?
- Are you reliving the emotions?
- Are you aware of the feelings and emotions you experienced at the time?

Where do you think?

- Where do you think about the activities of the day?
- Where do you do your daydreaming?

Do you have time and space to reflect on the activities of the day?

Thinking becomes our tool of reflection.

Schön (1983) suggested that as practitioners we may only implicitly know what we are doing. This knowing in action is made up of our abilities as practitioners to make judgements and decisions almost spontaneously. Sometimes we are unaware of how we know how to do something; we may have known at one time but cannot remember the reasoning behind our actions or we may have not known in the first place! Whatever the reason, we do things simply because we do.

This is not to say that we do not think about what we are doing. We think about our actions as we do them; this reflection in action is constant and ongoing, or we may think back over our actions, by reflecting on our action.

To improve our practice Schön says we need to reflect on our action by looking back over our practice. By reflecting on our practice we can evaluate and learn from what we have done. By reflecting on action we can acknowledge that we have reflected in action as well. We can analyse our practice, as well as our thought processes, in order to improve our practice in the future.

To reflect successfully on our practice we need to think about it in a structured way in order to evaluate, learn and improve. We also need to use this reflective process to develop as critical practitioners.

A number of different modes of reflection exist to help practitioners reflect upon their practice, which are all essentially methods for looking back on our practice. By looking at a few influential models of reflection you will be able to see which ones may be useful for your own reflection and we will be able to suggest some essential components in the process of reflecting on your practice. They all provide methods of evaluation and a way to improve or change your practice.

Jasper (2003, cited in Adams et al. 2005) sees reflection as being a three-phase sequence of 'experience–reflection–action':

- Examining and revisiting the experience by thinking about it. This involves concentrating and examining the event in the here and now or by looking back on the experience.
- Reflecting on the experience, by exploring feelings, and examining these to develop an awareness of their implications, their importance and how they effect the outcomes of our practice.
- Deciding on the action we take during the event or in the future when we encounter similar experiences.

Jasper's model corresponds to Schön's ideas of reflection in and on action. Most models are concerned with the process of reflecting on action. The Gibbs reflective cycle (cited in Quinn 1988), depicted in Figure 2.2, is seen as a popular and effective framework for reflecting on your practice. It provides useful headings to write about your experience if you are keeping a reflective journal.

The first part of the cycle is to describe the experience. You need to describe the events. In what order did things happen? Who did what and what was said?

The feelings that you experienced are important. What emotions did you experience? Were you happy or pleased? Angry or upset? What made you feel this way?

To evaluate the experience, the Gibbs model suggests you look at the experience in terms of what was good or bad about it. What was successful and what was not?

In analysing the experience you need to try and make sense of what happened. Why did things happen the way they did? Were the events predictable? Were you using a particular theoretical idea to guide your actions?

By coming to a conclusion you need to be able to formulate ideas about their courses of action. What else could you have done in this situation? Would they have made any difference to the outcome? Can you run an alternative course of events in your reflection?

As a result of reflecting on your practice you need to have an action plan. If a similar situation arose again what would you do differently?

The Gibbs cycle of reflection is a useful starting place, but it seems limited in its scope for analysing your practice in depth and it does not explore the nature of thinking about complex processes and events that are informed by a rich layer of thoughts, feelings, ideas and contradictory ideas.

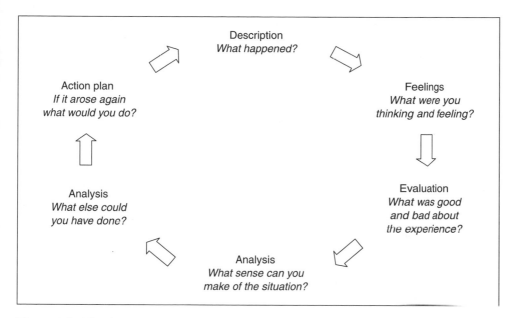

Figure 2.2   The Gibbs reflective cycle

Source: Gibbs, G. (1988) *Learning by Doing: A Guide to Teaching and Learning Methods*. Oxford: Further Education Unit, Oxford Polytechnic.

Boud et al. (1985) have developed a model of reflection that attempts to deal with some of these complex and abstract ideas. The model has two main components: the experience itself and the reflection on the experience. The experience includes what you thought, felt, did and the conclusions you came to about the event. This could be at the time and/or immediately after the event. The processing phase is after the event and it is here that conscious reflection takes place in three stages in which you:

- Return to the experience.
- Attend to feelings.
- Re-evaluate the experience.

Return to the experience is the retelling of the event or experience. It is important to describe the events without judgement, in chronological order. This describing of the events is so that the experience can be examined in terms of what actually happened. This seemingly detached mode of describing a situation does not mean that feelings are not acknowledged, because it is only by acknowledging both positive and negative emotions that you can move on to the next stage.

Attend to feelings is concerned with concentrating on the positive feelings associated with the event. In this model it is important to remove negative feelings as they may get in the way of reflecting on and analysing the experience in a rational way. It is not about ignoring the negative feelings and emotions, but about dealing with them so that they do not get in the way of reflecting on your practice and having creative ideas of how to develop your practice. Concentrating on the positive is also about providing the drive to persist in what may be a challenging experience.

Re-evaluate the experience in this model can only truly happen if the preceding two stages have been worked through. To re-evaluate the experience there are a further four sub-stages to work through:

- **Association** is about making links between the ideas and feelings of the experience with your existing knowledge and values. From making these connections the idea is that you should be able to make sense of the experience and develop an understanding of the event. It is also about challenging your previous knowledge and so developing your own knowledge about a situation.
- **Integration** is concerned with making further sense of the associations you have made. After making a series of links between feelings, knowledge, attitudes and values, the idea is to sift through all this information and begin to make further sense of it all. What connections can you make between the ideas you have generated about a particular event? What truth or insight can you come up with? What new ideas can you formulate?
- **Validation** becomes the stage where you test out your new idea. You can rehearse an event or test out a new strategy for an intervention. You do not need to test out your new idea or model in practice – you could replay and visualize the events to yourself or talk them through with someone. You need to check your new idea for any inconsistencies or contradictions. But even if your idea does not fit in with accepted practice, it does not mean that you are wrong – you could be breaking new ground.
- **Appropriation** is when the new knowledge gained from reflection becomes your own. This may involve a fundamental change in how you work or what you believe in.

The model ends with **outcomes and action,** a new way of practice and new knowledge.

This process of re-evaluating the experience may seem quite separate from everyday practice and experience, but the value of Boud et al.'s model is that it highlights the complex and abstract nature that thinking about your practice can create. To help the process it is useful to discuss each stage in a learning set, in a tutorial, or with your practice supervisor. Another person can help with exploring the situation and making links across a range of issues.

As an alternative to this abstract model the Johns model of structured reflection (cited in Quinn 1988) offers a series of questions and cues that you can ask yourself to guide your reflections. The questions can be used in a learning set to challenge each other so that you and your fellow learners can help each other to develop your reflective skills. The questions can also be the basis of a learning journal.

The Johns model of structured reflection

Description:

- Phenomenon – Write or give a description of the experience.
- Causal – What essential factors contributed to this experience?
- Context – What are the background factors to this experience?
- Clarifying – What are the key processes for reflection in this experience?

Reflection:

- What was I trying to achieve?
- Why did I act as I did?
- What are the consequences of my actions for:

  o The person and their family or carers?
  o Myself?
  o People I work with?

- How did I feel about this experience when it was happening?
- How did the person who uses the services feel about it?
- How do I know how they felt about it?

Influencing factors:

- What internal factors influenced my decision making and actions?
- What external factors influenced my decision making and actions?
- What sources of knowledge did influence or should have influenced my decision making and actions?

Alternative strategies:

- Could I have dealt better with the situation?
- What other choices did I have?
- What would be the consequences of these other choices?

Learning:

- How can I make sense of this experience in light of past experience and future practice?
- How do I now feel about this experience?

Have I taken effective action to support myself and others as a result of this experience? How has this experience changed my way of knowing:

- Empirics
- Aesthetics
- Ethics
- Personal?

The Johns model offers more structure than the other models outlined here and Quinn points out that such a framework could be regarded as being imposed upon practitioners. It is important to view the different models as guides to frame your reflection; the model is external to the worker and you may wish to develop your own.

Action research as a model of reflection

The notion of reflective practice is linked to the idea of action research, which is developed more fully in Chapter 3. However, it is important to note in this context that action research can be thought of as a form of formalized reflective practice with an emphasis on investigating and acting to improve elements of practice. In this sense developing an action research approach can be an important element of work-based learning and a way of linking the academic and vocational elements of your course.

Critical incident analysis

One way of developing reflective practice in a systematic way is through the use of critical incident analysis. This involves using the approach outlined above in a particularly structured way by identifying an incident of particular significance (usually something that has gone very well or very badly) and thinking the incident through in a very systematic way. This involves considering (in addition to the things outlined above):

- What context the incident or event took place in.
- How you were feeling before and after the event.
- What you were thinking at the time.
- How other people involved perceived the event or incident (in so far as it is possible to ask them).
- What the consequences were for you or the other people involved (in order to do this you need to discuss the incident with the other people who were involved).

In many cases it is useful to write this up in the form of a report and discuss it formally with a colleague (perhaps your mentor).

ACTIVITY

Try to think of a 'critical incident' within your own experience and analyse it using the model outlined above. It may be useful to record this and discuss it with your tutor or mentor.

Developing a framework of reflection

These different models of reflection and a range of others have some common elements that can be extracted and combined to develop a workable model for reflecting on your practice while undertaking your Foundation Degree. This book contains a range of information and ideas about theoretical knowledge and practice, policies and procedures, values and ethics, and the possible future for health and social care. These can be utilized to aid and develop your reflection on practice. Using the above ideas we have put together a framework that can be used with the accepted models of reflection to help guide your reflective processes.

Common to all the models of reflection is the need to describe and replay the experience, so the first thing in our guide to reflection is to:

- **Describe the experience:** Describing the situation or piece of practice is an important element in developing your reflective skills. Replay the events in a conversation with yourself or within a learning set or a tutorial group designed to aid your reflective skills. Taking on board some of the messages from the models above on how to describe the events as they happened. Recount the order of events, tell your story and write it down as soon as you can.

In your descriptions pay attention to the minutiae of interactions, the perceived causes of behaviour, the antecedents, the behaviour and the consequences.

It is impossible to separate out your feelings and emotions, as they are an important part of the story, so acknowledge them. You can explore the reasons why later.

The need to attend to feelings is also part of many of the reflection models. This seems important, as identifying why you felt the way you did enables you to locate any conflicts in values, attitudes and beliefs. It may also enable you to identify areas of practice that worked well as well as pieces of work that did not go as planned. So the second part of this guide is to:

- **Acknowledge and explore your emotional responses:** How do you feel about your practice? It is important to explore how you feel about your work and what you hoped to achieve by your practice and work with people who use services. Taking elements from the Johns model, you can explore why you feel the way you do in terms of your achievements. Do you feel as if you have accomplished something or do you feel frustrated in your efforts?

It is important to explore not only your feelings but also how other people feel and view your practice – the people who use the service you provide, fellow workers, managers, and even the organization itself. Can you identify any conflicts between these different levels of your work?

All the models have an element of analysis and evaluation. The Gibbs model asks you to look at your practice in terms of what was good and how you can make sense of what happened. The Boud et al. model offers us some abstract thought process to make connections and the Johns model gives us a structured set of questions. To aid your analysis and evaluation we suggest you explore your practice in the following terms:

- **Values:** It is important to be aware of your personal and professional values. Identify the values and moral principles that inform your interventions in people's lives. What are the ethical and moral dilemmas that you are encountering in your practice? Are you able to work in an empowering way and act as a morally active practitioner and with moral courage? What is your position of power? Does this have a bearing on how you are feeling about your practice and interventions with people?
- **Theory, knowledge and practice:** It is important to identify and recognize the theories and concepts that underpin your practice. What theoretical knowledge informs your practice? Do you have a couple of favourites or is your practice theory-less?

Some of the theoretical ideas that you may be using could be suspect and open to criticism. How do you know that the knowledge you have is adequate for your practice and why are you using the theory that you do?

It is important to be able to link and use theory in your practice, but equally so it is important to be critical and not simply take theoretical ideas for granted. It is very unlikely that grand theoretical ideas can explain or inform all you actions.

- **The policy and legal context:** Social care agencies and health authorities are bound by national and local policy, legislation and procedures. It is important to acknowledge the policies that guide your practice and the legal context in which they exist. Are you performing statutory duties and what are the legal limitations of your actions?
- **The evidence:** An important part of reflecting on your interventions in people's lives is to be aware of the research evidence that can inform your practice. How do you know that your interventions in other people's lives will make any positive difference to their lived experience? An awareness of sound research evidence and its relevance to your practice is of paramount importance in your reflective processes, but equally so it is important to be critical of research. Ask yourself 'where is the evidence?' Is the research evidence any good? You need to question the research that is reported to underpin your practice.
- **Where you fit in:** You need to acknowledge your role in your practice. You may have already done so by exploring your emotional responses or your personal moral principles. You could take this further to examine how you have interpreted any of these points for reflection or the meanings that you have created from reflecting on them. You are an important player when intervening in people's lives, so how have you changed someone's life course? You also need to consider how you would do things differently.

The models all have as a final outcome an aim of learning from and improving your practice. From reflecting on your practice you should be able to identify what you need for your own personal and professional development. Set yourself some objectives to develop your knowledge to inform your practice. It is in this way that you can develop as a reflective and critical practitioner.

Learning journals

A learning journal is in essence a diary or a record of personal learning experiences. Different educational establishments may refer to them by alternative names such as learning logs or personal journals. Although the title may vary in different institutions, the purpose remains the same, which is to encourage students to reflect upon their learning experiences. A learning journal can be kept over a period of time as a way of reflecting on generic and specific skills and competences that are being developed through your studies and placement or work setting. This may be through recording significant incidents, events, views and opinions and then examining them to identify your strengths and weaknesses as well as your preferences to learning (Klug in Jones-Devitt and Smith 2007).

Many Foundation Degree courses encourage students to keep a learning journal throughout their course as part of their Personal Development Portfolio (PDP), to enhance learning during the course. If this is the case for you, the learning journals are for your own personal development and a means of self-discovery and reflection which will only be read by you (unless you choose to share or discuss them). However, other courses may require you to hand in your learning journals as an assessment component or encourage students to use the journal entries to inform an assignment. If the learning journal is part of an assessed component it will be read by the marking tutor or tutors. Therefore the journal entries may need to be written in a particular format and you will need to plan accordingly as to the format and style of writing. Guidance and examples of formats for journal entries will be given later in this chapter.

Purposes and benefits of keeping a learning journal

The main reasons for keeping a learning journal are:

- To keep an ongoing record of your experiences, thoughts and feelings
- To identify and reflect upon key skills and competences
- To identify strengths and weaknesses
- To consider and motivate strategies for improvement.

You may be someone who has always enjoyed keeping a diary or journal and the idea of writing about your experiences and emotions is appealing and a way of improving your own learning and practice. Others reading this book will find the very idea of 'naval gazing' as a challenging or onerous exercise. Unless you are naturally a reflective thinker, experience alone does not always lead to learning, particularly as the pace and pressure of work often denies us the chance to synthesize outcomes from each day's events. In fact we do not always stop to consider why something went well or we find that time and time again we make the same mistakes. Our lives are often so busy that we do not take time out to think to try and make sense of it all (Eraut 1994). Writing a learning journal on a regular basis will enable you to periodically explore and examine specific incidents and try to clarify your motives, actions and emotions. Establishing a habit of writing about issues, experiences and events enables it to become much easier to identify patterns and inconsistencies and then consider strategies for improvement (Schön 1983). This is usefully illustrated by J.K. Rowling in *Harry Potter and the Goblet of Fire*. In the book Professor Dumbledore describes to Harry a magical device called the Pensieve, a stone basin that contains a silvery liquid or gas. Dumbledore tells Harry:

> 'I sometimes find, and I am sure that you know the feeling, that I simply have too many thoughts and memories crammed into my mind ... At these times,' said Dumbledore, indicating the stone basin, 'I use the Pensieve. One simply siphons the excess thoughts from one's mind, pours them into the basin, and examines them at one's leisure. It becomes easier to spot patterns and links ... when they are in this form.' (Rowling 2000, in Moon 2006: 25)

Keeping a learning journal can be somewhat like the Pensieve. Incidents, thoughts and patterns can be recorded in a learning journal and examined at a later date. Patterns of behaviour and ways of thinking or acting can be spotted that you may not have noticed before (Moon 2006). These may be strengths that can be developed further or areas that you have identified that need improving. Furthermore a learning journal can be a more objective way of examining our thoughts, emotions and actions that we often avoid or overlook in the day-to-day flow of our lives (Tripp 1993). One of the benefits of developing your skills of reflective thinking and practice is that it motivates you to understand why you behave or think in a particular way. This in turn will motivate you to become proactive in trying to develop your thinking and skills. Students who develop these skills of critical reflection gain a deeper understanding about themselves and about their practice. This in turn leads to an increase in their knowledge and practice which not only benefits their studies but also clients and their work setting. An example of this can be seen from an undergraduate student reflecting upon keeping a learning journal during her first year at university. She comments on identifying ways to improve her learning and behaviour by 'noticing which strategies have worked most efficiently in the past' and then using her observations to 'accurately identify strategic methods in improving [her] learning, behaviour and all other aspects of [her] life'.

Learning journals are useful only if they go beyond description and become reflective. However, reflective thinking does not occur overnight (unless you are one of those people we mentioned earlier who are reflective by nature). For most people reflective thinking takes time and practice. It requires you to ask yourself questions and helps you understand your thinking and how you work. Reflecting upon specific incidents may be an uncomfortable experience although ultimately we hope that the experience will help you to become more proficient in your work and therefore find it more rewarding and fruitful. Whatever the purpose of the learning journal it is essential to be honest when you write. 'Write how you really feel and not how you think you should feel. Record what you really think, not what you believe you ought to think' (Klug in Smith 2007).

'Reflection ... by its very nature, questions whether there is ever a right answer' (Stroobants et al. 2008: 17). It challenges you to seek other ways of doing something and encourages you to seek answers for yourself. It is only by being honest with yourself about your achievements and practice that you will be able to consider steps for improvement.

Examples of learning journals

The format for learning journals can vary widely. Many students prefer the more traditional pen and paper way of recording, using either a notebook or a loose leaf folder, whilst others prefer to use electronic means and type or record their journal entries (Moon 2006). If a learning journal is a required assessment component then you should check with your module tutor what format is expected. However, if it is not an assessed requirement then the format is purely down to individual preference. It is useful to note that every learning journal will be unique even if you follow similar guidelines, as it will reflect your individual experiences, personality, purposes and intentions.

ACTIVITY

Examine the following three examples of formats for keeping a learning journal. You might decide to trial each of them for a week or two while on placement (although they can be used at any time), and then evaluate how they have promoted your ability to be reflective and analytical.

Learning journal example 1

Write regularly about events, issues and experiences. Here are some ideas and questions that you might try to answer:

- Are there any issues that confuse or cause you concern or that seem inconsistent or incongruous?
- Describe a situation or event (this may be an everyday occurrence or something that went really well and motivated you or did not go as planned and demotivated you).

Reflect on the events, issues and experiences by answering the following questions:

- What happened and when?
- How did you handle the situation?
- Who else was involved?
- How do you feel about it?
- What would have helped you to handle this better?
- What would you do differently next time?
- Any other thoughts about the event, issue or experience
- What skills and competences are you developing?

The above example provides a series of prompts that you may find useful to relate to the notion of becoming a reflective practitioner. It could be used initially to focus on individual events that may occur during a day at placement such as a client becoming upset and distressed or you not feeling confident enough to contribute to a team meeting.

Example 2 is similar in that it gives prompts for reflection and analysis. Each entry will need two pages or sections and is designed to provide a format that gives space for immediate reflection, as well as reflection and analysis at a later date when you may be able to detect patterns or triggers signalling achievement and success or causing concern.

Learning journal example 2

Description	Reflection

In this section record events, issues and experiences.
 	
Describe
    An issue, event or experience
    that is concerning you
 	
Include
    What happened and when
    Who else was involved
    How you feel about it
    What you could or would do
    differently next time
    Any other thoughts about
    the event, issue or experience
	This section could be filled in at a later date after a number of journal entries have been completed.
	
	Take time to go over your journal entries and look for patterns of behaviour and ways of thinking.
	
	Consider whether you still think or feel the same or has your attitude or opinion altered?
	
	Consider how you can develop your strengths and areas of weakness and put together an action plan.

The third example provides additional structure which you might find more helpful if this is the first time you have used a learning journal. The columns are only a suggested format, but they prompt you to write descriptively first, thus creating a context for reflection and analysis thereafter.

Learning journal example 3

Describe a situation or event (this may be an everyday occurrence or something	How did you handle the situation? How do you feel about it?	What would have helped you to handle this better? What would you do differently next time?

that went really well and motivated you or did not go as planned and demotivated you). What happened and when? Who else was involved?	Any other thoughts about the event, issue or experience.	What skills and competences are you developing?

Skills audit

The process of regularly writing and reflecting in a learning journal should help you to identify key skills and competences relevant to placement learning. We have already identified specific skills that are important to develop in order to work efficiently and competently with colleagues, clients and other professionals as well as for academic success. Carrying out a skills audit will help you to focus on a range of skills and competences that you may not have identified in your learning journal. An audit of your skills, whether these are generic transferable skills or subject-specific skills, will help you to recognize areas of strength as well as ascertain areas that need developing. Although carrying out an audit may be time-consuming it can be described as being an interesting and rewarding process as it enables you to build and develop current skills and practice and motivate you to improve. Consultation with your supervisor or regular meetings with your mentor can be advantageous in terms of training opportunities, as they can 'take account of your professional development needs, [as well as] the requirements of your practice and your personal ambitions' (SEHB 2003: 26). Honest reflection is critical in completing an audit that is not only accurate but also useful in helping you to become a more skilful practitioner.

An example of an audit can be seen in Table 2.3. It lists some of the generic transferable skills that you may be expected to demonstrate. However, you may have specific skills or competences that you may wish to include as part of your studies, work setting or placement that are not included here.

Create a similar skills audit to the example provided using generic transferable skills, key skills, academic skills or subject-specific skills you consider relevant for your work setting or placement and that you want to focus on for development.

Other skills that could be included in the format for skills audit are personal organization and time management skills, presentation skills, multi-tasking,

ACTIVITY

written communication and listening to others. Action plans can be more successful if they are written in terms of SMART (specific, measurable, achievable, realistic, time-limited) targets. Other acronyms are available to create a structure for action plans, but it is important that you are able to devise systems that work for you, and are flexible enough to respond to your way of working, and the formats presented in this chapter have been offered in a spirit of responsiveness and autonomy for you, as constructors of your own learning.

Table 2.3   Example of a skills audit

Skills	Strengths	Evidence	Areas of concern	Target for development	Action plan (what I can do to address this development need)
Oral communication	I communicate well on a one-to-one basis with both staff and clients I feel I am clear and that people understand what I am trying to say	Feedback from staff and clients. Appraisal highlighted this as being one of my strengths	I am nervous about giving presentations and speaking in staff meetings	To be able to give presentations and speak confidently in staff meetings	To contribute to discussions in daily staff meetings To help plan and deliver next presentation workshop
Working in a multi-disciplinary team or working with others	I am a good team player and I am able to work well with a variety of people. I enjoy motivating others	My mentor commented that I worked well with the young people at the centre, motivating and encouraging them to participate in activities	I do not always recognize other people's feelings	To become more empathetic and recognize how others might be feeling	To read, go to emotional intelligence workshop or read book about emotional intelligence
IT skills	I have a basic understanding of using Word. I can use Google to search on the World Wide Web	I avoid using the computer. I generally only use it to write assignments	I am not confident using the computer and often avoid using it	To become more familiar with using Microsoft Word and PowerPoint	Student support Sign up for computer course

Becoming a reflective and critical practitioner

In this final section we will try to make explicit the relationship between reflection and your broader role as a practitioner. As you progress through your career in health and social care it is important to develop your skills of reflective practice. This is a process of turning thoughtful practice into a learning experience. Developing your skills further to become a critical practitioner and developing your capacity for reflective practice is an essential element of personal and professional development. Your aim should be to develop an open-minded and reflective approach to your practice that considers 'different perspectives, experiences and assumptions' (Brechin 2000; Eby 2000a: 55). It also becomes important to acknowledge and reflect on your personal involvement as you engage and intervene in people's lives and the relationship you have with people you provide services to.

Reflection and empowering practice: praxis and Paulo Freire

Underpinning your reflective practice should be an awareness of the values and moral principles that underpin your practice. These are explored in Chapter 6. Within this process of reflection you should be able to reflect upon your practice in terms of whether it can be considered to be empowering practice.

Paulo Freire, one of the most influential educational thinkers of the twentieth century, emphasized the importance of dialogue in education and was very critical of many traditional approaches, which he saw as a one-way process of imparting knowledge from expert teachers to passive recipients. In addition, Freire saw education as explicitly concerned with change and with trying to improve the circumstances of those who are disadvantaged. It therefore needs to be underpinned by a particular and explicit commitment to values and action, known as praxis. This links explicitly with the notion of the morally active practitioner, as discussed in Chapter 6.

In this model, since education should be about empowerment, there needs to be explicit reflection as to whether or not any approach or intervention is underpinned by the values that support good practice in health and social care. It can also be argued that praxis suggests we should go a stage further and actively reflect on whether we can change our practice in ways that are commensurate with further reducing power differentials and disadvantage.

This model of praxis as informed committed practice is an important element in using workplace experience as a basis for learning. The process of linking experience to theory as a way of improving practice has a long and honourable tradition, not just in health and social care but also in related areas such as education. A key example of 'praxis' in action could be in relation to the debate around empowerment. The theoretical/moral issues about empowerment are discussed in Chapter 6.

As social care workers we are responding to the needs of people who require our services. This is undertaken under the umbrella of empowering people who use our services. Yet how far do organizations and practitioners empower people within a framework of tackling disabling barriers?

A model of empowerment based upon the social model of disability (see Chapter 6) is concerned with the breaking down of disabling barriers and the promotion of people's rights. Service users are seen as experts of their own situation and people are regarded as equal and in control of the services that are delivered. The structures and procedures of organizations need to be responsive to this. In undertaking work-based learning we need to be able to develop approaches that facilitate the empowerment of services users.

In taking account of the social model of disability practitioners need to be aware of disability issues and of the factors that create institutional discrimination. This means being aware of the attitudes and behaviour of others and ourselves and the wider structural reasons for the exclusion and marginalization of disabled people. The disability rights movement is a social movement that campaigns for the rights of people and it is this political action that can break down the underlying reasons of disabling barriers.

But as practitioners it is important to be aware of how practice may reinforce disabling barriers. It is important to use our professional power in a way that promotes people's rights and does not reflect the disabling barriers that people face. The social model of disability is inclusive and relates to all people who face disabling barriers (Goodley 2004).

ACTIVITY

Empowering practice

From your practice or placement you may have been involved with what is regarded as empowering practice.

This exercise enables you to explore your practice within a framework of values and empowerment, so you need to be familiar with the content of Chapter 6. You will also need to refer to the policies of the organization and how they promote service user rights and equality.

Find and explore your organization's mission statement and policies regarding the services it provides. You may need to access these through your agency's internal website and electronic resources.

Evaluate the organization's policy by referring to the social model of disability, the promotion of rights and implications of human rights legislation, the development of advocacy services and normalization.

You could ask yourself:

- Does the policy promote service user control of services?
- What is the attitude expressed by the policies towards the people who receive services?
- Are the policies that you have found accessible to people who use the services provided by the organization?

- Are service users regarded as passive recipients of a service or are they fully involved in organizational policy and practice as equal human beings?
- What model of empowerment do you think is promoted by the organization?
- Does the organization truly empower service users?
- How does your practice fit in with organizational policy?
- Can you be a morally active practitioner?

It becomes important to reflect on your role as a social and health care practitioner by looking at the wider social context of the work you are doing, the moral and ethical base of your work and your guiding moral and ethical principles. It is important to ask yourself if your practice is empowering practice.

Being morally active and having moral courage

Husband (1995) points out that as practitioners we need to take moral responsibility for our practice and we need to be morally active practitioners and Sarah Banks (2011) argues we need the moral courage to challenge oppressive practice. This means that we should act on the basis of our internal values and as an autonomous moral agent. To do this successfully requires practitioners to be able to reflect upon their values and moral principles and what they believe in when working with service users. It becomes important to understand and recognize the values and moral principles that underpin our practice and this is explored further in Chapter 6.

Summary

This chapter has explored how work-based learning is an essential part of your learning on your Foundation Degree and we have emphasized the practical arrangements you need to consider to ensure your practice placement provides you with the practice opportunities you need so that it is a successful learning experience.

We have covered various approaches to reflection on practice and you should be able to use the framework presented here to develop a structured approach to reflection which will enable you to make the most of work-based learning for yourself and to the placement itself.

By using the reflective models we have outlined and the framework for reflection you should be able not only to develop your knowledge and skills but also to develop your ability to engage with your practice. It is important to take into account the notions of praxis and being morally active for your continual personal and professional development.

By reflecting on your role within the workplace you should be able to develop an empowering approach to your practice and make a meaningful and positive difference to people's lives.

Conclusion

The aim of this chapter has been to help you explore aspects of skills that will support you as you undertake work placement in a health and social care context, but also as you progress in your studies and career. We hope the activities and discussion have promoted some analysis that enhances your awareness of the political, philosophical and organizational contexts for skills and professional development. Reflecting on the potential range of skills required for effective professional practice promotes a critical evaluation of thoughts, feelings and actions and their impact on others. The dimension of analysing how our actions affect others is particularly important in the health and social care arena. Learning journals are a medium for self-reflection and deeper learning, encouraging us to take responsibility for our personal and professional development. Action planning can provide a meaningful way in which to specify our strengths and targets for such development and we hope you trial some of the suggested formats to find ways that work well for you. Finally, we feel that the essence of some of the key points in this chapter are captured by Confucius, who said:

By three methods we may learn wisdom:

First, by reflection, which is the noblest

Second, by imitation, which is the easiest

Third, by experience, which is the bitterest.

Further reading

There is a very limited (though growing) literature available on work-based learning. On a more philosophical level the excellent and extensive materials on the Infed website are highly recommended. The address is www.infed.org.uk

On reflective practice see:

Schön, D. (1983) *The Reflective Practitioner: How Professionals Think in Action*. London: Basic Books. This is an accessible introduction.

Fraser, S. and Matthews, S. (2008) *The Critical Practitioner in Social Work and Health Care*. London: Sage/OU.

Fook, J. (2012) *Social Work: A Critical Approach to Practice*, 2nd edn. London: Sage. This book draws on ideas about critical reflection to explore postmodernism, critical theory, critical reflection and contextuality. It is relevant to a range of professions in health and social care.

3

Understanding Evidence and Information: Becoming Research Aware

Graham Brotherton

Summary Chapter Contents

- Sources of information
- Finding research and information
- Evidence-based practice
- Approaches to research
- Research techniques
- Ethics of research

Learning objectives

By the end of this chapter, you should be able to:

- Identify a range of sources where health and social care information and research can be found.
- Evaluate published research in terms of its methodological appropriateness.

(Continued)

(Continued)

- Understand the idea of evidence-based practice in health and social care.
- Discuss ethical issues related to health and social care research.

Sources of information

In this section we will be considering how to find the information that you need in order to study effectively. There are a range of sources of information available to you, whether you are at work, in your college or university, or at home. The problem now is not so much how to find relevant information but how to work out which information is the most useful to you. In this chapter we will look at some of the sources available to you and how to access them. We will also consider how to look critically at sources in order to judge the usefulness of what you find.

Workplace information

There are two sources of information within the workplace that are likely to be particularly helpful to you: policies and procedures, and the 'trade press'.

Policies and procedures are central to work in health and social care. They provide a framework for practice within any organization, but they are also much more than this: they provide a way of looking at a broad range of issues. Policies in many areas are the practical application of government and 'company' policy and as such they also reflect broader social values and attitudes. Evaluating organizational policies can give us considerable insight into these underpinning values and the way in which they influence the development of practice. The way in which policy at all levels is made is considered more fully in Chapter 7.

ACTIVITY

Look at the module structure for your particular programme and at the range of in-house policies your organization has. Try to identify which policies may be useful to you at different stages on the course. If your setting is part of a larger organization try to find out if there are policies with which you are not familiar (your manager/mentor/training officer might be able to help you locate appropriate policies).

Understanding policies

The policies and procedures that exist in your organization do not exist in isolation; they are influenced by a range of external factors. As you identify the key policies for your organization try to find out what has influenced them. Some key factors might include:

- Legislation, e.g. to comply with the National Health Service and Community Care Act 1990 or the Children Act 2004 or the codes of practice associated with legislation, such as the Special Educational Needs Code of Practice (Department for Education and Skills 2001).
- Current views of good practice in terms of working with particular groups.
- Organizational values, e.g. the provision of services in a faith-based context.
- Financial or other resource constraints.

Each of these issues is explored more fully in the chapters in Section Two of this book.

The 'trade press'

Every sector has a range of magazines and websites which are produced specifically for it. Within the health and social care sector there are a range of publications aimed at the sector in general or specific parts of it. These provide a very effective way of keeping up to date with current debates and issues. Among the most widely available are *Community Care* and the *Health Service Journal*. In addition there are magazines aimed at those working with particular groups, e.g. *Children and Young People Now* and *Mental Health Today*. The great advantage of the 'trade' press is that it is current, practice-focused and usually produced in an accessible writing style. However, for higher education courses there are some limitations: articles are often fairly brief and make limited reference to research, they are usually written by professionals or others with a particular interest, and may not always give a full or objective overview of the issues. This is not to say that the trade press is not an important resource, but that it is important to use it as one of a range of sources.

It is also important to note that the 'broadsheet' general press also offers extensive coverage of health and social care issues. Of particular relevance is the Society supplement which is part of the *Guardian* newspaper on a Wednesday, which is an invaluable source of material (and contains a lot of relevant jobs!). It is worth making sure that at a fairly early stage you have a look at the range of 'trade' titles and broadsheets available in your setting and college/university library and try to identify which titles might be useful to you. You might also wish to purchase a broadsheet newspaper; student discounts are often available.

Using email updates

Many of the journals, newspapers and organizations referred to in this section offer the opportunity to subscribe to regular email-based updates, which are usually free.

These can be a very efficient way of staying up to date with current issues. One example is the *Guardian* Society briefing, details of which can be found on the paper's website.

Online resources

Before moving on to consider many of the valuable resources available online it is worth reminding you about the excellent and fairly comprehensive glossary of key health and social care terms available at the Centre for Policy on Ageing website (www.cpa.org.uk). We will first consider the range of general online resources and then move on to the more specialized area of academic journals.

Online tutorials

If you are unfamiliar with looking for resources online (or if you want to make your searching more efficient) a useful place to start is the virtual training suite. This contains a range of subject-specific tutorials on finding the right resources online aimed at higher education students. They can be found at www.vtstutorials.co.uk/. There is a tutorial for Health and Social Care but you might also find the Allied Health and Social Work/Social Policy tutorials useful.

Government websites

Government websites provide probably the most comprehensive resource in terms of legislation, policy, research and practice guidance. However, the sheer size of some of the departmental websites can make information hard to find. One way of dealing with this is to use the 'public face' of the government websites, www.direct.gov.uk. However, not all information is available from here and it is sometimes more useful to go into the departmental websites at the Department of Health (health and adult social care) www.dh.gov.uk, Department for Education for most children's services (www.dfe.gov.uk) or the Ministry of Justice for criminal-justice-related information (www.justice.gov.uk). All of these websites have research sections containing details of government-funded research.

Research and policy organizations

There are a wide range of organizations which play a role on developing or influencing policy and practice. Those listed below are just a sample:

- Joseph Rowntree Foundation: www.jrf.org.uk. One of the largest independent social research organizations with an emphasis on health and social care research.

The 'findings' section provides excellent summaries of all the research that the foundation has commissioned.

- Sainsbury Centre for Mental Health: www.scmh.org.uk. This provides access to a range of research on mental health issues, plus a lot of other useful material on these issues.
- The King's Fund: www.kingsfund.org.uk. This is a large health-related research and policy organization.

'Think-tanks' are independent organizations with an emphasis on trying to influence policy. They are a useful source of information on current debates and thinking. There are think-tanks that operate from a variety of political perspectives and again this is only a sample (a full list can be found at www.policylibrary.com. Some of those with an active interest in health and social care policy include:

- Civitas: www.civitas.org.uk. A right-of-centre free market think-tank.
- Centre for Policy Studies: www.cps.org.uk. Another right-of-centre free market think-tank.
- Institute for Public Policy Research: www.ippr.org.uk. A centre–left think-tank.
- Demos: www.demos.co.uk. Another centre/centre–left think-tank.
- Compass: www.compassonline.org.uk. A left-of-centre think-tank.

(The terms 'free market' and 'left' and 'right' are defined in Chapter 7.)

Specialist organizations

There is a range of organizations that produce information relating to particular groups from both 'user' and 'professional' perspectives. The following are just a sample:

- Mind: www.mind.org.uk. A superb resource on mental health issues; in particular the fact sheets and briefings within the information section provide an excellent source of policy and practice information related to mental health.
- The Mental Health Foundation: www.mentalhealth.org.uk. Again, a large and well-organized resource with a broad range of relevant information.
- Foundation for People with Learning Disabilities: www.learningdisabilities.org.uk. This foundation has a large and easy-to-use site with lots of useful information about learning disabilities.
- Mencap: www.mencap.org.uk. A good range of resources, especially in the publications section. Also includes some good examples of material designed to be accessible to people with a learning disability.
- Age Concern: www.ageconcern.org.uk. Another large and easy-to-use website with a focus on older people's issues.
- Barnardo's: www.barnardos.org.uk. A range of resources for those working with children and families.

In looking at any of the materials described in this section it is important to bear in mind the need to read 'critically', which means thinking about the strengths and limitations of any source. It is not always easy to separate 'research' from 'policy' or even opinion and almost all of the documents you will look at are written from a particular perspective or value position. Practical ways of assessing information are discussed in the reading research section below. Before considering how to 'look at' research, though, we need to look at why research is so central to good practice in health and social care.

Finding published research

As suggested above, being able to read, evaluate and where appropriate recognize the practical implications of research is an important element of your studies. In order to do this, though, you need to be able to track down appropriate sources. This section looks at how to do this.

Many of the sources outlined at the start of this chapter are useful here, though in most cases they will provide only summaries of research. In addition, there are a number of more explicitly research-focused sources. The first of these is refereed journals, which are often considered to be the 'gold standard' in that every article that is published has been read and evaluated by experts in the field and articles therefore represent a current contribution to knowledge in the specific area as judged by those currently researching the area. It does need to be pointed out, however, that not all articles published in refereed journals are actually research reports and that some journals only publish work undertaken in particular ways, e.g. qualitative or quantitative research.

There is a wide range of journals available and they can be accessed in three main ways. Firstly, directly from your college or university library – the library is likely to have a list of the journals that are taken. Secondly, it is often possible to access journals online; again access varies between institutions and your library should be able to provide you with a list of the journals you can access. Thirdly, you can often obtain copies of articles through interlibrary loan, though there is sometimes a charge for this; again your library will advise on the way things work in your institution.

It is also possible in some cases to access the journals kept by other higher education institutions and there are particular schemes that enable you to do this (see www.sconul.ac.uk for details). In order to make effective use of journal material, it is advisable to become familiar with the use of databases. Once again, some of these are subscription-based, so you will need to check which ones you have access to.

Using databases

Databases are collections of referenced material usually put together by librarians. Each one works slightly differently and you have to 'get inside the heads' of the people that put them together, in the sense of working out how material is categorized. The following tips can help with this:

- Keep a record of search terms used in each database and whether they generate data: so, for example, you might find that the term 'learning disability' works well in one database but in another you may have to use 'learning difficulty' or even in the case of some international databases, 'mental handicap'. Over time you begin to build up a picture of which terms work best in particular databases.
- Try to think creatively. You may, as illustrated above, have to think of a number of variations on a search term before you find much material. Using a thesaurus can be very helpful here.
- Become familiar with Boolean searching. This is a way of refining searches which helps you to find precisely the material you want. Most academic databases (and some Web search engines) support Boolean searching, which is based around using key words or symbols to broaden or narrow searching (see Box).
- Keep a record of what worked in particular databases – it saves time for future searches.

Boolean searching

To give some examples: AND (Boolean words are always written in capitals) or the + symbol are used to combine terms, so 'mental health AND care' would include everything which includes both terms. NOT (or –) excludes specific terms, so 'care NOT mental health' would bring up material about care that does not refer to mental health. OR enables you to search for more than one term, e.g. 'learning difficulties OR learning disabilities'. Most databases have a help section which gives advice on using Boolean searching.

Your university or college librarians are also likely to be able to help.

Examples of useful databases

A freely available database can be found on the Social Care Online website at www. scie-socialcareonline.org.uk/. This is very much a social-care-focused database (as well as a range of other resources), which provides a very useful topic-based index, making it easy to search, though it may take a few attempts to work out what sort of information can be found in each topic category.

There are a range of useful databases that cover different aspects of health and social care. As an example you may well have access to Web of Knowledge (wok. mimas.ac.uk), but to access this you will need an 'Athens' password. Your library should be able to provide you with this. This is a massive database and you are likely to find the Social Science Citation Index the most useful section. As with all databases, it can take a while to get used to. See tips on using databases above.

Systematic reviews

Systematic reviews are an attempt to pull together all existing research/knowledge on a particular topic or issue. Some adherents of evidence-based practice consider them to be the 'gold standard' in terms of evidence to support practice. Systematic reviews attempt to identify, synthesize and analyse all of the literature on a particular topic and are based on the use of explicit criteria. In this way it is argued that they reduce the potential problem of conscious or unconscious bias. They emerged from quantitative research approaches and there are those who argue that they are not always as appropriate or as easy to utilize when qualitative studies are involved; this debate is considered more fully later in this chapter. Nonetheless they do provide a useful starting point for taking stock of the evidence in relation to a particular area (assuming you can find one that is relevant to your interests). A useful way of at least beginning to search is to type systematic review into the search box on the front page of Social Care Online (the address is given above in the section on databases). It has been argued that systematic reviews are essential to improve the evidence base of social care and in the development of best practice guidelines. While this view can be challenged on methodological grounds, it is important for practitioners to be aware of this increasingly important debate. A range of health-related reviews (though some also have significant social care content) and some very useful material, though primarily from the United States, can be found on the Campbell Collaboration website, www.campbellcollaboration.org/.

Evidence-based practice

Gomm and Davies (2000) point out that government policy and professional guidance are increasingly calling for practice to be 'evidence-based'. There is a need to justify the decisions that practitioners make that affect people's lives. This includes the need to develop an awareness of the scope and limitations of research through the use of critical appraisal skills.

This leads us to a consideration of what can be considered as evidence. Whilst there are those who would argue that only certain types of research are appropriate for basing practice upon, e.g. the use of randomized control trials, or methods that approximate to this and seek to apply 'scientific' rigour, it is not the intention to make this argument here. The suggestion here is that good practice evolves in a number of ways, but central to this is learning both from direct evaluations of practice and from more general research that is relevant to the setting or user group we are working with. Evidence-based practice is not simply about being able to make direct comparisons, but about having an awareness of and a mind open to changing views of good practice balanced with a healthy scepticism about whether these really stem from evidence. It therefore overlaps with ideas about reflective or reflexive practice (see Chapter 2).

What do we mean by evidence-based practice?

Evidence-based practice is about choosing the options that are most likely to lead to a good outcome for the people we work with. Or, to put it another way, using an evidence-based approach to practice will increase the likelihood that successful outcomes will occur (Centre for Evidence Based Social Services 2004).

In other words, an evidence-based approach claims to be:

- Systematic – it attempts to be aware of the research which is around and how this is relevant to practice.
- Open – it attempts to look at evidence openly and assess the strengths and weaknesses on the basis of the 'case' that is made.
- Empowering – it enables service users to receive currently accepted 'good practice' in partnership with staff who are themselves able constructively to challenge practice.
- As such it is based on the effective use of research to support practice and requires practitioners to be able to find and evaluate research and policy/guidance.

There is, however, a debate about the nature of and limitations of evidence-based practice and the arguments for and against, which cannot be explored in full here. Nonetheless it is important to be clear that we see 'evidence' in the broadest sense and are not seeking to privilege the claims made by 'scientifically' gathered evidence.

Reading critically

With the increasing influence of evidence-based practice it is increasingly important for practitioners to be able to read and evaluate published research or articles evaluating published research. Research is undertaken by a variety of agencies and for a variety of reasons, so it is vital to be able to assess the strengths and weaknesses of the claims made by research. There are a number of useful questions that can form a basis for evaluating research (and other academic writing):

- Who wrote this? Is the research being undertaken by an individual/organization that has particular expertise in the area? Has it been undertaken by someone approaching the research from a particular political/ideological/professional perspective?
- Why? Is it promoting a particular approach (or even a good or service)?
- For what reason? Is it making a claim for resources? Is it 'pure' research (if it is possible to do pure research)?
- When? How recent is the material? Has policy or practice changed since the research was undertaken/ or the material was written?
- Where was the research carried out? Does the social/cultural context of the research enable it to be used appropriately in the context you are thinking of using it, e.g. can American research always be easily applied to the UK context?

- Who was involved?
- Where is the research being reported? Is the research in a refereed journal? If not, is it being summarized? Can you be confident that the summary gives a clear overall picture?
- Was the method appropriate to justify the claims being made? (This is discussed more fully in the next section.) Does it seem to you that the method used would give the sort of findings/information being presented?
- How convinced are you by the evidence? What is your 'gut feeling' about the research? Why do you think this is?
- Being a critical reader is something you have to work on by being an active rather than a passive reader, as described in Chapter 1. The link between critical reading and practice is explored further in the next section.

Gathering information directly

As suggested previously, there is an increasing emphasis in health and social care practice on the need for evidence to support good practice. This happens on at least two levels: firstly as an element of quality assurance and inspection systems and secondly as a way of developing good practices. It is this second level that will be the focus of this chapter, though it must be made clear that there is of course considerable overlap between the two levels.

ACTIVITY

Think of the way in which information about the service you provide is collected.

- Who collects it?
- How is it collected?
- How is it used?
- Would you describe this as research? Why or why not?

We gather information in a variety of ways, e.g. as part of the assessment and care planning process and of monitoring its implementation, through satisfaction surveys and other forms of user feedback, as well as in putting together information for inspection and informally through conversations with colleagues and service users. In doing this we are often seeking to evaluate the appropriateness and effectiveness of what we are doing. In this section we will be considering how we can make these judgements on the basis of evidence and some of the problems in deciding what constitutes 'good' evidence.

   In order to gather evidence in a systematic and reliable way, we become involved in a process of research. For something to be called research we often think of its being gathered in a formal way and usually in order to address some pre-set question or problem (though this definition is not without its limitations). 'Experts', often from the academic community, are often called upon to undertake research of this kind. There is, though, a tradition within the health and social care community (and in related areas such as education) of research undertaken by practitioners in order to address workplace problems, usually referred to as action research, and this chapter will include a discussion of both approaches. In addition, as stated previously we often gather information for other purposes but do so in a systematic way and use it for 'official' purposes, e.g. an audit. We do need therefore to be aware of the strengths and limitations of the various approaches to gathering 'data'. In this section 'data' will be used to refer to anything gathered in a structured way, whether this is qualitative or quantitative information.

Qualitative versus quantitative approaches

There are broadly two approaches to social research, which stem from different approaches to how we can obtain and interpret information. Quantitative research, sometimes (and perhaps over-simply) called 'scientific' research, is concerned with obtaining measurable data, often for the purposes of comparison or statistical analysis. Its focus is upon obtaining 'factual' information in an objective and value-free way, which can then be used to develop models that can be tested in subsequent research in order to check their robustness. The basis of this approach is a set of ideas usually referred to as positivism, which suggest that true knowledge can only be obtained by scientific approaches and that research should focus upon that which can be directly observed. This can be contrasted with qualitative approaches, which are concerned with attitude and perception. They are concerned with how people make sense of the world around them and are less concerned with notions of neutrality and objectivity, highlighting that all researchers have preconceptions and values that will influence their approach. There is not time here to develop the arguments about the philosophical foundations of research, but there are a number of excellent introductory research books available, which are listed in the further reading section.

In recent years in health and social care research there has been a move towards using 'mixed methods', which often combines elements of both qualitative and quantitative research. One of the justifications for this is the idea of triangulation. This suggests that by using a variety of methods it is possible to check whether there is correspondence between the different sorts of data being collected and thereby gain a fuller picture, thus increasing the validity of the research. It has to be noted, though, that triangulation between methods is complex in practice and that great caution needs to be exercised when attempting to use triangulation to make more general claims for any piece of research.

Two terms that you will often come across in research are 'reliability' and 'validity' and it may be useful to define them here. Reliability is concerned with whether the results would be replicated by using the same instrument/approach in the same circumstances. Validity is concerned with whether the research can be said to be presenting an accurate picture of the area being researched. Both terms are subject to some debate and are somewhat problematic in practice, especially in relation to qualitative data. (At a very simple level, can research about opinion or perception ever be truly reliable or valid? But does that mean it is not important to carry out this sort of research?) However, they remain important concepts that need to be considered fully in research design, reporting and evaluation.

The key issue is that when undertaking any form of research, no matter how informal, it is crucial to be aware of the strengths and limitations of any chosen approach and the implications that this has both for the nature of any findings and for any conclusions that can be drawn. Some research will inevitably be more tentative, especially if dealing with, for example, complex issues of practice, or issues around service users' attitudes or perceptions. This does not mean that these are not areas worthy of investigation just that care needs to be taken in the way they are interpreted.

Within the context of all research it is important to note that a central consideration is that of appropriateness: it is not that one research method is right and another is wrong, but that different approaches generate differing kinds of information. The judgement of research needs therefore has to be based on a consideration of whether the research was of the 'right' kind to generate the sort of information that would answer the questions the researcher was asking.

You want to investigate the 'satisfaction' of service users with the services you offer. What would be the advantages and disadvantages of using: (a) questionnaires; (b) interviews? (Assume for the purpose of this exercise that your service users would be able to contribute effectively using either approach.)

Comment: It depends. Questionnaires (see next section) are easy to administer and easy to collate but in most cases give you only superficial information. For example, on a form produced by one health organization patients were asked whether they were not satisfied, satisfied or very satisfied with the service they had received. How can we judge how people distinguished between the latter two categories, and does it really matter, given that both indicate satisfaction?

However, if we want in-depth information, talking to people at length about their experiences is likely to generate much richer information, but information that is harder to collate in a simple form. Gathering information in this way is also much more time-consuming.

As suggested previously, the key question here is appropriateness: why are we gathering information? What do we want to use it for? If we are simply monitoring ongoing satisfaction at a particular setting or with a particular service, then it may be that a questionnaire is the most appropriate. However, if we want to reform or develop services it may be more useful to gather information through interviews.

Techniques of research in health and social care

Action research

As referred to previously, a particular approach that has been widely used in health, care and educational settings is action research. Action research has been defined as 'a form of research carried out by practitioners into their own practices' (Smith 1996/2001; citing Kemmis and Carr 1986). It is therefore explicitly work-related and linked to notions of developing good practice. The full process of action research is: to identify a work-related problem or issue, gather information about the problem or issue, identify collaboratively a strategy for 'solving' the problem or issue and then to implement and monitor the strategy. Where appropriate, this can prove to be the starting point for another cycle of action research. In practice many action research projects (especially those undertaken as student projects) only go as far as identifying issues that can subsequently be used as a basis for developing/improving practice. It can of course be argued that this is not genuinely action research, though it does provide an introduction to the approach. A good summary of approaches to and some of the problems with action research can be found through www.infed.org.

Before looking at particular techniques it is important to point out that these are different to approaches. Particular techniques may be used within either of the broad philosophical approaches outlined earlier; for example, a survey (see below) could be either qualitative or quantitative in approach depending upon the way in which it is designed (or even contain elements of both). It is therefore crucial that any research instrument is designed in such a way that the researcher is clear about what kind of data is being collected as this obviously has significant implications for how any data should be analysed.

Particular techniques of data collection will now be briefly outlined.

Surveys

Surveys are pieces of research that attempt to look at a representative sample of a particular 'population'. This can mean a specific population, e.g. the patients of a hospital, the users of a day service or the population as a whole. Because many populations are too large to involve everyone, in most cases a sample is used. Samples can be either *representative*, i.e. designed to reflect the population as a whole, or *opportunistic*, i.e. assembled from those who are available to the researcher. Samples become important if we are claiming that the research gives an accurate picture of the whole population we are seeking to research. This can be genuinely claimed only if we can demonstrate that our sample was of the representative kind. There are various ways of doing this and where this is likely to be an issue you are strongly advised to read a more specialized text. There is a very good introduction to the issues in Robson (2011). It is of course impor-tant to point out that being representative in this general sense may not be important for small workplace-based projects as by definition these are perhaps better considered as case studies.

Interviews

Interviews are widely used in health and social care research, but there can of course be difficulties in using them with those groups of service users who may find it more difficult to articulate their thoughts, though multiple communication systems, e.g. speech plus some form of physical or symbolic communication, have been used to try to minimize the impact of this. While interviews offer a valuable research tool, there are several important factors that need to be considered. Firstly, issues of design. There are three broad types of interview: structured, where set questions are used; semi-structured, where a loose list of questions/prompts are used as a basis for a conversation; and unstructured, where there are no pre-set questions or prompts. Each has advantages and disadvantages:

- Structured interviews are easy to compare and collate afterwards, but can be stilted to do and may lead to important information not being collected if any area is omitted from the schedule. They are also highly researcher-led.
- Unstructured interviews have the opposite problems. They are much more likely to lead to rich information, but they are difficult to collate and difficult (if not impossible) to do for inexperienced (and possibly most other!) researchers.
- Semi-structured interviews offer a methodological compromise, with a loose structure to provide researchers with a framework, but also the opportunity to let the interview flow into a variety of areas. They do still pose problems of comparability and collation.

Observations

Observations have been widely used in research with young children, but have a useful role to play in health and social care research. Again there are two broad categories:

- Unstructured observations, in which an attempt is made to capture as much information as possible about the whole of a situation.
- Structured observations, in which a decision is taken in advance to focus primarily on a particular range of features or issues, using some form of schedule or checklist.

As with interviews, there are advantages and disadvantages to both techniques. Structured techniques (assuming they are undertaken appropriately) give a clear picture of a limited range of activity. Unstructured techniques give a fuller picture but run the risk of missing key details in trying to gain a broad picture; similar issues also apply in terms of collating and analysing data to those described for interviews above.

Questionnaires

Questionnaires are a widely used technique that enables a large amount of data to be gathered reasonably efficiently. There are, though, both practical and methodological problems. The main practical problem is response rates. Questionnaires are notoriously difficult to achieve good response rates on, especially if they are administered indirectly. Postal questionnaires are particularly difficult to get returned and if you intend to use them, this needs to be built into the way in which any research is designed. Unless you have some way of ensuring a higher return rate it may be wise to plan around a response rate of around one-third for any form of questionnaire.

On a broader level particular attention needs to be paid to how questions are designed; there is no opportunity to ask for clarification or to develop points afterwards, so questionnaires are a 'one-shot' approach. It is important then to think carefully about wording. Bell (2005) includes a chapter that gives a clear and comprehensive guide to the practicalities of questionnaire research. The issue of sampling is particularly important in questionnaire research, especially if you wish to make any general claims based on your results.

Life story or narrative research

Life story or narrative research has been used very effectively, especially in social care research. This is a fairly specialized technique that often uses repeat interviews plus documentary research or photographs with a view to building up a picture of someone's personal history. It can be useful for understanding how and why people come to be users of care services and is also claimed by some people to have direct therapeutic benefits. This is an under-utilized approach but requires very careful planning and careful consideration of its appropriateness in terms of working with particular individuals or groups.

Case study research

Case studies are pieces of research that look in depth at a specific 'case', sometimes for an individual or group of people and sometimes for a specific setting, e.g. a residential home or a social work office. The purpose of case study research is to examine a particular 'instance' in a lot of detail. As a result it is always difficult to generalize from case study research, though its strength is that it gives insight into one situation that may be transferable into others. Case studies can also give useful 'pointers' for possible research into similar settings. When using case studies it is important to ensure that you are clear about the 'boundaries' of a case (i.e. are you researching all of a setting or a particular subset, e.g. a 'ward', 'unit' or particular group of people who use the service, as this again has implications for data analysis?). Case studies are not in themselves a research technique so data collection will need to utilize one or more of the other methods as described in this section.

Comparative research

Another commonly used approach is to compare aspects of practice within health and social care settings as a way of emphasizing similarities and differences and possible explanations of factors that influence this. This often takes the form of case studies of more than one setting. It is an approach which is potentially extremely useful but needs careful planning in terms of ensuring that the chosen 'cases' allow for meaningful comparison and discussion.

Documentary analysis

Most agencies in the health and social care sector produce a range of internal documents. These vary from policy documents to internal reports and position papers (see Chapter 7). They provide a very useful resource in terms of undertaking research, but need to be used carefully. The key questions for reading research later in this chapter can provide a framework for doing this. There is also a very helpful chapter in Denscombe (2007), the full reference for which can be found in the section on further reading.

The ethics of research in health and social care settings

A key issue in all health and social care research is that of ethics. In some senses research ethics should be a straightforward issue in an area where there is a constant emphasis on the concept of ethical practice. If something can be considered good practice in health and social care terms, it is likely to be an ethical approach in research terms. Ethics can be defined in a number of ways, which are discussed more fully in Chapter 6. One useful checklist for looking at ethical issues in the research context is presented in the box here:

Ethical issues checklist

Informed consent: Are all participants aware of the purpose of the research and what their own role within it will be?

Openness and honesty: Is the research being conducted in a transparent manner? That is, are all participants able to find out how their contribution 'fits' into the bigger picture and if appropriate to challenge any assumptions made?

Protection from harm: What steps have been taken to ensure that participants are not harmed by participation, e.g. by being exposed to inappropriate questions?

The right to withdraw: Are all participants clear that they do not have to take part and that if they do decide to withdraw from the research that data relating to them will be removed from the research?

Confidentiality: What steps have been taken to ensure that all data is stored and used in a way which does not allow the identification of any of the agencies or individuals involved?

Debriefing: Are all participants able to access copies of findings etc. if they wish to?

Compliance with institutional and professional codes of practice: Many health and care agencies have organizational codes of practice and may in some cases require that any research undertaken complies with these. Have you taken appropriate action to investigate and if necessary comply with these?

'Doing' research

As a teacher supervising research projects at a variety of levels over a number of years, by far the commonest problem that I have encountered is a lack of clarity about what is being researched. Crucial to any piece of research in the workplace or elsewhere is being clear about what you are trying to find out. It is therefore vital to have a research question or questions that fulfil two central criteria:

- It/they must be precise in terms of what you are seeking to investigate.
- It must be possible actually to answer the question/s through the research and using the chosen methods (sometimes referred to as 'operationalization').

Think back to the activity earlier in this chapter. Imagine you want to investigate how satisfied a group of older people are with the home care that they receive. How could you 'operationalize' this?

While there are clearly a number of ways in which this could be approached, the central issue is how do we make sense of 'satisfaction', as this could mean a number of different things? For example, for one person this might simply mean how well the various tasks that they require assistance with are undertaken, for someone else the key feature may be the quality of the interaction with the home carer, and for others it may be a balance between the two or indeed a range of other factors, e.g. how flexible the worker is etc.

None of these could be said to be 'right' or 'wrong' definitions of satisfaction but any piece of research needs to be clear about which single or multiple definition(s) of 'satisfaction' it is using and the consequences that this might have in terms of both the design and ultimate usefulness of the research.

ACTIVITY

Involving service users in research

As practice in health and social care has changed to take greater account of the views of service users, there has also been increasing interest in involving service users in all stages of the research process as active participants and partners rather than as passive subjects. Obviously the issues involved will vary from group to group and there are considerable differences in the issues around working with, for example, young children as opposed to mental health service users. A number of organizations have developed ethical codes which specifically address the issues of service user involvement (e.g. the Social Research Association, www.the-sra.org.uk). While there may be some ethical and practical issues that do need to be addressed, the arguments for involving those who use services are so strong in terms of good practice that there is an urgent need for more research of this type.

Summary

This chapter has considered the key area of finding and using information and research. In attempting to summarize such a broad range of information a couple of key points are worth highlighting. Firstly, there are a range of useful sources which are easily accessible to you in the workplace and elsewhere but it is important to read critically: do not take research or other writing at face value but try to think about factors such as perspective and appropriateness of method as discussed in this chapter. Secondly, it is important to recognize the increasing importance of evidence-based practice, but once again to engage with this in a positive but critical way.

Review questions?

- What is meant by evidence-based practice in health and social care?
- What are the main approaches and techniques of social research and what are the strengths and weaknesses of each?
- Where should you look to find relevant research for your course or setting?

Further reading

Bell, J. (2005) *Doing Your Research Project: A Guide for First-time Researchers in Education*, 4th edn. Buckingham: Open University Press. Though education-focused, this is an accessible introduction with an invaluable chapter on questionnaires.

Blaxter, L. et al. (2010) *How to Research*. Maidenhead: Open University Press. A clear and accessible introduction to research for first-time researchers.

Bryman, A. (2008) *Social Research Methods*. Oxford: Oxford University Press. Contains a more detailed discussion of the issues.

Denscombe, M. (2007) *The Good Research Guide*. Maidenhead: Open University Press. Another clear and helpful text – especially in terms of the practicalities of research.

Gomm, R. and Davies, C. (eds) (2000) *Using Evidence in Health and Social Care*. London: Sage. Gives a clear overview of the evidence-based practice debate.

Robson, C. (2011) *Real World Research*. London: Blackwell. Another accessible and helpful text.

Section Two

Key Issues

4

The Social Context of Health and Social Care

Robert Mears

Summary Chapter Contents

- UK government expenditure on health and social care and the 'mixed economy of care'
- The challenges to medicine from critics
- Health inequalities
- Acute and chronic illness
- Stigma
- Future social and cultural change and the challenges posed to the relationships between health and social care professionals

Learning objectives

By the end of this chapter, you should be able to:

- Understand what is meant by the 'social context' of health and the ways in which health and social care must be seen in its social context.
- See how sociological theory and evidence help to clarify some of the dominant issues in health and social care.
- Describe some of the contested areas in health and social care and be able to contribute to these debates.

Introduction

Wherever health and social care work takes place – in a hospital, hospice, residential institution or in the home – it is important to understand that beyond a particular encounter there is always a wider social context. This 'social context' can include the wider social determinants of health, prevailing epidemiological trends and the characteristics of the groups delivering and receiving care. What happens in health and social care takes place in a context that embraces social values and attitudes, economic decisions, political priorities and cultural beliefs. 'Caring' is usually a meeting between people who are likely to differ in terms of age, ethnic group, social class, religious affiliation, economic power and so on. Critically, it will also involve relationships between people with varying levels of dependence and independence. The challenge of this chapter is to set the 'caring' relationship in this wider social context.

The connections between the 'individual' and the 'social' were explored by the American sociologist C. Wright Mills. He argued that the sociological imagination involved the ability to make connections between individual troubles and broader social processes. This way of thinking is not typical because, 'In Western industrial societies the ethic of individualism has led to a concentration on the position and activities of the individual and to individualistic explanations. People have not perceived the regularities in the patterns of social behaviour but only the individual differences' (Hurd 1974: 6). This chapter introduces the idea that many aspects of health and social care can best be explained when we understand more about these prevailing patterns. Care does not take place in a vacuum but is shaped by social, cultural, political and economic factors.

A starting point is some grasp of the sheer scale of national and local government expenditure on health and social care. In 2011–12 total UK government public spending was over £690 billion. This is over £11,500 for every man, woman and child in the country and health and social care and social protection takes up nearly half of this. Around £121 billion is allocated to the NHS and other welfare spending is around £110 billion split roughly equally between central and local government spending. (HM Treasury 2012). It is obvious that such significant sums cannot be allocated without a wider debate about value for money, affordability, entitlement and what economists refer to as 'opportunity costs' – how those resources might have been spent differently to get better results. So, 'formal' health and social care is usually paid for by governments and delivered by state employees. State expenditure is often supplemented by private spending and contributions made by voluntary agencies and charities. It is usual for care to be delivered by a mixture of the public, private and voluntary sectors, and what family, friends and neighbours provide informally. The particular balance between 'formal' and 'informal' provision is always a matter of policy debate and is likely to shift over time for particular individuals and will depend, partly, on what kinds of political choices are made by the wider society. Government policy determines not just how much is spent but how it is spent and there is always likely to be controversy about the allocation of scarce resources. Government policies also shape decisions about the most appropriate location for the delivery of care – home or institution.

It is useful to make this distinction between the formal system of care provided by doctors, nurses, social workers, therapists, etc., who provide a paid professional service, and the informal care, advice and support provided by friends, neighbours and family members, so-called lay care. For most of human history lay care was all that was available. It is only in the last century or so in rich countries that the balance of care has shifted in the direction of state provided 'formal' health and social care. It is important for professionals to understand the changing balance between professional and lay care and the ways in which these are related. There is also a growing possibility of conflict between formal and informal carers. Lay people and professionals may have different (incompatible) beliefs about what is the best course of action and they may have different opinions of the role of the person cared for in decision making.

'Choice' implies priorities and this means politics. Professionals in health and social care may think of politics as little to do with their work. The word usually conjures up images of political parties and voting, and the decisions taken and policies adopted by councillors, MPs and governments. For social scientists, politics means the study of the distribution of power between and among individuals or groups. Power is an inevitable feature of all social relationships whether that is between two people in a marriage through to the relations between powerful nation-states. In this sense there are power relations between parents and children, carers and the cared for, professionals and lay people. Max Weber argued that 'power can emerge from social relations in a drawing room as well as in the market, from the rostrum of a lecture hall as well as the command post of a regiment, from an erotic or charitable relationship as well as from scholarly discussion or athletics' (Weber, cited in O'Donnell 1987: 512).

Politics can also refer to the value system that underpins our actions. It refers to the whole cluster of ideas that characterize what people think and feel we 'ought' to do. This raises important questions of duty, obligation and the 'appropriate' ways of responding to social problems or social need. Politics also encompasses the ideological options we choose. For example, once we say that something ought to be done, or there ought to be more spent on a particular problem, group or social issue, we reveal our ideological choices. In the world of health and social care this can cover a wide range of questions – who pays for services, who 'ought' to deliver them, and what is the balance between, say, care in an institution and home care.

Choose an area of health and social care with which you are familiar and identify the mix of provision in this area.

Consider whether this area of health and social care is currently a political/institutional priority - is the provision diminishing, stable or increasing?

Consider how it has been/is being shaped by economic, cultural and other factors.

ACTIVITY

To grasp the scale of demand, present and future, on formal and informal health carers, we need to understand the patterns of fertility and mortality that shape the demography of a society. The likely demand for care, at either end of the life cycle, is affected by the age structure of the population and the relative balance of old and young people. The UK, in common with most wealthy countries, has experienced a falling fertility rate and a falling mortality rate. This gives us the distinctive feature of an ageing population with, in the UK, more people over 60 than under 16. This has triggered widespread debate about the costs and other consequences of an ageing society with economists and social policy analysts articulating concerns about the 'dependency ratio'. This refers to the relationship between the economically active and the 'dependent' population of the elderly, the sick and disabled, children, students and people at home caring for others. In policy circles this is a pressing issue, as witnessed by disputes about state retirement pensions and the viability of other welfare payments.

Making sense of 'care'

Because of an ageing population and the rise of chronic illness, more people are involved in paid and unpaid care of others than in the past. In addition to around 2 million employees of the NHS and social services, around 5 million people were providing care in England. The burden of care has far-reaching effects. According to the 2009/10 Survey of Carers in Households, nearly a third of carers in England report feeling stressed and a quarter have disturbed sleep. One in three state that they are left tired from caring and just over one in five say they are short-tempered or irritable due to their duties. Meanwhile three in five anticipate the amount of time they spend caring will increase in the next five years. Two in five say caring responsibilities affect their personal relationships, social life or leisure time. Of those affected, nearly seven in 10 say they had less time for leisure activities, nearly a third say they are too tired to go out and just under a quarter are unable to go on holiday. Just over a quarter of carers of working age say caring affects their ability to take up or stay in employment. Less than one in five of all carers were aware of the right to request flexible working hours. Just over a quarter have been caring for the same person for at least 10 years and just under one in 10 have been caring for more than 20 years. NHS Information Centre Chief Executive Tim Straughan commented, 'Although most carers seem happy with their quality of life, there are a number of issues affecting them day to day; from their general health to the ability to go out with friends or take time out for a holiday. The survey also shows many people have spent longer than a decade acting as a carer, while a substantial number anticipate that the time they spend caring will increase in years to come' (NHS Information Centre 2010). Unsurprisingly, a greater proportion of women than men were carers, both in the population as a whole and in age groups up to 64 years. The men who 'care' are very likely to be caring for wives, while women are caring for husbands, children, parents and others.

'Care' is a deceptively simple word. What could be easier to understand and explain? Yet it elicits a host of different and sometimes incompatible emotions. It can be carried out for love, duty, payment, guilt or some other sense of obligation. In reality more than one of these feelings can co-exist. The different meanings of the word have been carefully analysed by Carol Thomas. She deconstructs care into seven dimensions covering:

- identity of carer;
- identity of cared for;
- the interpersonal relationship between them;
- the nature of the care;
- the social domain (private/domestic);
- the economic relationship;
- and the institutional setting, e.g. home, residential setting, hospital, nursery, etc. (Thomas 1993)

Prevalence of caring

According to the Office of National Statistics, in 2009/10, 12 per cent of people aged 16 or over in England were looking after or giving special help to a sick, disabled or elderly person. This is around 5 million adults. Half of these were caring for someone who was living with them, and the other half were caring for someone living elsewhere. Around 3 million households in England have a carer. Around half (46%) of carers were in paid employment, 27 per cent were retired from paid work and 13 per cent were looking after their home or family. Around two in five carers (37%) were the only support for the cared for person, while the remainder reported shared caring responsibilities. This means that around 1.7 million adults in England were the sole carer for their main cared for person; 48 per cent provided care for 20 or more hours per week. Carers with such heavy commitments had a different profile to those who were caring for fewer hours per week; they were more likely to be aged 65 or over (30% compared with 20%) and less likely to be in full-time employment (17% compared with 35%). Overall, 62 per cent of carers felt their own general health was good, while fewer than one in 10 (8%) felt their health was bad. In comparison with the Health Survey for England (2008), carers were considerably less likely to describe their general health as good (62% compared to 76%), though this reflects, in part, the older age profile of carers. Among 50- to 64-year-olds, a greater proportion of women than men provide unpaid care, and a higher proportion provide intensive care (50 or more hours a week). The majority of older people continue to live in the community well into later life. Even when we look at the data for people aged over 90, around three-quarters were living in private households (Office for National Statistics website). One measure of domestic support for people is the amount of home care provided by local authorities. The number of hours purchased or provided by councils in England has increased significantly over the past two decades. In 1994 it was 2.2 million hours a week but by 2008 this had risen to an estimated 4.1 million hours provided to around 328,600 households (340,600 people). This represents a 5 per cent increase in the number of contact hours since the 2007 figure of 3.9 million. The average number of contact hours per household was 12.4, compared to 11.6 in 2007 and the majority (81%) was provided by the independent sector. It seems as if more intensive services are being provided for a smaller number of service users, continuing the trend seen over the last 10 years. In 2008, the annual expenditure on home care services was £2.7 billion. While the overall number of hours supplied has increased, the number of households receiving council-funded home care services has fallen consistently since 1994. This suggests that councils are providing more intensive services for a smaller number of households ('Community Care Statistics 2008', 'Home Care Services for adults, England', Health and Social Care Information Centre, March 2009, accessed ONS website May 2012).

Reasons for undertaking caring responsibilities

Carers were asked an unprompted question to establish why they started looking after or giving special help to their main cared for person. Some of the (multiple) reasons mentioned indicated that, for some, there was little or no choice in becoming a carer: It was expected of me (54%); He/she wouldn't want anyone else caring for them (15%); No one else (was) available (12%). However, around half of carers did make the decision to undertake these responsibilities as 53 per cent said they were 'willing or wanted to help out' (NHS Information Centre 2010).

ACTIVITY

Take an example of 'caring' and analyse it using the seven dimensions outlined by Carol Thomas.
    Think of examples of the last time you carried out the care of another. What was the dominant motive for doing it? What emotions did it elicit?

Medicalization

For much of the twentieth century the actions of health and social care professionals were usually seen in a positive light. Doctors and nurses in particular tended to be rated highly in any survey of public opinion, and the value of their work was such that they enjoyed high levels of esteem. Indeed health services were generally seen as a 'good thing' and the public seemed to want higher levels of spending. Academic critics took a much more sceptical approach about the role of medicine in prolonging life and promoting health. Firstly, it was argued by McKeown (1976) that the contribution of medicine in conquering infectious disease and prolonging life has been exaggerated. He analysed falling death rates in England and Wales for infectious diseases after 1870 and claimed this had much more to do with improvements in nutrition, housing, sanitation and town and city planning (such as rubbish collection and clean air) and family limitation. Medical discoveries and treatments were insignificant because they were ineffective, harmful or appear when the death rates are already in decline. Other critics complained about a growing disillusion with medicine because of the escalating costs of health services with disappointing returns from investment in medical cures and treatments (Abel-Smith 1996). Research showed that medical interventions were of limited benefit and that for many treatments there was little evidence of their effectiveness (Cochrane 1972). In 2006 Professor Ian Roberts claimed that many emergency treatments for trauma in hospital A&E departments were of dubious benefit. He was quoted in a newspaper report saying that treatments had not been properly evaluated: 'If you have an injury you will be exposed to treatments that we really don't know whether they will do more harm than good.' After decades of use there was little or no hard evidence for the treatments' effectiveness. In 2004 Roberts published a study in *The Lancet* exposing the dangers of corticosteroids, used to reduce brain inflammation. Rather than improving the patients' condition it actually increased their chances of dying. *The Lancet* report estimated that 10,000 people had been killed worldwide by the treatment in the 1980s and before. It is now rarely used in the UK (*Guardian*, 7 September 2006).

In addition, the long-term, chronic 'diseases of affluence' turned out to be difficult to cure. The consequences of high-technology medicine also came to be seen in a more negative light and the doctor–patient relationship was seen as beset with problems. Even more radical was the claim that the medical profession was guilty of extending its power into areas of human life that should not concern it, and that many medical interventions were harmful, either because they led to further complications (such as drug side effects) or because they weakened the ability of people to manage their own lives (Illich 1976). The critics argued that medical professionals claimed jurisdiction over wider areas of human life. Matters that might once have been the responsibility of priests, teachers, social workers or philosophers come to be seen as 'medical'. This starts a process of labelling something as a 'disease' and developing treatments that are managed and controlled by doctors. The critics argued that this made people unnecessarily dependent on the medical profession. For example, medical professionals dominated debates about adolescent sexuality, control of contraception and access to abortion, when these are ethical issues. So-called 'natural' conditions such as childbirth, adolescence, ageing and death gradually became medicalized so that medical solutions become dominant. In recent times, childhood behaviour, sexual dysfunction, unhappiness, obesity and even shyness have become 'medicalized', with associated medical diagnosis, therapies and drug regimes. For Illich and other critics, this had the deleterious consequences of strengthening the power of the professionals at the expense of the ability of lay people to control their own bodies and their lives.

What is incontrovertible is the ever-rising demand for more health services. Most measures show a rise in demand for GP and hospital services of every kind. In England, for instance, the number of prescriptions issued by the NHS (excluding hospital prescriptions) has increased from an average of eight per person in 1989 to 12.5 in 2002 – an increase of 56 per cent. This is 'more than one prescription per month on average for every year of a person's life' (Busfield 2006: 297). Busfield claims that the pharmaceutical industry, in alliance with medicine,

> is shaping the ways in which society responds to a very broad range of problems. It is contributing to an extension of the territory of medical problems and the tendency to respond to problems by pill taking as if the problem will be solved by magic. This response often fails to grapple with the sources of these problems ... drugs provide an individualized solution to problems that often have social or structural origins, which are not tackled by pharmaceutical remedies. (2006: 310)

The critics of the growth of modern medicine claim, then, that we invest more of our resources into health care, demand more consultations, more treatments and more drugs without evidence of any real improvements in human health or happiness.

ACTIVITY

Give two examples of behaviour that has become medicalized in recent times.
   Are we becoming over-dependent on medical services?
   What are the alternatives to 'medicalization'?
   Are there drawbacks in turning everyday troubles into 'health problems'?

Health inequalities

There is a long history of research that shows the link between socio-economic position and health measured in life expectancy and sickness. The assumption of much of this work is that people who share a common economic position, with similar sources of wealth and power, will have similar life-chances. This view of 'life-chances' sees a person's health status as a sign of their past social position and, 'through the structured nature of social processes, as liable to selective accumulation of future advantage or disadvantage' (Blane, cited in Nettleton 2006: 186). In other words, lifelong inequalities impact on the chances of being ill and dying young or old. Although the class structure is in flux, there is robust research evidence that establishes a strong and enduring link between socio-economic status and disease. Ever since data has been recorded on death certificates it was clear that occupation is linked to life expectancy. In the UK people in the lowest social class (5) can expect, on average, to live around nine years fewer than those in social class 1, the professional and managerial occupations. There are also marked inequalities of gender, region and minority ethnic group. Low socio-economic status is linked with 14 of the major cause-of-death categories in the International Classification of Diseases as well as many major psychological disorders. One of the most experienced researchers into health inequalities in the UK, Professor Richard Marmot, has chaired a review of strategies to address health inequalities. The final report, 'Fair Society Healthy Lives', was published in 2010 and Marmot commented:

> We have a highly valued NHS and the overall health of the population in this country has improved greatly over the past 50 years. Yet in the wealthiest part of London, one ward in Kensington and Chelsea, a man can expect to live to 88 years, while a few kilometres away in Tottenham Green, one of the capital's poorer wards, male life expectancy is 71. Dramatic health inequalities are still a dominant feature of health in England across all regions. (p. 29)

The Report concluded that,

> People with higher socioeconomic position in society have a greater array of life chances and more opportunities to lead a flourishing life. They also have better health. The two are linked: the more favoured people are, socially and economically, the better their health ... Consider one measure of social position: education. People with university degrees have better health and longer lives than those without. For people aged 30 and above, if everyone without a degree had their death rate reduced to that of people with degrees, there would be 202,000 fewer premature deaths **each year**. (2010: 29)

Establishing that health inequalities exist does not tell us what causes them or what, if anything, could or should be done about them. Competing explanations include so-called structural and cultural explanations (Mears 1992).

Structural explanations emphasize the material advantages and disadvantages of different socio-economic groups. The unequal distribution of resources – money, property, power, knowledge, status, etc. – is replicated in the distribution of health. One of the reasons for such persistent associations between economic position and ill-health is the fact that access to resources helps people avoid risks to health or to minimize the consequences of disease once it occurs.

Cultural explanations concentrate on the beliefs and behaviours of different groups, so-called 'lifestyle' factors.

There are also differences in people's access to what sociologists call 'social capital'. The American sociologist Robert Putnam defines it thus: 'social capital refers to connections among individuals – social networks and the norms of reciprocity and trustworthiness that arise from them' (Putnam 2000: 19). The degree of social support enjoyed by people and the extent and quality of their social networks are seen as critical in understanding health status and coping with the consequences of disease. This idea of the beneficial health effects of strong social networks has generated a great deal of research recently. It has been shown that the extent and quality of social relationships – how strongly we are bonded to others – can have powerful influences on physical and mental health. According to Chris Yuill, 'Social capital has established itself as one of the most pre-eminent concepts in health and social policy' (Yuill et al. 2010: 67).

It may challenge 'common sense', but there is widespread agreement among researchers that expenditure on health services makes very little difference in terms of health outcomes. According to a recent review of the international data, 'beyond a certain threshold of expenditure, long since surpassed by most industrialized countries, one would be hard-pressed to conclude that spending more on health care leads to better health for a population' (Lewis et al. 2000: 510). Many of those concerned with health inequalities have argued that the most effective steps that could be taken to prevent ill-health would probably not involve medical expertise at all because the determinants of ill-health are rooted in economic and social structure.

ACTIVITY

Take some time to reflect on the following questions:

- Why should health inequalities concern health and social care professionals?
- What explanations for health inequalities are more persuasive?
- What measures do you suggest might be taken to address these inequalities?
- Is this a matter for central government only?

There are also debates about the extent to which social class inequalities of health are narrowing or getting worse, and why it matters. It has been argued that they matter for three reasons. Firstly, how long we live and how sick we are is the ultimate measure of wider trends in socio-economic inequality. 'The size of our car or the desirability of our house and the number and type of exotic holidays are all a consequence of socio-economic inequalities. But none are as potent as life and death' (Carr-Hill 1987: 87). Secondly, health inequalities provide a guide as to how effective health and social welfare services are. The persistence of such inequalities is a negative commentary on decades of 'free' health care and a welfare state. A third reason is to guide policy decisions so that we have a better idea of where to direct resources so they have maximum impact. Blaxter argues that inequalities at the start of life may be particularly controversial: 'It would appear that we have some feeling that that variability becomes inevitable with time, but at least there "ought" to be as much equality as possible at the start of life' (Blaxter 2004: 5).

Bartley (2003) gathers a wide range of evidence that shows how health is affected by socio-economic status, gender and ethnicity, but that stressful life events of a social nature (e.g. the death of a loved one, loss of a job, or being a victim of crime) are implicated. The impact of such stressful life events can be mediated by the level of social support enjoyed by people, but it is clear that there are marked differences in the levels of social support enjoyed by different groups. It is often claimed that men and women, for example, can draw on different types of social support and 'having social support is generally associated with better health – but appears to be more important in shaping women's health' (Payne 2006: 53).

Women and health

The improvements in life expectancy in the twentieth century have impacted on men and women differently. In the UK, life expectancy is higher for women than for men. In 2001 female life expectancy at birth was 80.4 years compared with 75.7 years for men. Although this seems like good news for women, the gap between men and women is smaller in terms of the number of years they can expect to live in good health, and women consistently report slightly higher rates of limiting and long-standing illnesses than men. In addition, 'Women of all ages report more use of GP and outpatient health services ... and women report higher levels of psychiatric morbidity' (Baggott 2004: 25). As well as obvious biological differences between men and women which account for gender differences in health, sociological research has focused on material factors (levels of pay and pensions etc.) and social roles and relationships. The gender gap in terms of ageing and care is marked with, currently, more older, disabled women, and many are reduced to poverty in later life (Arber and Cooper 2000). A key difference – and an example of 'social context' – is that generational changes may be very important. Older women are less likely to have had a lifelong career and less likely to have enjoyed further or higher education. Just a couple of generations ago women were a tiny minority in many of the better paid and more prestigious professions. The relative poverty of older women today is partly, then, a consequence of lifelong exclusion from careers that makes them much more likely to be dependent on benefits and state pensions.

The dominant picture of men's and women's health has been that men die earlier but women are sicker! Researchers are now a little sceptical about this simplistic claim. According to Payne:

> this conventional wisdom has been challenged by research which suggests that variations in patterns of ill-health between men and women are rather more complex. Studies exploring the health of men and women have reported a narrower gap than before, with little evidence that women suffer more health problems overall during their lives. (2006: 9)

The changing social roles of men and women also impact on mortality levels and morbidity rates. Social and cultural changes have an impact on lifestyles. As younger women have enjoyed greater economic independence and cultural freedom, consumption of alcohol and tobacco has increased and women are more likely to suffer from eating disorders. So some social and cultural changes may confront women with greater health risks.

Typically, men are more likely to engage in risky behaviour, which sees higher rates of death and injury from suicide, accidents and crime. So there are 'risk factors' and 'protective factors' that impact on the health of men and women (Brown and Harris 1978). For example, research has suggested that women have stronger social networks than men and can, more easily, rely on contact with close friends and relatives in times of crisis and stress. Marriage may provide a major source of social support, but in a differential way for men and women and across societies. In terms of social support, marriage may be good for men but less so for women. Men tend to rely more on their wives for social support and a confiding relationship, with divorced and widowed men reporting particularly poor health (Payne 2006).

Make a list of risks and protective factors that may impact differently on men and women.

What examples of social and cultural change may impact on the health of women.

What do you understand by 'social support' and how might it differ in the lives of men and women?

In the domestic setting of the home there may be disputes about power and the control and management of resources. Pahl showed in a number of studies in the 1990s that in households where men managed and controlled money there were serious consequences for women and children in terms of access to money to spend on food, leisure, clothing, etc. (Pahl 1990). Her research showed that women and children were most disadvantaged when men controlled and managed household income. In the poorest households, where women had control of money, more was spent on children and on food. In households with male control and management, more was spent on alcohol and male leisure pursuits. Where women's life expectancy is lower than men's it is usually associated with much lower social and economic status. Arber and Thomas (2001) provide a thorough review of the gender inequalities in mortality across different countries. They cite research that shows that excess female mortality is found in countries where women's social status is very low. They write: 'Women's lack of power and influence in the home, and lack of access to valued resources of food, opportunities for leisure, income, may have adverse health consequences' (Arber and Thomas 2001: 61). International studies show that where women's life expectancy is on a par with men's they are also more likely to be involved in politics, the labour market, and enjoy generally higher levels of economic independence. The national and international variations in morbidity and mortality rates between men and women are a powerful insight into the importance of 'social context' on heath. Despite obvious biological differences, the impact of structural and cultural factors is critical in explaining women's health and the variations between men and women.

Gender and 'emotion work'

In most countries the majority of providers of health and social care are women. This is not an accident but reflects deeply held beliefs and prejudices about the nature of men's and women's personalities, and the most appropriate work for each of them to do. Traditionally, caring roles have been seen as an extension of the 'natural' roles of women. It is they who have usually had major responsibility for the care of children, old people and the sick. Such beliefs are being challenged with the advent of greater equality between men and women.

An obvious example is the changing pattern of paid work in the UK and other countries (Gallie et al. 2001). For example, not only are there many more women in paid work, but they are no longer confined only to 'women's jobs'. More men are entering nursing and the majority of medical students in the UK are now women. Health and social care involves a great deal of what has come to be called 'emotional' labour. The term was coined by Hochschild in her study of the working lives of American flight attendants (Hochschild 1983). They were required not just to show people to their seats, instruct passengers in safety procedures and serve food and drink. A key part of the job was dealing with the anxieties of passengers while portraying a smiling and confident exterior. They were required to manage their emotions in order to display something they did not necessarily feel.

Social scientists have pointed out that women undertake the bulk of emotional labour in families. Examples of such 'emotion work' include planning household routines, patching up quarrels, arranging family events, remembering birthdays and special occasions, negotiating conflicts, etc. In other words, the domestic work undertaken by women does not just entail physical labour such as housework, but also includes emotional labour. It is obvious that the concept of 'emotional labour' has a great deal of usefulness in understanding the work of provision of health and social care professionals. The delivery of care is not a mechanical process. It involves dealing with people's bodies and their feelings. This may elicit a range of emotions from pity to disgust, fear and sadness. All these emotions must be managed in the encounters between patients, clients and carers.

If you share your household with others, think of examples of emotional labour being carried out and by whom.

   When did you last carry out 'emotion work'?

   Are there changes occurring in the amount or type of 'emotion work' being done by men?

   Think of examples of how it may be more acceptable for men to display emotion.

ACTIVITY

From acute to chronic illness

A striking feature of health patterns in rich countries is growing life expectancy for all groups. With this comes the inevitable rise of chronic as opposed to acute illness. Acute illness typically has rapid onset, a fairly predictable course and a clear resolution (death or cure!). Chronic illness on the other hand is more likely to have a slow and insidious onset, sometimes surrounded by uncertainty about diagnosis, prognosis and outcome. The role of professionals is more likely to be about ameliorating the condition and helping to manage its effects. The rise of chronic illness and disability is the dominant characteristic of health care in all industrialized countries. It is obvious that getting a diagnosis of diabetes as opposed to sustaining a leg fracture will have far greater consequences for the person, the professionals who treat them and those who care for them. For the person, a chronic condition might involve a profound and difficult period of adjustment to their new selves. A serious chronic illness involves 'biographical disruption' as many of the expectations people have of their lives and their futures, what they can do in terms of jobs, independence, etc., may have to be rethought and renegotiated. Chronic illness can introduce uncertainty and unpredictability which makes planning all aspects of daily life much more difficult. Chronic and disabling illness may necessitate, therefore, a deep reassessment of oneself as a person (Bury 1982). In learning to live with a chronic illness it may also be necessary for the sick person to develop a degree of expertise in handling both the illness and the drug treatments. It sometimes comes as a shock to people when they realize that early expectations of medical control over their condition must give way to a recognition that some control of drug balancing lies in their hands (Allott and Robb 1998).

One of the consequences of this shift from acute to chronic illness is on relationships between professionals and those they care for. There is a strong possibility that people with chronic conditions become so familiar with their own condition through their daily lived experiences that the traditional model of the passive patient is no longer appropriate. In addition, the promotional activities of self-help groups and/or accessing information on the Internet means that many more chronically sick people become expert in their own conditions. If a condition is relatively rare, and professionals encounter it infrequently, it is even more likely that the patient will know more about prognosis and newly emerging treatments than the professionals he or she encounters. This has been acknowledged in the NHS by the 'expert patient' initiative. The changing power balances between professionals and patients/clients means there is potential for much more conflict as the question of 'who knows best?' comes to the fore.

One writer expresses the challenges of chronic illness thus:

> Chronic illness poses more social, interactional, and existential problems than acute illness because it lasts. However, preconceptions of acute illness permeate ideas about chronic illness and pervade institutional practices for handling it. Through analyzing the experience of chronic illness, we learn what chronically ill people's actions mean, when and how they come into conflict with practitioners, and what it means to face loss and reconstruction of self. (Charmaz 1999: 277)

This author reminds us that the pain, distress and adverse effects of medical procedures cause suffering, but if we concentrate only on physical discomfort we ignore the broader suffering experienced by people who must come to terms with the loss of self felt by many persons with chronic illness. In other words, a narrowly medicalized view of suffering might overlook the challenge of coming to terms with a changed self in the context of a society which makes things more difficult than they need be. The disabling effects of wider social expectations are spelt out very clearly by Scambler:

The lives of the chronically ill are sometimes more restricted than they need to be. The world is set up for the healthy and the able, a fact the ill and disabled usually do not question. Hence, they judge themselves and who and what they should be by yardsticks applied to the healthy and able. In that way, they contribute to the restrictiveness of their own lives. (2003: 166)

In a society that is organized around the healthy and the young, being chronically ill can be a dispiriting experience not just because of the physical limitations caused by the illness. Social attitudes add to the negative experience of chronic illness because 'experiences of being discredited, embarrassed, ignored and otherwise devalued also contribute to the growing isolation of ill individuals and to their subsequent reappraisals of self' (Scambler 2003: 169).

Sociologists have also pointed out that we live in an era when the physical appearance of the body has assumed greater significance than ever before for our sense of identity: 'Contemporary society's emphasis on the body makes it a location where much of selfhood is grounded. This emphasis makes it difficult for individuals to dissociate identity from corporeal experience and physical appearance, even when that appearance is flawed' (Gimlin 2002: 72). If our sense of self and identity is more and more tied up with bodily appearance, it is obvious that physical decline, disability and visible deviations from the 'perfect body' will impact on how we see ourselves and others see us. In Western culture conditions that impact on the physicality of the body can lead to negative self-image. This is not invariably the case but there are factors that make it more likely: negative reactions from the outside world, lack of control of bodily functions – we live in a culture that places great emphasis and value on bodily control – or if there is a fear of social or sexual rejection.

Seeking help – the problem of stigma

Decisions to seek help or treatment for particular conditions are not always straightforward. These decisions will be made in the context of quite complex calculations that we all make about the likely costs and benefits of making an appointment to see a doctor or other professional. Among the calculations people are likely to engage in are to weigh up the perceived level of severity of the condition, an assessment of risk and culpability and to what extent there is access to informal care. The visibility of the condition, the extent to which symptoms are 'normalized' and the likelihood of its impinging on functional capacity are also important factors in decisions to seek help. The level of social disapproval of a condition, and the fear of stigma, is one reason why some diseases may be under-reported.

Goffman drew attention to the fact that certain human conditions carry with them the danger of stigma. A stigma originally meant a mark or a scar made with a branding iron that marked out a criminal or a slave. This was a clear sign of outsider or deviant status, visible and unambiguous. Nowadays the term is used more widely to describe any condition or status that marks off a person as 'discredited' in some way. Goffman has shown how these forms of deviance pose particular problems for the sufferer. Because certain conditions, such as mental illness, have been seen as deviant and shameful, it is widely regarded as a stigmatized condition. Some diseases such as HIV/AIDS, leprosy, epilepsy or syphilis are surrounded with vague feelings of disgust or embarrassment and the sufferer has to endure the added problem of a sense of shame or guilt.

Erving Goffman, 1922–82

American sociologist and author of *Asylums*, in which he describes the process of institutionalization as a response by patients to the bureaucratic structures imposed on them in total institutions such as mental hospitals, prisons and concentration camps. In 1963 he published *Stigma: Notes on the Management of Spoiled Identity*, which outlines his ideas about the management of stigma. Goffman claims that interpersonal encounters involve performance – hence his use of the term dramaturgical.

The experience of stigma can pose severe barriers to normal social interaction. It can lead to isolation of the individual and discrimination against them and interrupt the extent and nature of their everyday relationships. Stigmatized individuals experience particular problems in their relations with 'normals'. Victims of stigmatized conditions have suffered abuse, isolation and ridicule. Even if there is no evidence of discrimination, people who are 'discredited', to use Goffman's phrase, will try to manage situations that are made tense or awkward because of their conditions. They have the added difficulty of coping with the reactions of others, in addition to managing their own condition. Public reactions to different diseases will vary in terms of their visibility, obtrusiveness and prevailing attitudes. Of course not all conditions are stigmatized, or those that may be are not stigmatized equally. The onset of chronic arthritis in late middle age is unlikely to lead to the imputation of negative characteristics. Public reactions to different diseases will vary in terms of their visibility, obtrusiveness and prevailing attitudes.

ACTIVITY

List three conditions that elicit social disapproval and/or shame and embarrassment.
  How might the stigma of a condition be combated?
  What are the consequences for the patient/client of suffering from a stigmatized condition?
  Think of a condition in which the level of stigma has been reduced in recent times. How has this been achieved?

Even something as common and apparently without stigma as blindness can be seen as a form of deviance. In a classic American study Scott (1969) discovered that the organized socialization of the blind by medical and welfare agencies was so strong that even some who could see a little came to regard themselves as dependent and adopted the blind role.

In his description of cultural stereotyping in the United States, blindness was seen as something that involved docility, helplessness, melancholy and gravity of inner thought. However farfetched or misleading such stereotyping may be, blind people cannot ignore these beliefs in their interaction with others. How did blind people adapt to such cultural stereotyping in the Scott study? There were a range of reactions, from concurring with the dominant view of blindness through to active resistance. Scott also showed how professional interpretations of blindness, and the ways that health and social care workers dealt with blind people, differed across the three countries in which he conducted field work. In the United States the basic goal of the caring professionals was to bring about a therapeutic resolution of the anger of the blind through counselling therapies. The key assumption was the need for the blind to confront and deal with the 'feelings' associated with the loss of their former sighted self. In the UK, at the time of this study there was little effort aimed at therapeutic adjustment. Instead there was an unrelenting cheerfulness in which the professionals saw themselves as combating the melancholy and depression of the blind by always trying to 'keep up their spirits'. In contrast, in Sweden, sight loss was seen as a technical handicap to be addressed by new techniques and aids to daily living. Instead of dealing with the person, effort was directed at changing the external physical environment and training the person with new coping skills. Indeed this approach characterizes much of the Scandinavian approach to disability and handicap.

The value of the Scott study is that it shows how varied the responses to a 'deviant' condition can be. Reactions ranged from those who stubbornly resisted the beliefs of health and welfare professionals, through to those who completely accepted their dependent status. Some blind people absorbed or internalized the dominant definitions of the wider society. If professionals and carers, charity workers and friends and family tended to believe that blind people are dependent then that is what they became. Others were able to insulate part of their self-concept from these views and others were able to adopt deliberately a facade of compliance for reasons of expediency. The 'resisters' challenged the stereotyping but this required considerable reserves of power as one of the consequences of rejecting the allotted role is the charge of ingratitude or even bitterness. In the campaigns over disability rights there have certainly been examples of such reactions.

Future challenges and relations between clients and professionals

The term 'professional' has a long and confusing history. It can simply mean the opposite of amateur – as in sports or music. More often it has come to mean work that differs in some important ways from 'just doing a job'. It is also used in an evaluative or judgemental way – to comment negatively or positively on someone's actions or even as a way of commenting on how people dress or speak. This use of 'professional' is not very helpful. It seems best to stick with a definition that stresses 'expertise' and the extent to which people enjoy a degree of freedom in their work, and are able to control the work of others. At one extreme a production line worker or someone responding to enquiries in a call centre enjoys very little autonomy. What they do and say will be the result of careful training, there will be close monitoring and there is almost no scope for individual decision making.

At the other end of the spectrum are jobs that enjoy a high level of choice and discretion. Typically medicine has enjoyed high status as a profession and historically doctors as an organized professional group have enjoyed high levels of self-regulation, control over their education and training and control over the work of others.

ACTIVITY

Give two examples of occupations that are regarded as 'professions'. Why do they enjoy social prestige?

Give an example of an occupation that is or has been trying to 'professionalize'. What did this involve?

How is it possible to reconcile professional expertise with the wish to involve people in decisions about their care?

Health and social care systems in all rich countries are confronted by a growing 'consumer culture' which has the unintentional effect of eroding traditional deferential approaches to professionals. A generation that endured deprivation and war may be less demanding than a generation brought up during periods of growing affluence and choice. Changing expectations from lay people mean that the scope for tension in the relationship between carers and cared is bound to grow. Certainly doctors have reported much higher levels of dissatisfaction and more conflict in the doctor–patient relationship than in the past. Recent data from the ONS, for example, showed that although around 70 per cent of people were very or quite satisfied with their local NHS doctors or GPs, levels of satisfaction have declined since earlier periods when they were usually around 90 per cent.

Linked to satisfaction is the apparent decline of trust in professionals. A prominent British sociologist has argued that we live in a period in which traditional institutions and authority figures have been undermined (Giddens 1991). Changes in the status order, raised levels of public education and easier access to information via the Internet mean that many lay people are better equipped than in the past to challenge professional knowledge. As a consequence all professional groups feel the pressure of public scepticism, with their views being treated with much less respect than formerly. There are consequences that flow from this – professionals in health and social care cannot treat their clients and patients as supplicants with the expectation of gratitude. The language of rights and entitlements means that the delivery of care is more likely to be negotiated, and the existence of pressure groups covering every condition and illness gives patients/clients access to information and advice that they can utilize in a power struggle with professional carers. At a time when there is greater scepticism about professionals, and less trust in them, there are also important developments in the training and education of staff to enable them to become more 'professional'. The growth of qualifications such as Foundation Degrees for Health and Social Care professionals, which aim to improve the professional practice of health and social care workers, is part of this process. The relentless professionalization of all occupational groups may have benefits in terms of skills, expertise and efficiencies but it can have negative consequences. The complex division of labour in health and social care, with the inevitable involvement of different professionals, each with a specialized task, may mean that care is experienced as fragmented with no one person having a grasp of the whole person. As professionals deal with a part of a person or one part of an issue, and delegate to others, there is a price to be paid by patients. As Bradby points out, 'From a patient's point of view, trying to make sense of an illness, reconstruct a life story and adjust his identity, there are serious disadvantages to this delegation of care and communication: there is a sense of dislocation when a clinic consultation is held with a doctor who did not carry out the surgery or recommend the treatment plan' (Bradby 2009: 194).

How health and social care is funded, organized and delivered in the future is a matter of intense controversy. There will certainly be a very public debate about the relative balance of public and private provision. This underlines a point made at the opening of this chapter that economic, social, ideological and political themes cannot be avoided in future arguments about the funding, organization and delivery of health and social care. The whole policy area of health and social care is much more contested than in the past. Arguments over NHS and social services rationing are likely to rise up the policy agenda. In the case of the NHS, the President of the Royal College of Surgeons has said that he no longer believes a tax-funded NHS, free at the point of delivery, is sustainable and that it should be abandoned in favour of a social insurance model. According to one newspaper report, 'Many doctors will be surprised and disappointed by his stance, but many also see the need for an intelligent debate about what should be affordable within the NHS' (*Observer*, 14 August 2005). Although the NHS enjoys high levels of public support, and political parties are reluctant to question the funding of health care from taxation, there are voices, particularly on the political right, who note the rising demand for health and social care in the UK and claim that it is unlikely that taxation can continue to be the main basis for funding such services. Research has also shown that people have very high expectations of health and social care services. A poll for the Institute for Public Policy Research found a third believed that the NHS should provide 'all drugs and treatments, no matter what the cost' (*Sunday Telegraph*, 3 September 2006). If state services become more difficult to secure, the burden may well fall more squarely on families, and that usually means women.

The study of the social context of health and social care in coming years will involve recognition of the tensions between differing trends in society. On the one hand we have a growing dependent population as people live longer and more people live alone. There is also evidence of people wanting and expecting more from the health and social care sector as well as being discriminating consumers exercising choice. Professionals in the health and social care sector may be keen to 'empower' the people they care for, and this, along with the rise of the expert patient, challenges deeply held notions of professional superiority. Workers in health and social care face a number of critical challenges over coming decades: How much information to share with those they care for and their families? How can 'clients' become involved in their care? What is the appropriate balance between professional and lay knowledge in decisions about therapy? How might rationing and disputes about priorities affect relations between different professionals? There is no simple answer to any of these dilemmas. What is apparent is that the social trends that affect the demand for health and social care – an ageing population, the rise of disability and chronic illness, smaller families, geographic and social mobility – are likely to continue. This occurs at a time when fewer women are prepared to take on uncomplaining the caring role of the past. Add to this a vigorous consumerism in which we are encouraged to see public services as an entitlement, and it is clear that the social relations of health and social care can only become more contested.

Summary

Health and social care consumes a large and growing proportion of state resources, whether in health spending, social services or on benefits and pensions. Although the state is the main provider in the UK, we can distinguish between care provided by the state, the voluntary sector, the private sector and by lay people (families, friends and neighbours). This is usually referred to as the 'mixed economy' of care. When such large numbers of people (and resources) are involved, it is highly likely that decisions about health and social care will involve debates about values, priorities and choices and these are inevitably political. It is also important to differentiate between paid and unpaid care and clarify the different meanings of care. It encompasses a wide variety of relationships and emotions and includes notions of duty, obligation, love, as well as paid care.

Critics of medicine have claimed that the historical benefits of medical interventions have been exaggerated. Some also point out that many treatments and procedures have not been shown to be beneficial. The concept of 'medicalization' was advanced to draw attention to the extension of medical power and the broadening of the scope of medical interventions in our lives. Critics claim that the medical profession has extended its power and control in societies by claiming jurisdiction over wider areas of life and, in the absence of countervailing sources of moral authority, become the arbiters of how we should live and die. Another facet of the medicalization argument concentrates on the ever-rising demand for treatments, therapies and drugs to assuage the ills of modern living. There is ample evidence of escalating demand from the public for more consultations, more therapies – conventional, 'alternative' and 'over-the-counter' – as well as more prescriptions. Some critics see this as evidence of socio-cultural trends towards an individualization of problems that have their roots in social and cultural changes. This rising demand for health intervention may be unrelated to any improvements in life expectancy of quality of life but may tell us something about the ways in which, at a societal level, we approach the problems of human living.

Good health and a long life are not distributed equally through societies. Patterns of morbidity and mortality reveal the impact of social class, gender and ethnicity. Inequalities of health are not fixed but fluctuate according to social factors. Although there is real debate about the causes of these inequalities, most explanations come down in favour of either 'structural' or 'cultural' factors or some mix of the two. Rapid social and cultural change impacts on health. Many of the things that impact upon health status are beyond the influence of health services, health professionals or health managers. Deeply rooted gender differences are also seen when we examine 'emotional labour' and the realization that a great deal of 'emotion work' is done by women in families – and this has obvious relevance for the delivery of health and social care.

Most formal and informal health care in the UK is concerned with managing chronic illness and disability. Because chronic illness is of long-term duration, medical intervention is often about ameliorating symptoms and managing the condition. The consequences of chronic illness can be huge for individuals and their self-identity. It also impacts hugely on their families and friends, and for those who care for them. It has the potential to destabilize traditional relationships between professionals and those they care for, and it calls into question the very basis of 'expert knowledge'. Chronic illness carries with it the threat of stigma. The Greek word stigma meant originally a mark or brand burned onto a body to mark a person as a slave. Since then it has come to mean anything that is seen as discreditable about a person. Social and cultural beliefs about particular conditions may impact upon help-seeking behaviour and certain diseases (such as HIV/AIDS) and other conditions (such as mental illnesses) carry with them a degree of shame and/or embarrassment. Professionals need to be aware both of the wider social and cultural understandings about diseases as well as their own beliefs when dealing with patients and clients.

Health and social care professionals face a number of challenges and dilemmas in the early years of the twenty-first century. Important social and cultural changes are occurring that have the potential to transform the relationships between health and social care professionals and those they care for. The rise of a discourse of 'empowerment', human rights and the championing of the 'expert patient' confront professionals with difficult challenges. These ideas challenge traditional notions of professional power and expertise. This could lead to more conflict in the relationship between professionals and those they care for, especially in the context of rising expectations, the rationing of services and a culture of entitlement and 'consumerism'.

Review questions

- What do we mean by the 'mixed economy' of care?
- Why do health inequalities exist and how might they influence health and social care practice?
- How is the shift from an emphasis on dealing with acute illness to responding to chronic illness affecting health and social care practice?
- Why do health and social care students need an understanding of the concept of medicalization?
- How might an understanding of stigma help us improve practice?

Further reading

Albrecht, G.L., Fitzpatrick, R. and Scrimshaw, S.C. (eds) (2000) *The Handbook of Social Studies in Health and Medicine*. London: Sage. This is a comprehensive collection covering the main areas of the social context of health and social care with each chapter written by an expert summarizing research in areas such as disability, gender, patient satisfaction, medical authority etc.

Baggott, R. (2004) *Health and Health Care in Britain*, 3rd edn. Basingstoke: Palgrave Macmillan. This is a comprehensive and readable account of health care in the UK. It has solid, well-written chapters on the development of services and policy dilemmas in health, but with useful summaries of recent policies on community care and patient involvement.

Ham, Christopher (2009) *Health Policy in Britain*, 6th edn. Basingstoke: Palgrave Macmillan.

This is an outstanding review of policy during one of the most interesting times in the history of the NHS. It is written with a strong sense of 'telling the story' of the NHS, without ignoring the extraordinary complexities of delivering health care to the whole population, free at the point of contact.

Klein, R. (2002) *The New Politics of the NHS: From Creation to Reinvention*, 5th edn. London: Prentice Hall. A classic study of the politics of the NHS since its creation. It is invaluable because it puts into historical context much of the hype around the 'crisis' of the NHS.

Nettleton, S. (2006) *The Sociology of Health and Illness*, 2nd edn. Cambridge: Polity Press. Highly regarded, clearly written sociology textbook in an up-to-date second edition that covers many issues of relevance to health and social care including social inequalities, lay-professional interactions and chronic illness.

Payne, S. (2006) *The Health of Men and Women*. Cambridge: Polity Press. A more advanced summary of the theories and evidence about the differences and similarities in the health of men and women. The book discusses a range of health-related behaviours such as diet, exercise, alcohol, smoking and drug use.

Wainwright, D (ed.) (2008) *A Sociology of Health*. London: Sage. A lively collection of papers covering issues including medicalization, health scares and the 'feminization' of health.

Yuill, Chris, Crinson, Iain and Duncan, Eilidhe (2010) *Key Concepts in Health Studies*. London: Sage. From ageism to public health, gender to obesity, this excellent book covers most of the concepts likely to come up in discussions about the social context of health.

5

Developing a Professional Identity

Graham Brotherton and Gill McGillivray

Learning objectives

In this chapter we will:

- Explore the concept of professional identity for health and social care workers.
- Consider influences on professional identity.
- Look at the implications of professional identity for inter-professional working.

(Continued)

(Continued)

- Examine barriers to developing a professional identity and how this affects role of students on placement or in the work place.
- Reflect on the idea of a professional journey and its continuation after your initial course.

Introduction

This chapter encourages you to take an analytical perspective on aspects of professional development, particularly the notion of a professional identity. It encourages you to be critical of concepts, constructs and influences related to being a 'professional'. The following activity is intended to help you begin to reflect on this.

Consider what, in your view, is needed to become a 'professional' practitioner. Talk to others to explore their views.

You may have identified specific criteria, qualifications, personal qualities or a level of education in your response. Did others offer similar responses? Was the focus on qualifications, or other requirements such as having effective interpersonal or transferable skills? What it means to be a professional practitioner is complex, and the range of responses may have indicated some of the difficulties in its analysis.

Ideas about what it means to be a 'professional' are contested, especially during the period of economic uncertainty and restructuring of health and social care services which are taking place at the time of writing. Many health and social care practitioners are currently required to have a degree or equivalent, such as nurses, social workers, and speech and language therapists, for example. Workforce reform is creating change for some groups of practitioners in terms of the level of education and qualification required of them, and such change can create uncertainty and be unsettling.

Terminology relating to the term 'profession' is confusing itself, even before looking at what it means to be a professional. You may have already encountered the terms 'professionalism', 'professionality', 'professional identity', 'inter-professional' and 'professional' in your learning and work experiences so far. This chapter will focus on professional identity and the next section examines potential influences on its construction. It is intended to allow you to apply these influences to your own work and practice to facilitate an increased awareness of how they can have an impact on your day-to-day professional life.

What is professional identity?

In this chapter we will take professional identity to mean how you perceive yourself as a professional practitioner and how others perceive you and your role. It therefore includes status and the level of 'discretion' granted to particular groups, as well as the values and attitudes that underpin practice and how these are reflected through codes of practice and principles of practice, for example.

Factors that can be considered to influence professional identity include discourses, the language that is used in popular culture (images, language), as by the general public, but also by those in power such as politicians. It also includes historical events and discourses, societal need and demand; structures and hierarchies and expectations within and beyond the workforce, as well as education and training. Our individual life experiences, work history and personal dispositions contribute to professional identity too.

A model that introduces aspects of discourse, among other influences such as ideology, education and training, has been proposed by Tucker (2004: 88, see Figure 5.1). The model proposes specific influences that have a directional impact on professional identities.

Tucker (2004) also proposes that roles, relationships and expectations can create tensions for professional identity. An alternative model might represent 'core' and

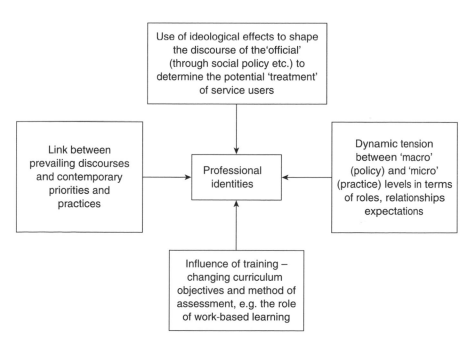

Figure 5.1   Factors involved in the construction of professional identities (adapted from Tucker 2004)

'peripheral' influences on professional identity. Core influences are those that affect the day-to-day lives of workers, having a direct impact on their way of working with clients and colleagues on a daily basis. These could include relationships with clients and colleagues, places of work, pay and conditions, for example. Peripheral influences are those that might seem more distant to workers, but still have an impact on their work. These could include policy, inspection regimes, education and training, and sociological influences. The interplay of core and peripheral influences is explored in more detail in the final section of this chapter.

In the context of interplay between influences, it is useful to consider what the expectations of those who work and learn in the health and social care field are in terms of being or becoming a professional (which will be explored from a theoretical perspective later in this chapter) as well as what the general public expect of those who work in the health and social care sector. Those who work in health and social care undertake a wide range of work roles, each with a particular construct or perspective of what it means to be part of that group of workers. For example, nurses, residential child care workers, those who work in care homes for the elderly, and child care workers, will each have their own sense of what it means to be part of that group of workers. In other words, they will carry a label of child care worker, nurse, physiotherapist, and attribute certain qualities to that label. They will have expectations and constructions of what it means to become a member of that particular workforce.

ACTIVITY

Using work and placement experiences identify some expectations attached to becoming an employee in a specific sector of health and social care work (such as child care, a nurse, or carer for older people) in terms of training, prior experience, personal qualities, for example.
  What impact have such expectations had on your career choices?
  Have you had to make changes to your plans, attitudes and expectations?

Images are powerful in our society, influencing how specific individuals or groups are constructed. Images are portrayed through television, magazines, newspapers, advertising and the Internet, and often perpetuate stereotypes. Images of families, children, young people and people undertaking their work are numerous in such media, and those who work in a health and social care context may reinforce constructs that the workforce is gendered (female), low paid and does not require high levels of education or training. Historically, such images and stereotypes have prevailed and are thus difficult to challenge and change.

Research (Fealy 2004; Gillis 1981; Griffin 1993; Weber and Mitchell 1995) has been undertaken into how images and discourse have influenced constructs of nurses, youth workers and teachers respectively. Images and discourse provide shared understandings for those who have direct contact with nurses, doctors, teachers and youth workers, or those who are considering entering such professions. You may have been influenced in career choices you have made because of such shared or dominant discourse. Weber and Mitchell (1995: 130–1) suggest that popular culture can 'provide a way into ourselves individually and collectively, a stimulus for self-interrogation that can sharpen our professional identities'. There is a need for introspection and a desire to examine our identity on an understanding that it is partly self-determined and partly influenced by others, but never assigned or allocated by others. It is a dynamic and unsettled concept, responding to the external influences outlined above as well as internal dispositions and attitudes.

Other chapters in this book outline models of reflective practice, and it is through such ways of working (by taking time for introspection and reflection) that we can interrogate who we are and who we want to be, thus creating and informing a notion of our professional identity.

Identify some images, such as characters on television, well-known people in the news currently or historically, that perpetuate particular constructs of what it means to be a health and social care practitioner. Consider specifically the individual's appearance, personality, behaviours and attitudes. How helpful are such constructs to the health and social care workforce?

ACTIVITY

Gender, as an aspect of self-identity that impinges on professional identity, perpetuates inequality in health and social care work. The majority of the workforce is female. Figures suggest that 85% of the hospital and community health workforce were women in 2005 (Information Centre 2005), and those who work in child care, or care for the elderly for example, are often low paid (Low Pay Commission 2011). There has been legislation to ensure equality for men and women, but inequality remains for now in terms of women and men being equally represented in all levels of work within the sector as well as women being able to compete equally for senior level posts (Doyall 2005). It has been suggested that in order to progress to higher level posts, women need to adopt male stereotypical attitudes and behaviours (Bogg et al. 2005). Such change indicates the tensions and dynamic forces that you may have to respond to in your professional life and aspirations, particularly if you are female.

Gender constructs, particularly feminine constructs, have certain qualities associated with them that are perceived by society to be desirable when taking on a caring role. Similarly, other personal qualities have associations with health and social care work, and have repercussions for professional identity. Research with practitioners working in residential care with children and young people in England, Denmark and Germany (Petrie et al. 2006) found that staff and managers of homes valued specific personal attributes and qualities in workers. This was more apparent in England, and a particular quality noted was 'the ability to cope with stressful situations' (Petrie et al. 2006: 55). 'Empathy, caring, involved, committed, assertive, thoughtful' (2006: 56) were qualities of the carers noted by the researchers themselves. The researcher in Denmark noted similar attributes: 'calm, involved, reflective' (2006: 56) and thus there has been consensus in this research as to what specific personal qualities might contribute to the professional identity of this group of practitioners. When individuals make decisions about career choices within health and social care, are an implicit set of values and attributes considered as part of the associated role, responsibility and identity?

When you made a decision, if you have already done so, about which aspect of health and social care you chose to specialize in, did you consider whether you understood, and possessed, the attributes required to undertake the role? How much has gender influenced your decisions?

While at work or on placement, how have you reflected on values of professional practice (as separate from the training, education and qualification requirement) that underpin what it means to be a child care worker, a nurse, a carer for older people, for example?

Different areas and roles of work within health and social care have a common goal of seeking better outcomes for service users. It is worth taking time to consider the extent to which common goals, consensus within principles and codes of practice and shared experiences bind groups together and create stronger, more defined professional identities or whether obstacles and change preclude identities having the space and time to be established.

Inter-professional practice and professional identity

Working with other professionals adds another dimension, in addition to the reflections of ourselves and the way we are seen by colleagues and service users. Legislation and policy such as the Children Act 2004, or the Adult Social Care Outcomes Framework (Department of Health 2012a) require those working in any capacity with children, young people or other groups who may need support to have an understanding of inter-professional working and to be able to work effectively with other professionals. For example, The Common Core (DfES 2005) sets out the skills and knowledge required by those working with children and young people, and includes multi-agency working and sharing information. Such ways of working can challenge the professional identity of individual pro-fessions for them to understand the potential contribution they uniquely, as a profession, have to make to inter-agency working for effective outcomes for clients.

Reflect on work experience situations when you have been working alongside other professionals (a team meeting or case conference, for example.) What was expected of you as a health and social care practitioner? Did you, or other health and social care colleagues, have a particular role to play that complemented others? Was there a sense of equitable contribution for all who attended or participated?

Professional identity is inevitably influenced by the norms, behaviours and culture within the professional group. Individuals are initiated into the professional group by adopting the attitudes and behaviours that are considered acceptable by the group. Pietroni (1994) draws on the analogy of tribal behaviours and norms existing within professional groups in the field of health and social care, suggesting that members are expected to conform to maintain membership status (Anning et al. 2006). The behaviours and attitudes of those within vocational groups are a significant aspect of how identities are constructed and sustained, both within such groups and beyond, impinging on peripheral groups and clients (and 'communities of practice', which are considered later in this chapter). Where there are discrepancies in the attitudes and behaviours within inter-professional groups who are required to work together, however, barriers to establishing a professional identity can be created, and some of these are explored in the next section.

Barriers to establishing a professional identity

Sociological barriers such as gender, social and historical constructs, have already been identified. Other barriers arise through relatively contemporary ways of working such as multi-professional partnership within health and social care, and the activity above may have elicited some experiences that illustrate such difficulties. Hudson (2002, cited in Anning et al. 2006) suggests significant barriers to effective multi-professional practice in health and welfare services are professional identity, professional status and professional discretion and accountability. Anning et al. (2006: 72), in their research, found that it was important that 'individual professional identities, related to their specialisms, were acknowledged and retained within team functions'. Times of transition for practitioners are potentially de-stabilizing for their identity. Newly appointed practitioners, practitioners who are undertaking a different role, or who are joining a team for the first time, all require time and support in order to adjust to the professional demands of their new role. A practitioner's title and their role may have multiple connotations to others, including clients, and thus identities can become compromised and muddled. Frost (2005) suggests that workers may have to re-shape their professional identities as a result of working alongside others. Self-assurance can be eroded through such change and adaptation, thus reinforcing the need for support from managers, mentors and supervisors. It is important that identity is not dissipated or eroded by multi-professional working, but that different professionals sustain a complementarity of identities.

Lines of communication, management, accountability and responsibility and status may jointly or separately blur identities. One of the respondents in the research conducted by Anning et al. (2006: 74) talked about those who wear 'tall hats' as a metaphor for practitioners with high status. Anning et al. (2006) concluded that inter-professional working can break down barriers that might have been created by the apparent superior status of some practitioners. The opportunities to work more closely with other professionals can create familiarity and demystify who they are and what they do. However, issues of terminology and jargon, hostility, and different ways of working, remain as barriers to effective multi-professional working and can create confusion for those making transitions into new teams, new work roles and new experiences. Professional identity can be blurred and challenged in such situations.

ACTIVITY

The above points reinforce the importance of effective mentoring or supervision for students and employees alike in order to help people cope with transitions. What are your reflections on how you have been supported through transitional phases in your work experiences? Have issues such as conflicting roles, ways of working and status been discussed, for example?

How have you felt in a student role in the work setting? How included and integrated into teams do you feel you have been and why?

Barriers can emerge from internal as well as external influences (but these are simplistic categories). How we react to discourse, education, colleagues, expectations and experiences, all of which could be considered as external forces, will, to a certain extent, be determined by traits that are inherent to our personality. Our identity as an individual cannot be separated from our professional identity. Kelly (1963) argues that our personality is determined by learning, however. In other words, it is the nature of our prior experiences that determine who we are. He proposes that learning is 'not something that happens to a person on occasion; it is what makes him a person in the first place' (Kelly 1963: 75).The cyclical nature of learning creating the individual reinforces the notion that 'external' forces cannot be extricated from internal constructs. It is beyond the scope of this chapter to debate theories of personality, but our dispositions to be confident, resilient, motivated, enthusiastic, open-minded and good communicators are likely to interact to a significant extent with the range of factors already identified in this chapter that contribute to our professional identity.

Theoretical perspectives on professional identity

Having considered a range of factors that can affect our professional identity we now move on to consider some further theoretical perspectives that contribute to understanding how our identity is formed as a 'professional'. We have already encountered Kelly's personal construct theory (Kelly 1963); other perspectives include those of Goffman (1969) and Lipsky (1980).

ACTIVITY

Try to think about your own identity by exploring what has contributed to making you the person you are now.

Then think about what attracted you to working with people. Have there been key people or experiences that attracted you to a career in health and social care?

Finally, do you have one 'identity' or does your identity change in different contexts? If you are at work, at home or socializing, how aware are you of adopting different behaviours; ways of speaking or ways of interacting with others for example. If you are aware of adapting to contexts, what characterizes you in your professional context?

When we begin to address the issue of identity, as the above activities are intended to do, it becomes apparent that we are talking about a complex set of ideas. Self-identity is influenced by a broad range of factors, psychological, social, cultural and historical, and by the interplay of these factors. Professional identity is no different, so any attempt to analyse professional identity requires us to acknowledge that we are dealing with a dynamic concept rather than a fixed entity.

Another way to explore professional identity is through Goffman (1969: 202), who saw identity as being defined through roles, traditions and expectations. He states: 'Sometimes the traditions of an individual's role will lead him to give a well-designed impression of a particular kind and yet he may be neither consciously nor unconsciously disposed to create such an impression.' An example may help illustrate Goffman's ideas.

Imagine you have undertaken a self-diagnosis for an illness using information from the Web. You then visit the doctor, deliver your diagnosis and state what treatment is needed.

Now explore the role, tradition and expectation of a patient–doctor relationship, by reflecting on what your doctor's reaction might be. Whilst different doctors may respond in different ways, it is highly unlikely the response will be to simply confirm your diagnosis. Why?

How have you acquired such expectations of the role of doctor and patient?

How are other work roles in your place of work, or work experience, defined by such traditions and expectations?

How have these influenced you, your behaviours and attitudes (and thus your identity)?

ACTIVITY

There are expectations about the roles of doctor and patient with a significant two-way implicit, interplay of behaviours. The example illustrates how professional identity is contributed to through training and education; we begin to develop a professional identity through 'modelling' ourselves on the behaviours, attitudes and judgements of other professionals and our interactions with them. Work-based learning is therefore clearly integral to the development of professional identity as it provides us with a supported opportunity to construct such expectations. An alternative perspective on how ways of working influence professional identity is explored in the next section.

Street level bureaucracy

Amongst the implications of Foucault's (1972) conception of power are that the development of professional identity is in many cases linked to the acquisition of power, through the gaining of 'expert' status and the ability to control resources. This is a point highlighted in the work of Michael Lipsky (1980) who analyses the complex position of front-line workers in health, social care, education and related areas (for example housing or benefits staff). Such practitioners are there to implement formal policies and procedures, but the nature of their role, which often involves individual contact in unsupervised contexts, also gives them an element of discretion and autonomy in the way they choose to interpret their role. For Lipsky (1980), this discretion is a 'dilemma' for practitioners, the organizations they work within and for policy makers.

ACTIVITY

If you have been in a work situation when you have been able to make autonomous decisions, using your own discretion, what were the outcomes for you, for your colleagues, for clients?

Were you aware of working within policy guidelines precisely, or were you able to make your own interpretations? Reflect on your response, in terms of why you did, or did not, adhere precisely to policy.

For practitioners the dilemma relates to how to approach practice. The nature of health and social care practice in particular means that much of it takes place unsupervised in private space giving practitioners considerable room to interpret their task in ways that may not reflect those intended by policy makers. In particular Lipsky highlights the way in which the pressures often associated with being a front-line worker in health and social care, for example the pressure to provide services that in reality are scarce resources, can lead to workers responding to service users in routine and stereotypical ways (Hill 2005). Such autonomous work can lead to the creation of a 'micro-culture' which can be at significant variance with formal organizational policies and cultures.

Case study

Simone is a child care worker, employed in a private nursery. She left school at 16, gained employment as an unqualified child carer and, now aged 22, is in her first year of an early years Foundation Degree, studying part time. Simone completed NVQ Level 2 and Level 3 qualifications during her first three years of employment.

There have been numerous changes for Simone in her day-to-day work, such as new day care standards and curriculum frameworks, more emphasis on working with parents and pressure to undertake higher level qualifications.

As part of her Foundation Degree, Simone is reflecting on how her ways of working with children, colleagues, parents and other professionals have changed.

She realizes that, when working in the baby room, she now works with the babies in a very different way compared to when she first started her job. She understands the importance of relationships between carers and babies, as well as the need for space, play and routines. Simone plans carefully for each baby's well-being and development on a daily basis. How she sees herself as a professional has changed with experience, training and education; she is more confident in her work and talking to the babies' parents.

Using the ideas of Goffman (1969), Lipsky (1980) and Tucker (2004), for example, explore how and why Simone's reflective professional journey has taken the trajectory it has.

Are there parallels between Simone's professional learning and yours? How has your programme of study contributed to your professional journey?

Trajectories and progression are significant for the ever-changing notion of professional identity. What would you project for Simone in the future, beyond her current employment?

Supervision, mentoring and management

For management within organizations and for policy makers the 'challenge' is to create a context within which policy is implemented in the way in which it is intended. The consequence of this is a range of approaches that seek to define and prescribe professional practice. We can broadly categorize these approaches into three strands (though there is overlap between them). The strands are supervision, performance management and codification. Each has significance in terms of professional identity. Professional supervision covers a range of activities and can mean different things in different professional contexts, but can be loosely defined as a process of reviewing the effectiveness of particular interventions or cases. Mentoring also takes on a variety of guises in different professions, but for simplicity will be tied in with the notion of supervision here. Supervision creates a context for the discussion and promotion of particular philosophies or approaches which can be interpreted both as a form of peer review by a professional colleague and a policing of the appropriateness of specific ways of working in particular situations and is likely to both create and reinforce particular professional identities.

Performance management can be considered to be the process of defining workload through the allocation of particular roles and activities and the measurement of these through the setting of particular goals and targets. This can be said to shape professional identity through the prioritization of particular aspects of a particular individual or group's role and by attempting to quantify this; for example a target that said '75% of initial assessments of new service users should have been completed within 10 working days' is likely to lead to a particular focus on the completion (but perhaps not the quality) of initial assessment – perhaps to the detriment of other areas of professional activity.

Codification sets out guidelines for practice in the form of either standards such as National Occupational Standards or in specific framework guidance, for example 'Transparency in Outcomes: A Framework for Quality in Adult Social Care' (Department of Health 2011) or 'The Common Core of Skills and Knowledge for the Children's Workforce' (Department for Education and Skills, 2005), described previously. A second form of codification is the development of more general codes of practice to govern professional practice such as the General Social Care Council Code of Practice for Social Workers or the Nursing and Midwifery Council's Code of Professional Conduct.

ACTIVITY

Think about your experiences in a work setting, and how supervision, mentoring, performance management and codification have affected your professional development and your sense of professional identity.

Look at the documents outlined previously and at codes of practice on the Skills for Care (www.skillsforcare.org.uk) and Nursing and Midwifery Council (www.nmc-uk.org) websites.

How might they influence you development as a practitioner?

Communities of practice

A way of making sense of professional identity which has gained considerable popularity in recent years is the idea of communities of practice, as developed by Lave and Wenger (1991). This model has particular relevance to work-based learning and Foundation Degrees as it emphasizes the continuous process of informal learning that takes place between people who work together. Identity is developed through an ongoing process of interaction and is partly negotiated and partly created by context. Communities of practice are not necessarily the same in particular settings but they do require that 'members' have regular interaction. Wenger (1998) suggests that communities of practice have three dimensions:

- Joint enterprise – a shared sense of 'purpose' about the community and why it exists.
- Mutual engagement – interaction that makes the community a shared reality for its 'members'.
- Shared repertoire – a range of routines, approaches, understandings etc. which are shared by participants.

For Lave and Wenger (1991) the key to understanding learning is not about the knowledge required to undertake a work role, but about the relationship between forms of knowledge and their application in particular contexts. In this model, learning is acquired through a process of participation, which requires us to move from 'legitimate peripheral participation', where we are learning through being on the fringes of a particular community and where new practitioners have a greater licence to observe, ask questions and explore explicitly the 'dimensions' of particular communities of practice, through to a more central position in the community of practice, where we have picked up the 'rules' of the particular community and are able to fully engage with it.

A person's intentions to learn and the meaning of learning are configured through the process of becoming a full participant in a socio-cultural practice. This social process includes, indeed it subsumes, the learning of knowledgeable skills (Lave and Wenger 1991: 29, cited by Smith 2003).

It is important to note that this is not simply a process of experiential learning, though it clearly has an experiential element. It is described by Lave and Wenger (1991) as 'situated learning', learning that can only meaningfully take place in the context of a community of practice. The assumptions made in the model are open to challenge, and critics have highlighted that the notion of communities of practice is somewhat idealized and fails to address issues of power. Furthermore the move from periphery to centre is perceived to occur without internal barriers (which exist, in reality) and may not take account of interpersonal factors.

Do you perceive yourself as part of any 'communities of practice' both within particular settings and perhaps as part of a multi-agency or inter-professional team?

How useful is Lave and Wenger's model (1991) in helping you to make sense of your work experiences?

ACTIVITY

The model of communities of practice can usefully be developed by linking it to the ideas of Pierre Bourdieu (Bourdieu and Passeron 1990). In this particular context, it is Bourdieu's ideas about 'habitus' and 'field' which can be useful. Habitus refers to the way in which our background predisposes us to act and respond in particular ways in particular contexts and situations. It is not a process that we are fully conscious of, but stems from the way in which we have internalized previous experiences and made sense of them. 'Field' refers to areas of activity within our lives so work places or education settings are particular 'fields'. For Bourdieu, our habitus predisposes us to act and respond in particular ways in particular situations. Brooker's (2002) research, for example, illustrates the way in which professionals' personal habitus reacts to, or is influenced by, particular organizational cultures (which some writers call institutional habitus). On a practical level the consequence of this is that we approach the work place (or placement) with a stock of previous knowledge and experience that will influence us in ways we are not always conscious of. Bourdieu felt that it was possible for us to develop new ways of approaching particular contexts through becoming reflexive. For Bourdieu we are likely to become reflexive when there is a mismatch between our disposition (the way in which habitus is manifested through our behaviour) and our position (the context we find ourselves in; see Mouzelis 2007).

Reflexivity is a complex and much discussed concept in Bourdieu's work and Bourdieu uses the term in a way that is both more specific and detailed than when used in the term 'reflexive practice'. For Bourdieu, reflexivity is the process of seeking to obtain an objective 'view' of a context or situation (field) and the way in which others perceive it whilst acknowledging the limitations created by our own habitus and position within particular fields. The implication of habitus and field for professional identity is that reflexivity is a way of attempting to be objective about the nature of practice or the work place, taking a critical look at the social reality that underpins this.

Towards a model of professional identity

The model developed by McGillivray shown in Figure 5.2 attempts to present a model of factors that can influence professional identity. It is best seen as a web of influences and highlights the way in which factors both overlap and potentially conflict. It is also useful to highlight the way in which different levels can act as filters promoting or inhibiting particular professional discourses, for example a very strong 'culture' in a particular workplace might have a significant impact on the way in which professional values are perceived. The representation of each of the factors as overlapping with the others is intended to highlight the fact that these are not separate domains of activity but are inextricably linked and that at any point in time each factor will have some influence (though these may change over time). A student may well find that the stronger influences on identity are training and the values and attitudes which stem from it. On the other hand, an experienced practitioner may well find national policy and the culture within their own work setting to be particularly influential. In this sense particular factors may be 'core' for us at particular points in our career and peripheral at other stages and vice versa.

ACTIVITY

Think about your own experiences and how influential each sphere of influence has been in promoting/developing your own sense of professional identity.

Have different elements or levels been more or less important at different stages of your professional journey?

If you are relatively new to this area of work, what influences you most now in terms of your professional identity? What might change this?

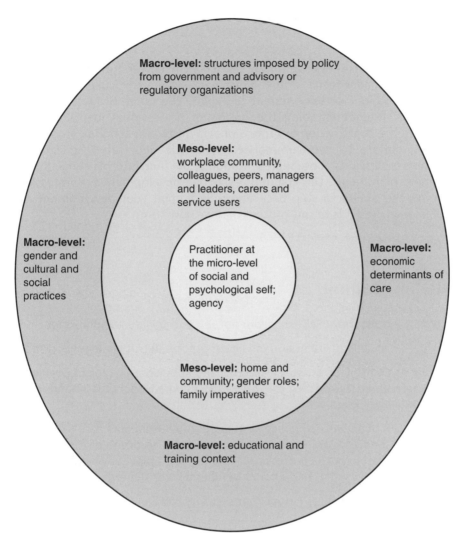

Figure 5.2   Influences on Professional Identity

Summary

Professional identity is perhaps best thought of as a journey rather than as a fixed position, shaped by our own experiences and individuality, the roles that we find ourselves in, the settings we work within, the colleagues we work

(Continued)

(Continued)

with and the policies of governments which are in power during our career, as well as the broader social context which pertains at a particular time.

In this chapter we have sought to explore the range of factors that are important in understanding the notion of professional identity. Having described the construction of professional identity as a complex process, it is not appropriate to over-summarize. The model illustrated in Figure 5.2 attempts to provide a loose representation of the fluid interplay and interface of spheres of influence. Understanding your own development as a professional requires the ability to step back and reflect upon your development as a professional, and it is to this process that we now turn.

Further reading

Burkitt, I. (2008) *Social Selves: Theories of Self and Society*. London: Sage.

Provides an excellent discussion of the concept of identity in a general sense.

Anning, A., Cottrell, D., Frost N., Green, J. and Robinson, M. (2006) *Developing Multiprofessional Teamwork for Integrated Children's Services*. Maidenhead: Open University Press.

Provides an overview of policy and a research-informed analysis of the changes in services working for children and families. Some of the dilemmas that are emerging for the professional identity of employees working in multi-disciplinary teams with children and families are considered.

Weber, S. and Mitchell, C. (1995) *That's Funny, You Don't Look Like a Teacher*. London: The Falmer Press.

Although the book focuses on teachers, is not recent and the research it reports was undertaken in the USA, it provides an accessible and illustrated text that conveys how significant societal influences such as media and popular culture are in constructing identities.

6

Values in Practice

Steven Parker

Summary Chapter Contents

- Exploring values
- Understanding values, moral principles and ethics
- Ethical principles in health and social care
- Empowerment and power
- A practice model for working with values

Learning objectives

By the end of this chapter, you should be able to:

- Engage with the debate around the moral principles and values that underpin good practice in health and social care.
- Develop an awareness of the origins and diversity of values.
- Understand the idea of power, empowering practice and the ethics of care.
- Reflect on what it means to be a morally active practitioner and act with moral courage.
- Uphold the fundamental rights of people who use care services.
- Recognize how practitioners have to work with conflicting values, opinions, beliefs and attributes, and the resulting ethical issues that influence practice.

Introduction

As practitioners we intervene in people's lives. We need to know that our interventions do no harm and that we are doing the 'right' thing; our practice thus becomes a practical and moral activity.

Our practice becomes guided by values (Beckett and Maynard 2005). Dawson and Butler (2003: 237) make this clear when they say that to be morally active is 'to act on the basis of internal values' rather than solely rely on externally imposed codes of conduct.

Tensions and conflicts may exist between values resulting in ethical dilemmas and problems (Banks 2006; Eby 2000b). Importantly, this chapter will enable you to examine how as practitioners you may have to work with conflicting values, opinions, beliefs and attributes, and the resulting ethical issues, and develop a value-based framework to reflect upon your practice.

By making links between a range of issues this chapter should equip you with a sound understanding of the moral principles that underpin practice and you will have a clear understanding of empowering practice and the ethic of care as central moral principles. Students will be in a position of being morally active practitioners who believe in the fundamental rights of people who use care services.

Exploring values

The language of values, ethics and morals is all around us. From political parties, high street fashion houses, to supermarkets, banks and social networking sites. The films we watch, the music we listen to, all contain messages related to sets of values. With a stroll along the high street and the scroll of a touch screen or the click of a button we are subject to the language of values and ethics. The Conservative Party (2006) claims 'to cherish freedom, advance opportunity and nurture responsibility'. Ed Miliband claims that his vision for the Labour Party is built on his own values of 'family, fairness, community and decency at work' (Labour Party no date a), which are reiterated in the Labour Party values of social justice, community, reward for hard work, decency and rights matched with responsibility (Labour Party no date b). The Liberal Democrats (no date) 'seek to balance the fundamental values of liberty, equality and community and in which no one shall be enslaved by poverty, ignorance of conformity' and the Green Party (2001) believes in humankind and a sustainable society with a fundamental message of equality, devolved power and peace. The language of values, morals and ethics is increasingly used to justify political rhetoric.

On the high street, Monsoon (no date) say they are 'Living Our Values and Ethics', with a commitment to ethical trading, sustainability and the creation of the Monsoon Accessorize Trust to help the lives of women and children, and Marks and Spencer (2012) aim 'to become the world's most sustainable retailer' and face the challenges of social injustice and inequality. In the world of banking, the Co-operative Bank (no date) has an ethical code based on consultation with customers and covers human rights, the arms trade, corporate responsibility and global trade, genetic modification, social enterprise, ecological impact and animal welfare. In popular culture Lennon and McCartney's (1967) message that 'love is all you need' continues to infiltrate popular music, meanwhile Facebook has become a place where ideas about values and ethics are exchanged and explored across the world.

Exploring values and ethics

Using a search engine such as Google, search for the values of a range of organizations that are not usually associated with the world of health and social care. You could start with some of the organizations in the above discussion or ones that you are familiar with.

What terms do organizations use to describe their values or ethical code?

Choose a particular organization or company and make a note of what they claim to be their values.

Carefully read through the value statements and consider how precise they are and what they are trying to achieve.

Consider the reasons for having a statement of values.

Try to relate the values of commercial organizations to health and social care.

Commentary

You may have found a wide range of organizations claiming to have a set of values or ethical codes. They may be within mission statements, policy documents or statements of procedures which outline what the customer should expect from the organization or company. Some statements may be precise in the service to be expected, giving details of timings, while others may contain statements claiming to be trustworthy and honest, with promises of working with integrity and being committed to providing a professional service, and having a close working relationship and keeping customers informed, being enthusiastic and understanding your needs.

Other companies may include wider statements of ethical trading, donations to charity, supporting good causes and having sustainability targets reflected in a commitment to recycling. There may be a genuine commitment to issues such as human rights and social responsibility.

You may have come up with a range of reasons why a particular company has a particular statement of values. It may reflect genuine principles of working in an ethical way and doing the right thing. A real concern for society. You may have decided that they provide guidance for people working within the organization, so that they have a benchmark to set their work against. They may also provide guidance to customers and clients providing a degree of accountability and setting expectations.

(Continued)

ACTIVITY

(Continued)

You may have thought that the statements are just a very good marketing tool presenting an ethical image of a company that customers want to buy into. They may even create a positive image by giving an impression of status and credibility.

Some of these reasons behind a statement of values and ethics may be applicable to health and social care organizations, but there is a fundamental difference in that an understanding of values and ethics is fundamental to the provision of services to people. It is not simply a marketing tool or about presenting a positive image to the world. Practitioners in health and social care should have a set of values that they should work to and that permeate professional practice.

Values are fundamental to the provision of welfare services. Dawson and Butler (2003) suggest that social care workers need to be aware of the importance of values and so have an ethical framework to do their job. This is about developing an understanding of what is right and wrong and ideas of what is good practice. Banks (2000) argues that a practitioner would need 'to be aware of the societal and professional values underlying her work and her own values' (2000: 64).

ACTIVITY

Considering the origin of our values

Take some time to consider what you believe to be right and wrong.

Compile a list of actions that you would consider to be your personal values.

Think about the extent to which they guide your daily life.

Having thought about your list of values and principles take some time to think about where they have come from. Have they changed over time?

Consider how your identity as a person is linked to your values and beliefs.

How do these ideas of right and wrong come together to create your moral position?

Commentary

In thinking about what you believe to be right and wrong you may have thought that it is wrong to hurt someone or even kill someone. You may have thought that it is right to help other people or donate your time or money to charity. You may have considered it wrong to steal or damage property. You may have come up with ideas such as equality, rights, respect and sustainability as principles that you believe in.

It may be difficult to think about how your ideas of right or wrong guide everyday actions, yet on the other hand you may have come up with a clear set of principles that you think to be right and you can see how your life is guided by them. In considering where our values come from you may have thought about how we are brought up, the society we live in and our shared culture and our community. You may have also thought how values change between places, cultures and time.

In looking at the origin of your values you may have linked them to your identity. Our values and identity are made up of a range of factors including our relationships with other people, background, the society we live in and our upbringing. Perhaps religion and faith has provided you with a set of values and beliefs about what is right and wrong. It is not only important to understand the origins of our own values, it is also important to understand that different people will have different personal values based on their own experience and identity.

Martin and Henderson (2001: 57) tell us that 'values are deep seated beliefs about what is right or wrong'. It is this central belief of what is right and wrong that guides our daily life and professional action.

Religion and Values

In thinking about the origin of values, you may have considered that religion is an influential factor, whether it is your own belief system or simply in general terms where religious ideas have influenced your upbringing through socialization and the society in which you live. According to the Office for National Statistics (2012) about 70% of the population in England and Wales said they had a religious affiliation in the 2011 census. The religion question was the only voluntary question on the census and about 7% of people did not answer it. Almost 60% of the population identified themselves as Christians. Nearly 5% of the population identified themselves as being Muslim. Of the other main religious groups 1.5% of people identified themselves as being Hindu, 0.8% as being Sikh, 0.5% as being Jewish, and 0.4% being Buddhist (see Figure 6.1).

The census results suggest that religious belief continues to play an important part in society, and religious leaders themselves have an influential moral voice not only at a local level, but also on a national and international scale. Religion provides people with a strong belief system and a unique view of the world, with particular moral and ethical codes governing behaviour. For people who have a particular faith the world we live in can be seen in various ways, with different calendars used to divide time both for pragmatic reasons and to identify religious events, where particular days have specific meaning.

Religion provides people with a set of beliefs, in doing so religion says what is true in the world. Religion provides guidelines for how to act and behave whilst being alive and it also says what will happen after death. So how people behave is not only governed by the rules, truths and expectations of religious belief, but also the prospect of what happens after death. For some people this is about threats of punishment in this world and the consequences of our behaviour in the next. For some it is about the existence of heaven and hell, and for others it is about the ending of continual rebirth.

Different religions provide ethical codes and influence the lives of millions of people across the planet. Religious belief is not just limited to the spiritual or providing moral guidance for everyday life. It has influenced wider society at a community, social, economical and political level, within local, national and international contexts across the globe.

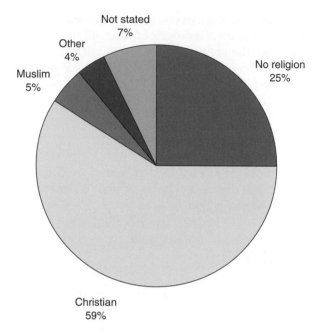

Figure 6.1   Religious affiliation in England and Wales 2011

Source: Office for National Statistics (2012)

Understanding different religions is important in health and social care for different reasons. Religion has had a significant influence on our moral framework. It is not the sole influence as we shall see as we progress through this chapter, but the values of religion have a resonance in health and social care and wider moral ideas. It is also important to understand the different religious traditions of people who we may provide services to. In trying to understand the beliefs and practices of different religions it is important not to make ethnocentric assumptions, and draw conclusions about the different religions based on poor information. It is important to understand different religious traditions on people's own terms, what is believed, how it is practised, and how it influences daily life. We will briefly explore some of the values associated with the six main religions of the UK. This is not a definitive guide, yet it should provide us with some basic understanding.

Judaism

Judaism is the original of the three monotheistic religions stemming from the prophet Abraham and originated in the Middle East over 3,000 years ago.

The history and development of Judaism as a monotheistic religion is complex; it is linked to disillusionment with ancient Mesopotamian religions and arises out of a clash of cultures and religious beliefs (Cohn-Sherbok 2003). The biblical story presents Abraham as the original patriarch of the Jewish nation and, over 1,000 years after Abraham, Moses is regarded as the primary instigator of monotheism. Moses led the Hebrew slaves out of Egypt, receiving the *Torah* including the 10 commandments on Mount Sinai, and it is from this time that Judaism is seen as an organized and structured religion.

The Early Israelites were trying to encourage people to worship only one God, and to worship that God in one way, to treat each other in certain ways and to follow certain rules. Eventually these ideas became accepted, including the idea that the temple in Jerusalem was the only place where the one true God could be worshipped. When the temple was destroyed by the Romans, Judaism needed to change, and ever since this time Judaism has constantly responded to historical events, including the Roman Empire, and the rise of Christianity and Islam. The history of the Jewish experience over the past 2,000 years makes what Judaism is today.

Being Jewish is about having a shared history and a shared cultural identity based on sacred texts which have been written by God. It is about living out daily life in accordance with being God's chosen people who have a covenant relationship with God.

The main texts in Judaism are the *Torah* and the *Talmud*. The *Torah* is believed to have been dictated to Moses on Mount Sinai and contains information on how God wants his chosen people, the Jews, to live their life. The *Talmud* contains the *halakhah,* the Jewish law and various commentaries on it.

The *halakhah* contains the rules and legal aspects of Judaism. It shows people how to behave and provides them with a set of rules, procedures and ethical guidelines. The *halakhah* is about the covenant relationship between Jews and God. This means for the good things that God does, Jews will keep God's laws and live life in a holy way, in this way Judaism is a faith of action. The important thing here is also how the *halakhah* is interpreted.

At the same time Judaism recognizes that there is human free will. Consequently, the person is seen as being in conflict with two opposing forces: the force of evil, (*yetser ha-ra*) and the force for good (*yetser tov*), which de Lange (2000) equates with conscience. So, it is up to each person to recognize *yetser ha-ra,* and with the help of God, control it, or change it into an action for good. *Halakhah* is also about charity, generosity, hospitality and compassion.

According to Neusner (2002) God admires acts of selflessness. These are acts that go beyond simply the obedience of the *halakhah,* or the *Torah.* They are seen as acts of love and can be a single remarkable action which results in God's divine favour or *zekut.*

There may be sets of rules, but Judaism has developed to respond to changes over the past 2,000 years. There are different subdivisions with Judaism, such as Masorti Judaism, Reform Judaism and Modern Orthodoxy which respond in different ways to the modern world. In this way Judaism can be seen as a religion that is flexible and open to new ideas.

Christianity

Christianity started as a small Jewish sect in Palestine about 2,000 years ago and has developed to become the world's largest religion. Christians are the followers of Christ, who is believed to be the Messiah prophesied in Jewish Texts. The Christian holy text is the Bible which contains the 'Old Testament' and the solely Christian texts of the 'New Testament'. The New Testament contains the four 'canonical' gospels of Matthew, Mark, Luke and John which tell the story of Jesus' life. The New Testament also includes The Acts of the Apostles, letters to early Christians giving advice on how Christians should behave and worship, and The Revelation of St John the Divine.

The 'synoptic gospels' of Matthew, Mark and Luke tell the story of Jesus' life and, for Ford (1999), show that Jesus' message and what he did were totally intertwined with him as a person and with what happened to him. Each gospel tells the story of his life, culminating in Jerusalem, where Jesus is put on trial and executed by crucifixion. Jesus entered Jerusalem at Passover riding a donkey. This was a fulfilment of a biblical prophecy about the coming to Jerusalem of the messiah to bring peace. He then drove out the money-changers from the Temple and this was seen as an attack at the centre of religious and political power. He was arrested, accused and executed on charges of claiming to be the messiah who predicted the destruction of the temple.

Jesus was crucified by the Romans because they regarded him not just as a rebel or trouble maker, but also because he was seen as a political threat. Ford (1999) suggests that Jesus regarded his death as fulfilling his mission. The Last Supper was the critical event where Jesus ate a meal with his disciples, where bread and wine were identified with his body and blood in remembrance of himself.

The teachings of Jesus are open to various interpretations, but it is generally accepted that he challenged social values, such as wealth, power and hierarchy and social inequality. His teachings also ask his followers to give up such things as power and wealth as well as have a 'commitment to righteousness, forgiveness, care, mercy and the willingness to be persecuted' (Open University 2006a: 26). The Christian ethical code comes from the central idea of love (from the command to love God and love your neighbour), and from this arises the idea that injustice and inequality in all its forms should be challenged and fought. Fighting oppression and challenging inequality is a central message in the Christian tradition.

Jesus was asked what he judged to be the most important commandment, in reply he said:

> 'You shall love the Lord your God with all your heart, and with all your soul, and with all your mind.' This is the greatest and first commandment. And a second is like it: 'You shall love your neighbour as yourself.' On these two commandments hang all the law and the prophets. (Matthew 22:34–40)

By saying this, Jesus is showing his commitment to Jewish law, but he is also emphasizing the importance of love. From this and his other sayings and actions in the Gospels, Jesus demonstrates his belief in the equality of all human beings, and he emphasizes this by associating himself with the poor and social outcasts and being critical of those in power.

The Christian Church has three main branches – Orthodoxy, Roman Catholicism and Protestantism, with numerous subdivisions. Christianity has adapted to different cultural, historical, political and social traditions around the world and, like other religions, Christianity has needed to respond to the challenges of modern times. As a result Christianity has become a diverse and pluralistic religion.

Islam

'Islam' is the third monotheistic Abrahamic religion. It was revealed to Muhammad over 1,400 years ago and means 'submission to the will of God'.

A Muslim is able to recite the basic statement of faith which is called the *shahada*. It is the first 'Pillar' (or 'duty') of Islam: 'There is no God but God and Muhammad is his Prophet'. When reciting the *shahada* a Muslim is saying that they believe this to be true, and that they will obey the commitments of Islam. A Muslim also practises four other duties to God. These are the remaining Pillars of Islam which must be adhered. The Pillar of *salat* is 'prayer' and it is necessary to pray and worship in the proper way. The Pillar of *zakat* is about paying alms and giving a proportion of one's assets (2.5%) to charity to help those in need. *Sawm* is about fasting during the holy month of Ramadan and *hajj* is about undertaking a pilgrimage to Mecca in Saudi Arabia, which every Muslim must do at least once in a their life, if they are able to do so. A central message in Islam is 'peace' and this can be heard in the everyday greeting *'as salaam alaikum'* ('peace be upon you').

The Qur'an is the Book of God, and is regarded by Muslims as the final word of God sent down from heaven to the Prophet Muhammad. Esposito (1988) points out that for Muslims the Qur'an is regarded as a guide for humankind and that it does not invalidate, but rather it corrects the Jewish and Christian Scriptures. In the Qur'an each person is accountable before God for their own actions.

Muslims are guided by the word of God in the Qur'an to create a moral social order and to develop a society based on acting in the right way and by forbidding what is regarded as bad. So in Islam there are rules about what to do and not to do and the importance on correct behaviour has had a significant impact on people's daily life, on Muslim societies and communities. *Sharia* governs how Muslims are to live their lives and, as Rabbani (2009) outlines, it provides divine guidance and covers all aspects of human life and it is the intention and sincerity of behaviour is seen as paramount in judging the worth of that behaviour. The aim of *sharia* is to promote people's welfare.

Sharia provides protection for women, but it also maintains gender inequalities. The view that the Qur'an is the unchangeable word of God creates a significant problem for a range of issues where gender inequalities and differences are specified. Some of these have historical and cultural origins and differences, especially around dress. Issues around gender inequality and the role of women continue to be debated and are challenged by a range of Islamic scholars (Open University 2012).

Islam is a diverse religion with its own rituals, scriptures and ethics. As with other religions it faces challenges in the modern world, and a pluralist view of Islam is consistent with individual religious choice and modern lifestyles. Pluralism and diversity have been noted to be among the core values Islam and the Qur'an acknowledges diversity and accepts differences of gender, colour, language, belief and rank. The Qur'an stresses that 'humankind is one community' (*Ummah*), it also praises harmony between people and communities, while condemning competition and control by others (Open University 2012).

Hinduism

Hinduism is India's most popular religion, yet is complex and it is difficult to trace its beginnings. It has no historical founder, yet for many Hindus the religion is seen as being *sanatana dharma*, or eternal and is 'beyond human history' (Knott 1998: 5). Some of the more ancient traditions within Hinduism could go back several thousand years (Flood 2009), though many of its traditions can be traced back to at least the second millennium BC. Hinduism itself is a variety and complex cluster of beliefs and practices and, like other religions, has its own scriptures. There are two types of scripture, those which have been divinely revealed (*shruti*), and those that have been handed down (*smriti*)

The **Veda** is the earliest known *shruti* scripture and has four parts containing hymns, mantras, spells and charms and is about creation and various sacred rituals. The other important *shruti* scripture is the *Upanishads* which has influenced Hindu religious thought. The *smriti* scriptures include the *Epics* of the *Mahabharata* which contain the poems of the *Bhagavadgita* and *Ramayana*, telling stories of Krishna and Rama; the *Sutras* containing information on the core religious principle of *dharma* and other Hindu traditions and the *Puranas*, relating stories of gods and goddesses (Knott 1998).

Hinduism assumes a process of continual rebirth or reincarnation until liberation from this cycle of being reborn is achieved (*moksha*). This is about being able to understand the ideas of *karma* and *samsara*, which is underpinned by the unifying principle of *dharma*.

Knott (1998: 20) defines dharma as 'truth, law, duty or obligation', where the 'harmony of the world must be maintained and an individual's dharma must be fulfilled'. Flood (2009) sees *dharma* as the power that maintains the universe and society and provides people with the opportunity to act in a moral way. So *dharma* is about natural and moral order, justice, righteousness and personal duty. It becomes a person's duty to order society and maintain personal conduct in a way that corresponds with the design of the universe. This brings integrity, harmony and balance, both at a social and personal level.

Karma is the 'chain of cause and effect linked to action' (Knott 1998: 37). It originally referred solely to the performance of rituals; more generally, it now includes the performance of ritual and behaviour according to a person's *dharma*. Its performance, therefore, is seen to be of inherent value, which brings merit (*punya*) to a person. So good behaviour will fit in with a person's *dharma* and have good consequences, either in this life or in the next life. So it is important as it is the way rebirth is determined.

Samsara is the process of reincarnation, the cycle of birth and rebirth and is closely linked to *karma*. Acting together they provide justice as a person will receive the consequences of their good or bad actions in this and the next life. So following the moral path of one's own *dharma*, *karma* can be understood as a law of moral cause and effect. It also provides an explanation for life's inequalities.

Moksha is 'to gain liberation' (Knott 1998: 23) from the endless cycle of rebirth. It is the performance of selfless actions which based on a person's own dharma that leads to *moksha*.

Hinduism is amazingly complex with many traditions, beliefs, practices and divisions. Knott (1998: 112) uses the ideas of Sarvepalli Radhakrishnan, who says that Hinduism is a way of life and fully integrated with society and with what a person does. In this way *dharma*, 'the law, order, truth, and duties of the Hindu people' (Knott 1998: 112), are central to Hinduism.

Buddhism

Buddhism is a complex and large system of practices beliefs that have developed from the teachings of the Buddha who lived in what is now present day Nepal in the fifth century BCE. Buddhism is seen as one of the most ethical religions (Keown 1996). It is a religion which encompasses a way of life, a philosophy and a strong ethical code.

Buddhism is about enabling people to become enlightened and leave behind the unenlightened state of greed, hatred and delusion. Liberation from this endless cycle of rebirth (*samsara*), is the goal and in Buddhism this goal is to reach *nirvana* or enlightenment.

The *dharma* is seen as the truth in Buddhism and anyone can find it if they are ready to understand it.

The Buddhist idea of *karma* does not mean that people should simply accept that what happens to them is inevitable. For Buddhists, living in a way that accepts that one's current life is simply down to the past and ones own *karma*, means that it is likely that what they do in this life will continue to be motivated by greed, hatred and delusion, rather than by the opposites: non-attachment, benevolence and understanding (Keown 1996). A person's life circumstances can be determined by past deeds but, as Keown (1996) explains, for Buddhists, some things can be accidental, but also 'Karma that has been accumulated but not yet experienced is carried forward to the next life, or even many lifetimes ahead' (Keown 1996: 39). So it becomes important to behave in new ways based on Buddhist teachings and practice, and living as a human being provides the opportunity to live a moral life, gain wisdom, and accumulate good *karma* or *punna*.

The end of the cycle of rebirth is to reach *nirvana* and so end of the problem of suffering, confusion and delusion, hatred and greed.

At the centre of Buddhism is a strong ethical and message, and this can be summarized as: 'Cease to do evil, learn to do good, purify the heart' (Dhammapada, v. 183).

In Buddhism five ethical precepts for lay people can be identified:

- Abstain from harming or killing living beings.
- Abstain from taking what is not given.
- Abstain from misconduct concerning sense pleasures, including inappropriate sexual activity, and overindulgence in eating or sleeping.
- Abstain from lying.
- Abstain from intoxication or unmindful states due to drugs or alcohol. (Buddhist Scriptures Trans: Conze 1959)

Buddhism can be seen as a religion with an emphasis on love, equality and spiritual freedom.

Sikhism

Sikhism was founded by the first Guru Nanak (1469–1539) in the Punjab in India. Sikhism has had 10 gurus through which the word of God has been revealed. The last guru was Guru Gobind Singh, who died in 1708. It is a monotheistic religion which developed within a context of Islam and Hinduism.

Guru Nanak's life is documented in the *janam-sakhis*, and it is these scriptures which provide guidance on how Sikhs should live their lives. Guru Nanak had a particular understanding of God and emphasized the religious state of a person and the importance of experiencing, understanding and thinking about God. As in Hinduism and Buddhism, Sikhs believe in the cycle of rebirth and *karma*. Freedom from the cycle of death and rebirth results in the union with God.

One very important feature of Sikhism is singing and music and these are the main way to worship. By concentrating deeply (*samadh)* on the music the mind can be cleared of negative thoughts, and be at one with God.

Being a Sikh is about behaving in a good way, doing good things and living a good life as part of a community. This is about keeping God in mind all the time (*Nam Japna*), being honest and hardworking (*Kit Karna*), treating people equally, being generous and serving others (*Vand Chhakna).*

Sikhs should also try and avoid things which prevent a person from concentrating on God and so becoming self-centred. These are identified as being lust, greed, attachment to things, anger and pride.

Sikhism is characterized by the importance of a single human family and equality, tolerance and democracy, upholding the rights of others, respect for life, and social responsibility and community involvement (Open University 2006b).

If someone is causing harm Sikhs are asked to kiss the feet of those causing it, which is similar to the Christian response of turning the other cheek (Open University 2006b). But Sikhs have a duty to intervene when violence or injustice is directed at the weak or disadvantaged, and as a last resort the sword can be used. Violence can only be used if all else fails, as the gurus emphasized non-violence and peaceful protest (Open University 2006b). Sikhs also have a duty to make things in the world right and make the world a happier place for everyone.

From this brief outline of the different religions we can see that each faith has its own divine message, practices and traditions. At the same time there seem to be common values such as peace, love, doing good, challenging injustice and caring for others. Religion does not hold a monopoly on ethical principles, as we shall see later in this chapter, but it is important to recognize where some of our own personal values may come from and the commonality of values between the different faiths. Health and social care work occurs within a multi-faith and multi-cultural context so it becomes important that we have some understanding of the religion and beliefs of people we provide services to. This raises issues concerning the appropriateness of services being delivered to people and places an obligation on health and social care workers to understand the values and ethics of people who have different faiths.

To discover more about different religions and current debates the BBC religion and ethics pages are a good place to start (www.bbc.co.uk/religion). The Open University also provides free access to some of its religious studies material through OpenLearn www.open.edu/openlearn/).

Our values and identity arise from the influences of our family and culture during childhood and continue to develop into our adult life as we encounter other people and enter the world of education and work. Our values can be individual to ourselves on a personal level or shared at a community or society level. This process of primary and secondary socialization helps form and shape our values first at a personal level and later at a professional level. For Eby and Gallagher (2008: 114) values are 'beliefs, ideas, and assumptions that individuals and groups hold about themselves and their society'. There is a complex interaction between our personal values and the culture and norms of society and the community in which we belong, so our values both inform and are informed by our surroundings. Values also change over time and Inge (1940) suggested that crisis and catastrophe such as war has the power to hasten changes in our values that may have otherwise come about gradually. Inge examined the rise of values such as pacifism and humanism, and as our world continues to change we see the rise of new values based on concepts of sustainability and respect.

Understanding values, moral principles and ethics

Health and social care workers are dealing with the practicalities of people's lives and so make practical decisions that have ethical consequences. The decisions we make when intervening in someone else's life are informed by our moral position. Parrott (2010) suggests that this becomes a practical–moral activity and so an understanding of ethical principles becomes important when thinking about how to respond to people who are in need of services. Dawson and Butler (2003) suggest that to think and act ethically and morally right requires a set of values, and so practitioners need to develop an ethical perspective to their work. This means that we need to think ethically about our actions and interventions, so that we can clarify and resolve practice issues. Thinking ethically does not provide immediate solutions but using an ethical framework can provide reasons for our action and enable us to think about ethical issues in a more structured and critical way (Open University 2009).

Practitioners in health and social care hold sets of values or ethical principles that can be understood in terms of moral philosophy which has its historical roots in the works and ideas of Socrates (269–399 BCE), Plato (c.427–328 BCE) and Aristotle (384–322 BCE). These fundamental ideas of moral philosophy concerning why we act in certain ways remain relevant today and continue to inform our action in health and social care.

Raphael (1994) defines moral philosophy as exploring ideas of right and wrong, good and bad, what should and should not be done. This moral philosophy of practice is used to guide practice, it cannot tell practitioners what to do, but it can enable practitioners to explore the dilemmas of practice decisions. By exploring the different ethical approaches practitioners can reflect on ethical dilemmas they encounter and clarify the issues that are created when intervening in people's lives. The choice of what decision to make remains with you, the health and social care practitioner.

To understand and reflect on the ethical issues in practice to enable practitioners to be morally active it is useful to explore some general approaches to understanding the area of moral principles and ethics that have developed over time. The principles that exist within the domain of moral philosophy can act as a framework to examine our own values and the professional ethical principles that have come to influence our practice. The differing moral theoretical approaches attempt to provide an answer to what is the morally right thing to do, or even what should we think about a particular issue. Consequentialism, reflected in the ideas of utilitarianism, looks at the right action in terms of the greatest good and on the surface provides a framework for action. But on the way to reaching such a decision we may have to do things that could be seen as in conflict with our values. Another way of looking at ethical decision making is deontological theory which says that the right action is the one which accords with duty. In this sense you have a range of duties that you and other people adhere to. Virtue Ethics has become increasingly influential, with the suggestion that the right action is done by a virtuous person. More recently the progressive agenda of empowerment, including a feminist approach that challenges oppression and discrimination, and the ethics of care, has influenced health and social care. Principled approaches have also been developed to aid practitioners to work through ethical decisions.

Utilitarian approach

The basic premise of utilitarianism is that the right action is that which produces the greatest balance of good over harm. As Raphael (1994) points out, the right action is the action that produces most happiness. So actions are right if they result in good and remove or prevent what is bad. The principle of utilitarianism has been discussed and debated over the past 150 years or so and has resulted in a range of variations.

Traditional utilitarianism, according to Raphael (1994), attempts to simplify the concept to the idea that 'things are valued for the sake of pleasure, either the pleasure they themselves contain or the pleasure they are likely to produce'. Other notions of utility, such as hedonistic utilitarianism, suggest that the pursuit of pleasure alone is to be regarded as good. Ideal utilitarianism would say that other things could be regarded as good other than pleasure, such as love, virtue, knowledge and beauty.

The consequences of actions can be linked to utilitarian principles in that the morality of an action can be determined by whether or not its consequences are seen as good (Beckett and Maynard 2005). This can be broken down into act and rule utilitarianism. Act utilitarianism is where the morality of a person's actions is judged by its consequences and whether the result is the greatest amount of good. Rule utilitarianism is where the rules that cover actions can be judged as contributing to the greatest good (Beckett and Maynard 2005).

The principles inherent within utilitarianism seem to offer an overarching framework for action: that what we do in our practice should produce the greatest amount of good and happiness for the people we work with. It is about exploring the possible consequences of our choice of actions and choosing the action that in our opinion produces the greatest amount of good. On the surface, the ideas of consequentialism seem to provide a clear framework for deciding moral issues. Acting in a way that maximizes 'good' seems a sensible course of action. For Banks (2000), though, the principles of utility 'tells us nothing about whose good' we should be promoting. In the delivery of health and social care services should we be promoting what people who use the service regard as being good, to promote happiness and utility as defined by the people who access the services they need? Or should we be promoting what others view as good, such as society, or what we as practitioners would call 'in someone's best interest'? Utilitarianism itself has been criticized in that following a course of action which maximizes good or happiness may involve actions that are viewed as simply wrong and going against our duty.

Deontological approaches

Deontological approaches are concerned with our duties towards ourselves and other people, and Immanual Kant (1724–1804) suggested that ethical duties could be derived from reasoned argument. At the centre of Kant's idea is the categorical imperative. This can be roughly explained as follows. In our performance of any action that we do, we would expect everyone else to do the same action; in this way our action would become a universal law. So when we are in a particular situation we may find there are a number of different possible actions to take. To establish which action could be considered our duty we could consider the consequences of everyone doing the same action. If we consider that it is acceptable that everyone does the same action, it then becomes our duty to act in this way (Open University 2009).

Raphael (1994: 34) believes that Kantian principles are more satisfying in suggesting a single moral framework, other than when it comes to conflicts between rules. For Raphael, Kantian principles are about three things:

- When making a moral decision we should treat everyone in the same way.
- We should treat people as always having 'ends' and not merely as 'means'. By this Kant is saying that we should regard people as having a purpose, a purpose made up of 'desires' and 'choices' and an ability to make decisions. It is a moral duty to enable people to carry out their own decisions. It then becomes morally wrong to dominate other people, to exert power over others, to treat them as a 'means'. It also becomes morally wrong to fail to help where help is needed.
- We should be collectively making decisions. We should accept that other people are competent, suggesting a concept of equality. Thus, 'every human being equally has the power to make choices and decisions'.

For Kant there is recognition that everyone has unconditional worth and the power to make decisions and the moral capacity to determine their own moral destiny. It would also seem that we all have a moral duty to enable this to happen.

Deontological approaches are greatly influential in health and social care with the belief that health and social care workers have a duty to do good as well as having a duty of care. Eby and Gallagher (2008) suggest that deontological approaches may avoid looking at the consequences of our actions and this could lead to 'disastrous results'. Health and social care workers may also face a conflict between duties towards service users and the state and face a dilemma over which duty takes precedence. Banks (2000) suggests that neither deontological nor utilitarian approaches can provide a single principle for determining the right action. Instead she notes that authors on professional ethics draw upon both when thinking about moral issues.

Virtue ethics approach

Deontological and utilitarian approaches for understanding moral decision making have been criticized for being directive and used to predict courses of action. Acting within a Kantian framework of obligation, an individual may be accused of simply doing one's duty, and using a utilitarian framework you may determine your actions after considering the consequences of your action rather than because of wanting to do the right thing.

The virtues approach to ethics is different as it suggests that if people were to be virtuous then people would act according to their innate goodness (Eby and Gallagher 2008). To be a virtuous person is to do the right thing because you want to do the right thing. It is not simply because it is your duty to do the right thing, or because of the consequences of your action.

As an alternative approach, being virtuous is based on moral character and capacity. The right thing is done because of a fundamental belief in the right thing. It is, as Beauchamp and Childress (2009) say, about doing the right thing from 'the right state of mind'.

Virtue ethics has its origins in the work of ancient Greek philosophers. Socrates, through the work of Plato (1935) explores the idea of justice, arguing that acting in a just or moral way is in itself virtuous and that a just life is 'the happiest in this world' (p. xlii). The idea of acquiring happiness by being virtuous is developed by Aristotle (1929: 5), who regarded it as the 'best of human things'.

McBeath and Webb (2002) point out that virtues are 'acquired inner qualities' that when applied 'contribute to the realization of the good life' (equivalent to Plato and Aristotle's notion of happiness). So the idea of having a virtue is a concept that makes the person good. Being virtuous could be synonymous with being a morally good person, of having a moral character. Adams (2009) regards virtue ethics as defining a virtuous person as someone who has and demonstrates certain virtues which are seen as being needed to 'flourish and live well as a human being'. For Plato and Aristotle there are four virtues consisting of wisdom, courage, self-discipline and justice, and the idea that health and social care workers should reflect such qualities remains relevant today.

In health care Beauchamp and Childress (2009) identify 'central virtues' of:

- Compassion: being an active regard for another person's welfare and an ability to have empathy.
- Discernment: being about the ability to make decisions with sensitive insight.
- Trustworthiness: concerned with being able to be relied upon, of having the moral character and competence that other people can rely upon.
- Integrity: concerned with being a morally reliable person and able to stand up for the principles that one believes in.
- Conscientiousness: being about doing the right thing because it is right and having given some thought to what may be the right action.

Virtues in social care have been explored by McBeath and Webb (2002: 1015), who identify social (care) workers as being able to apply the virtues of:

- Justice
- Reflection
- Perception
- Judgement
- Bravery
- Prudence
- Liberality
- Temperance.

For McBeath and Webb (2002) social (care) workers require these virtues to make judgements based on the worker's perception and judgement and not on an automated response based on organizational requirements. Virtuous social care workers are able to reflect on their action and to strive to do the right thing.

Adams (2009) regards social (care) work as a virtue-guided profession. The focus of health and social care is the promotion of the well-being of people and society and for Adams (2009) the virtues promoted by Aristotle and Plato, which result in happiness, reflect the mission of social care. Banks (2011) seems to reflect Plato and Aristotle's virtues of courage and justice. She argues that social (care) workers need to take responsibility for just practice and challenge unjust practice. She also argues that courage is a vital virtue for social (care) workers as moral courage is needed in many areas of practice, whether it be challenging prejudice, making difficult practice decisions or speaking 'out about inadequate resources and policies that impact disproportionately on people who are in need or difficulty' (p. 19).

Virtue ethics is criticized in that it is unable to guide action and resolve ethical dilemmas. Holland (2010) argues that the approach is not useful in terms of professional ethics, arguing that utilitarian and deontological approaches are more useful, but as Adams (2009) points out a virtuous approach does not mean that other approaches are disregarded. The importance of virtues is advocated by Putman (2012), who points out that there is a clear distinction in actually being concerned about a person's welfare and simply acting concerned out of duty. Working in both health and social care requires virtues and also develops virtues. The virtue of a person motivates practitioners to think ethically about practice situations and becomes the basis for ethical decision making and taking action.

Progressive approaches

As well as being a profession, Banks (2011) views social (care) work as a social movement where ethics need to underpin practice that is seen as 'anti-oppressive, critical, structural and radical'. Such values are concerned with challenging discrimination, oppression, power and the promotion of equality (Thompson 2003, 2006) and are seen as radical or progressive approaches.

Radical values have been differentiated from traditional values, which seem to focus on the individual relationship between the professional practitioner and the person requiring a service. Traditional values could be said to reflect an individualization of supporting or even empowering people. A progressive approach recognizes the role of health and social care workers as agents of control on behalf of an oppressive system and so by working in ways that challenge structural oppression, health and social care workers need to be aware that the 'very rules and structures within which society operates reflect basic inequalities in power' (Banks 2000: 59). This can be a challenging concept.

Radical approaches focus on the structures that cause problems such as poverty, poor housing, patriarchy or racism. Interventions in people's lives become part of a wider agenda of working collectively for social change. Traditional values are seen as a system of rules and principles that maintain the oppression of people because they reflect the interests of the powerful dominant groups in society. Radical values reflect the idea that social (care) workers should enable people to exercise more choice, be part of the decision-making process, and be in control.

Feminist and ethic of care approaches are separate but linked. Care-focused approaches identify the failure of deontological and utilitarian approaches to understand the attitudes of women and feminist approaches look at the patriarchal oppressive aspects of society (Eby and Gallagher 2008). For Tronto (1993 in Tronto 2010) ethic of care is based on the notion that action should be guided by the need to care for others. As people we need to provide and receive care, and we exist in a network of relationships with responsibility for each other. Tronto (1993 in Tronto 2010) suggests four phases of care:

- Attentiveness, which is about recognizing the need for care: *'care about'*
- Responsibility for responding to a person's needs: *'care for'*
- Competence in caring practice: *'care giving'*
- Responsiveness, being an awareness of how people receiving care respond to the action of care: *'care receiving'*.

Within this perspective it becomes important to understand the effect of power in relationships and the idea that we are all interconnected and have a shared human experience stressing the importance of community rather than individualism. There is also the importance of recognizing the significance of different points of view and knowing and acknowledging the importance of everyday life (Eby and Gallagher 2008). Using an ethic of care, Tronto (2010) warns that care could be subject to 'paternalism, in which care givers assume that they know better than care receivers what those care receivers need, and parochialism, in which care givers develop preferences for care receivers who are closer to them'. Tronto raises a number of issues to consider from an ethic of care perspective. She suggests that people need to be recognized as having different capacities and needs, where needs are not fixed and narrowly determined by experts. She is critical of regarding care as a commodity, as purchased rather than as a process, where treating people as consumers is to deny them the right to make judgements about their needs. Tronto is also critical of how service users could be viewed as incompetent because they are dependent and of care work itself being devalued. The four phases within the ethic of care suggest that care needs to be understood as a full process.

In developing the ideas that inform the radical agenda Banks (2011: 17) takes the core of the human relationship in care and places social care work alongside service users and people who experience poverty and injustice, where practitioners need to have a radical view of 'social justice, a sense of solidarity and willingness to speak out and take action'. In doing so Banks (2011: 19) argues for a 'situated ethics of social justice', where social justice is taken as the starting point and is embedded in practice and everyday life and in the human relationship at the centre of health and social care. In proposing a set of values for a situated ethics of social justice Banks (2011) outlines a progressive model of values consisting of:

- Radical social justice
- Empathic solidarity
- Relational autonomy
- Collective responsibility for resistance
- Moral courage
- Working in and with complexity and contradictions.

With this set of values Banks is suggesting that workers need to take seriously the social justice agenda and work for equality of outcomes and challenge unjust policy and practice. Radical social justice is about challenging oppression in the form of 'exploitation, marginalization, powerlessness, cultural imperialism and violence' (p. 18). To do this, Banks is saying that workers need to have a sense of empathic solidarity with people who use services and have a collective commitment to social change that requires a critical approach to practice and having a hopeful attitude that sees the possibility for a better world. Banks also suggests that individual professional autonomy needs to be reframed as relational autonomy where autonomy is seen within a social context of oppressive and constraining structures and institutions that influence individual autonomy. By being collectively responsible for resistance workers should take responsibility for good practice and resist unjust practice and policy. This resistance involves challenging how individuals, families and communities are made responsible for the causes and solutions to social problems. To fulfil some of these progressive values, the virtue of moral courage is needed. In health and social care we are working in a complex area full of contradictions and uncertainty and the ethics of practice need to reflect this. To act in an ethical way it is important to question our practice and to be aware how health and social care is becoming dominated by a managerialist agenda. So for Banks (2011: 19) 'ethics is definitely not about simply following rules – it is about questioning and challenging, feeling and acting' .

Ethical principles in health and social care

Banks' model of progressive values is not designed to replace existing sets of values. She is suggesting that they already exist within the ethical principles that guide ethical decision making but that they need to be re-claimed if they are to avoid being diluted. Ethical principles in health and social care provide practical advice to aid decision making in a wide range of circumstances. There is a history of ethical guidance and principles which enable practitioners to develop what Beauchamp and Childress (2009) regard as a professional morality. A profession shares this morality as it is common amongst practitioners who acknowledge their moral responsibilities.

In the area of health, Beauchamp and Childress (2009) outline a framework of moral principles. They regard their set of moral principles as 'guidelines for professional ethics', namely:

- Respect for autonomy
- Non-maleficence
- Beneficence
- Justice.

In social (care) work Banks (2000, 2006) believes that it is possible to determine four principles:

- Respect for and promotion of individual rights to self-determination
- Promotion of welfare or well-being
- Equality
- Distributive justice.

The principles above have similarities and differences and are relevant to the practice of health and social care workers.

Respect for autonomy: the promotion of individual rights to self-determination

By autonomy at a personal level Beauchamp and Childress (2009) mean the freedom to act as people wish. An autonomous person is able to choose and is not controlled by others. Ideas around autonomy link to notions of freedom and liberty so that individuals are free from controlling influences. For Beauchamp and Childress being autonomous means that people have a right to 'hold views', 'choose, and act on their own beliefs'.

Banks' principle of self-determination is similar. She regards self-determination in two ways: as allowing people to do what they choose, and creating the conditions that enable people to become more self-determining. So, as practitioners this means that we need to practise in a way that promotes and enables people to be autonomous. It also means that our practice should actively enable people to be autonomous.

Both authors point out that it is important to determine a person's capacity to be self-determining. For Banks this will be limited by judgements of the person's competence, the need for protection and the right to participate. She also suggests that being self-determining may not be without its limitations, as in the interests of justice it may not be possible to promote the rights of service users at the expense of others.

Beauchamp and Childress (2009) argue that agency, or the capacity for intentional action, is essential for autonomy. So Beauchamp and Childress believe that the obligation to respect autonomy does not extend to people who cannot act in a sufficiently autonomous manner and therefore cannot be regarded as autonomous. This would include people who, as health and social care practitioners, we would be working with.

Reflecting on respecting personal autonomy

Consider how the principle of respecting autonomy could apply in a health and social care setting.

What do you think would limit personal autonomy?

Should 'incapacity' limit autonomy?

Does a person's incapacity extend to all the decisions they may want to make?

Who defines who is capable or not in having the right to make decisions and choose?

Commentary

The area of autonomy raises a number of thought-provoking issues challenging aspects of power and control. In looking at the principle of autonomy you may have concluded that is about respecting a person's decision about their service even if it is not what you would recommend. This seems straightforward, but when deciding to limit a person's autonomy it becomes a difficult and complex issue. Perhaps you thought that it would be legitimate to limit a person's autonomy if the decisions they made may result in harming other people. You may think that a person's cognitive ability may reduce their decision making skills. This raises issues about a person's right to make decisions, regardless of whether we view it as a reasonable decision. It also raises issues about a person's assumed ability to be autonomous and the power and authority of people providing a care service. You may have concluded that even if someone is assessed as not being competent to make decisions about some aspects of their life, everyday choices can still be made. The ability to consent is essential in determining a person's capacity.

Beauchamp and Childress (2009) suggest that a person's autonomy is reduced by their capacity to make decisions for themselves. In social and health care, practitioners need to respect the autonomy of individuals to make decisions and choices for themselves. Beauchamp and Childress limit this autonomy on grounds of mental capacity, suggesting that people with learning difficulties may not be able to be autonomous due to 'limited capacity for intentional action'.

These views of autonomy and self-determination raise a number of issues for practitioners working with people with cognitive impairments. Do people with dementia or learning difficulties have the same rights as other people to be autonomous? How much power does a person seen as having cognitive impairment have to determine or make decisions about the service they are involved in? To deny a person's right to be autonomous may be about maintaining the discrimination, oppression and marginalization of powerless people which is hidden behind an ethical principle.

Shopping

Belinda is a young woman living in the community after spending over 10 years in a long-stay hospital. The staff who work with her have a professional remit to encourage Belinda's independence. This includes learning how to go shopping. For the care workers working with Belinda this means encouraging her to shop at the local supermarket.

Belinda says she does not want to go shopping. She has found the experience stressful and uncomfortable. The organizational response is to help Belinda go shopping by using established learning methods, breaking down the process task by task, teaching it in small stages and eventually withdrawing, so that Belinda can shop independently.

It is assumed that Belinda does not have the cognitive ability to make an intentional decision not to go shopping. The justification behind this is that Belinda needs to be independent in the community and she does not understand this. Being able to shop is an essential skill to live in the community. It is the professional remit of the care staff to encourage her independence and develop her living skills. It is also an organizational aim of community care.

- Consider to what extent Belinda's views need to be taken into account.
- Is Belinda's decision not to go shopping intentional?
- How far do you think Belinda should determine her lifestyle?
- To what extent do you think there could be a conflict between Belinda's assumed autonomy and the authority and expectations of her care provider?
- What are your views concerning independence?
- What alternatives are there?
- Consider the wider issues raised by this situation.

Commentary

Belinda's circumstances may seem superficial, and you may quickly conclude that her views should be considered, that she is making an intentional decision not to go shopping and that she should be fully involved in the decisions affecting her lifestyle. Taking on board some of the earlier discussions concerning radical approaches to ethics you may think that by continuing to encourage Belinda to go shopping and not take into account her wishes she is in a position of powerlessness. That the right cause of action would be to support Belinda in her decision and work with her to develop alternatives. Perhaps you considered Internet shopping and a home delivery service as a realistic option. Independence is not the most important thing in health and social care, enabling people to live a chosen lifestyle with support may be the best way forward.

(Continued)

(Continued)

The view that people with cognitive impairments, including dementias, do not have the capacity to be autonomous and make decisions is a view that needs to be challenged as it continues discrimination, oppression and marginalization of powerless people which is hidden behind an ethical reasoning. This includes challenging the view that people are unable to make decisions concerning their everyday living as well as more significant decisions concerning where people live and the service they receive. Both Tronto's ethic of care, and Banks' model of progressive values could inform our action.

Non-maleficence

For Beauchamp and Childress (2009) the principle of non-maleficence is an obligation to do no harm. As practitioners we need to know that our actions when we intervene in people's lives do no harm, so it is about not implementing any action that may cause harm to anyone. The implications of a principle of non-maleficence is that we should not kill, harm, cause pain and suffering, incapacitate, or even offend someone. In practice situations it may be difficult to establish how this translates into action. In attempting to clarify this Campion-Smith (2007, in Open University 2010) suggests that in doing no harm, health and social care workers need to be aware of their own limitations and only intervene when they have sufficient knowledge and skills and to avoid interventions that have not been proven to work. It is also about communicating effectively with people and being transparent about interventions and treatments and taking into account people's beliefs and personal values when working with them. Difficult situations could also arise in practice situations where withdrawal of a service may cause harm, and the role of health and social care workers may be to speak out, challenge and resist unjust and even harmful practices and policy.

Beneficence and the promotion of welfare or well-being

Beneficence and the promotion of welfare is about providing benefit and 'good' to people. This is different from the ideas of non-maleficence as beneficence is a positive act to help other people, not simply to refrain from harming them.

Beauchamp and Childress (2009) argue that practitioners should contribute to the welfare of people and make a positive contribution to help other people. They see the principles of beneficence as being distinguishable from the virtue of benevolence and being a positive action where intended to benefit another person. There are two aspects of beneficence.

- Positive beneficence requires that a person provides benefit to someone else. Here the health and social care worker must make sure that the service being delivered will benefit the person receiving the service.
- Utility beneficence is about balancing risk and benefit with cost to bring about the best possible outcome. In this aspect beneficence and the delivery of services are linked to utilitarian principles in that they may involve a balancing of cost and benefit to determine the action that provides the greatest benefit.

The principle of beneficence may seem straightforward, that the services we provide create good outcomes for people. In deciding the best course of action, beneficence may become an abstract idea that is difficult to put into practice. On a practice level Campion-Smith (2007, in Open University 2010) suggests that beneficence could be about supporting a person's decision about refusing treatment, considering the best course of action, consulting with service users, remaining up to date with the effectiveness of interventions and using the care relationship with service users effectively.

However, the principle of beneficence and the promotion of good is open to interpretation. The definition of what is good can be socially and culturally determined. There are different views and definitions of what a good quality of life is and what may be in a person's best interest. Making assumptions about acting in people's best interest could result in paternalism which continues the marginalization and powerlessness of people. In this way beneficence could be used as an ethical approach that continues to harm people through oppressive practice. It therefore becomes important to challenge benevolent claims of acting in people's best interest.

Justice and distributive justice

The general principle of justice is linked to ideas of treating people equally and is also seen as fairness (Rawls 1972). General ideas of treating people equally may not be helpful in health and social care, so justice also becomes linked to ideas of entitlement and what is deserved. For Beauchamp and Childress the moral principle of justice is concerned with inequality in accessing services and is about the equitable distribution of care and the delivery of appropriate treatment and services and the equal treatment of people.

Distributive justice is about the fair, equitable and appropriate distribution of all rights and responsibilities in society, including civil and political rights. For Banks, distributive justice can be according to certain rules and criteria, which can be selected from people's existing rights, 'desert' and need. To help with the distribution of resources Beauchamp and Childress outline material principles to consider for each person, suggesting that to each person resources can be distributed in equal share, according to need, effort, contribution, merit and free-market exchange. These material principles may conflict and each one may be more appropriate in certain situations. Issues are raised whether or not resources should be redistributed equally in equal share, or people in greatest need take priority. Resource allocation could depend on who has taken more personal responsibility for their own welfare (effort) or contributed more to the service (contribution). Some people may be considered as more deserving based on merit, and others may be able to help with the purchase of their own services (free-market) and so become a priority for service allocation (Open University 2009).

The principle of justice is about treating people equally and fairly yet acting in accordance with it is challenging and creates problems in the allocation of time and resources. This is a fundamental part of social and health care: that practitioners are involved in and are responsible for the distribution of public resources according to set eligibility criteria and assessment of clinical and care needs. At a practice level Campion-Smith (2007, in Open University 2010) suggests that an attempt to apply the principle of justice may influence practitioners in a number of ways. They may distinguish between a person's wants and needs, and find themselves accounting for the distribution of limited resources. In promoting fairness and justice it may be necessary to enable less powerful service users to express their interests and use the time they have equitably to do so. In this way a principle of justice is linked with the principle of equality and the removal of disadvantage.

Equality

Equality is usually linked to the removal of socially created inequalities. There are inequalities reflecting the social stratification of society where different groups have more power, influence, prestige and wealth and it is important to distinguish between socially created inequalities and social stratification. Social equality is linked to the principle of justice and can for some be within the concept of justice. For Banks (2000) it is about 'the removal of disadvantage' and can be regarded in different ways.

The idea of equal treatment may provide some basic principle that people should not be treated disadvantageously by discrimination and prejudice, but as Bagihole (1997) points out, this does not tackle the complex interaction between the social, political and economic issues surrounding the concept of equality. Equality of opportunity is the 'provision of equality of access to institutions and social positions amongst relevant social groups' (Bagihole 1997: 32).

For social care workers this may include 'the removal of disadvantage in competition with others, giving people the means to achieve socially desired ends' (Banks 2000: 39). This would for instance enable the same access to information for people who do not read as people who do read, information about services being made available to people in symbols, for instance.

Enabling equality of access does not tackle issues of equality of condition. Equality of condition is about recognizing the material and cultural disadvantages that some groups in society have. So Bagihole (1997) suggests that inequalities of condition can obstruct real equalities of opportunity as people are not starting from the same position.

Equality of result or outcome is a radical approach to equal opportunity that is about applying differing policies and procedures to different social groups in an attempt to remove past discrimination and disadvantage. This becomes the application of preferential treatment to different groups because 'past disadvantages require us to treat people unequally' (Jenks 1988, quoted in Bagihole 1997: 33).

For Banks, social (care) workers are involved in the differing forms of promoting equality. She suggests that equality of treatment is easier to achieve, and this also fits in with the moral principle of respecting the person. Equality of opportunity may require policy decisions while equality of result involves practitioners with the radical agenda of tackling oppression and discrimination. Thompson (2003) regards equality as essentially concerning itself with human rights, and that as health and social care workers an essential component of the work we do is to challenge inequality and promote social justice.

The concept of equality itself is complex. Promoting equal treatment through equal opportunity and tackling inequalities of condition are essential. For Dahrendorf (1968) the absolute equality between people is simply not possible due to social stratification. Inequality will continue to exist and he is suspicious of governments or policy makers who promise equal societies, as political promises are often 'a thin veil for the threat of terror and constraint'. He suggests that the very existence of social inequality is an 'impetus towards liberty'. Taking Dahrendorf's message, we need to be aware that a principle of equality is not used as a veil by policy makers to continue the oppression of the people we work with and that oppressive practice and policies need to be challenged.

Working with ethical approaches

The idea of using ideas from moral philosophy and having a set of principles to guide practice is not without its problems. How do we know which moral theory or set of moral principles we should be using at any one particular point in time or in any one situation? The different ethical approaches, whether they are utilitarian, deontological, virtues, or progressive, and the moral principles of autonomy, non-maleficence, beneficence, justice and equality, are not separate entities. They have a relationship with each other in that they overlap and conflict with each other. The principle of autonomy is apparent across the range of the ethical approaches and this has led Dawson and Butler (2003) to suggest that principles concerning the autonomy of people tend to be concentrated upon at the expense of the others. Yet Beauchamp and Childress (2009) make it very clear that in terms of moral principles, they all have equal importance. There is a need to be aware of the competing values and moral principles because, unless we are, it may be easy to favour one over all the others without fully recognizing the ethical issues presented in our practice and interventions in people's lives. The skill of the practitioner is to be able to use them in a combined way. It is important to engage with the ethical issues in the practice context and recognize the moral principles at play, recognize the dilemmas these create, assess the strengths and weaknesses of possible ethical decisions and to act in a way that reflects what you think and believe to be the right action; to challenge the notion that as health and social care professionals we do not need prescriptive codes to guide our actions and interventions in people's lives. What is needed is an understanding of morals and values that enable practitioners to reflect upon interventions within a moral context so that as practitioners we can be morally responsible for our actions and act with moral courage within a framework of an ethic of care. Bauman (1994, quoted in Hugman 2003), suggests that to act morally is to take responsibility for another person and that person's well-being is a 'precious thing' that should be preserved and enhanced. Hugman (2003) explains that from the perspective of Foucault, to act ethically is not to deceive and to take as a starting point not to deceive oneself. So it becomes important to scrutinize oneself and be aware of one's own perspectives. This is important, as Carritt (1930) suggests that to act morally is to act in a way that you think is right.

Ethical frameworks

Working with the complexity of ethical approaches can seem daunting. To help social and health care practitioners work through ethical issues, ethical frameworks have been developed to provide a process and a structure to systematically work through. Using ethical frameworks can help not only in making decisions but also in justifying action.

The Open University (2009) has devised an ethics framework that is based on a reflective model.

The ETHICS Framework (Open University 2009)

Enquire about the facts of the case – You will need to consider what facts or descriptive claims are relevant and how they bear on the case or situation.

Think (and, if appropriate, talk) through the options available to those involved – Consider what options are available to the different people in the situation; for example, the option to refuse or accept treatment, to tell or withhold the truth, to maintain or breach confidentiality, to respect or disrespect wishes of others.

Hear the views of those involved – Where possible, this would include the patient or service user and professionals and, where appropriate, the views of family members or friends (if the patient/service user agrees or is unable to express a view).

Identify relevant principles and other values – Here you can engage with the repertoire of ethical theories and approaches you have learned about so far; for example, consequentialism, duty-based theories, and principles. This is a normative enquiry to suggest what ought to be done. Select those theories that appear most relevant to the situation.

Clarify the meaning and implications of the key values – If, for example, autonomy is one of the key values, you should identify the key features (acting intentionally, with understanding and without controlling influences) and what follows from this.

Select a course of action, drawing on the ethical values and arguments you have considered – You might, for example, argue that a doctor should maintain confidentiality in a particular situation and present arguments based on:

- consequences (there are better consequences, for example, from maintaining than breaching confidentiality in this situation)
- duties (doctors have a duty to maintain confidentiality in this situation), or
- principles (respect for autonomy is, for example, a key principle supporting confidentiality).

The Open University ETHICS framework (2009) does not provide a clear cut answer to working with the competing demands of conflicting values. It highlights the complexity of working with people and working with a set of often conflicting and competing values. Despite this the framework enables us to focus our attention and consider a range of options based on an understanding and awareness of values and ethics.

There are other ethical decision making frameworks. Seedhouse (2009) has developed a practical ethical grid to guide ethical decision making in health care. He has also developed a values-exchange community, which enables people to work through ethical problems on-line and to solve ethical conflicts. The values-exchange can be found at www.values-exchange.com/ and is free to use and access.

Seedhouse's Ethical Grid (adapted from Stutchbury and Fox 2009)

Seedhouse suggests that ethical dilemmas are like a spider's web where ideas are all connected. The grid is in four concentric layers, where the layers represent four aspects of comprehensive ethical analysis in terms of: external, consequential, deontological and individual perspectives (see Figure 6.2). Each layer represents an ethical 'aspect' to a situation and each 'aspect' approaches the situation from a different perspective. The outer (bottom) layer for example encourages us to think at an organizational level whereas the inner (uppermost) layer concentrates on individuals. Within each layer there are boxes that identify different issues within that aspect. For any given dilemma, all, some, or even just one of the boxes in a particular layer, might be relevant in that context. The position of the boxes in one layer relative to those in the next layer is not significant.

(Continued)

(Continued)

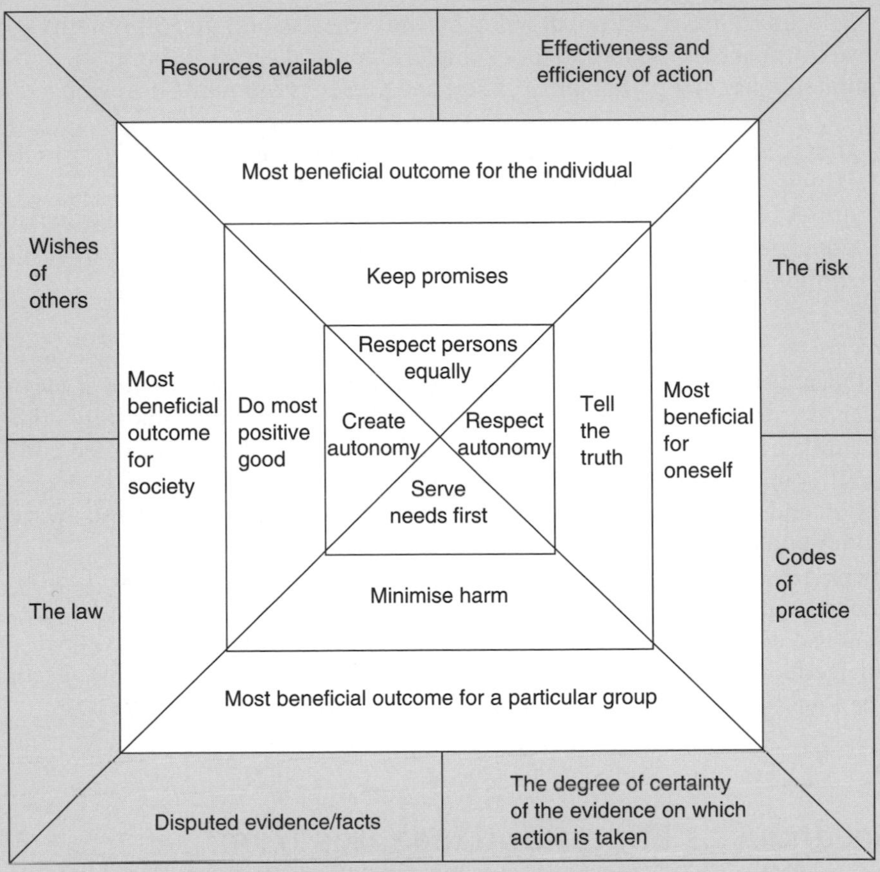

Figure 6.2   Seedhouse's Ethical Grid

Source: Seedhouse, D. (2009) *Ethics: The Heart of Healthcare*, 3rd edn. Chichester: Wiley-Blackwell.

The layers can be summarized as follows:

- The *External layer (outer layer)* includes all the external issues, such as the law, codes of practice, and use of resources available and the context of practice.
- The *Consequential layer* is about the consequences of possible actions for society, for individuals or for particular groups of people.
- The *Deontological layer* covers issues to do with 'duty' and consideration of possible actions.
- The *Inner layer (uppermost layer)* covers the 'core rationale' and includes issues of respect for the individual and autonomy.

The grid is not intended to be an exact representation of the mental processes that make up moral reasoning but it provides, through its language, a practical and accessible route into the processes of moral reasoning. The point of the grid is not that it will solve ethical dilemmas, but that it provides a moral framework for thinking about them.

Competing values, ethical issues and dilemmas

Working through the different ethical approaches and ethical frameworks it becomes apparent that working with values and ethics is complex. This is compounded where values compete because they are held at different levels. Martin and Henderson (2001) point out that values are held at a societal, organizational, team and individual level and that these different levels interact and influence each other. It will be inevitable that tensions and conflicts may exist between values at the different levels. These tensions will sometimes result in ethical dilemmas and problems for social and health care workers.

Societies and cultures across the globe have a diverse range of values, of what is believed to be right or wrong. This diversity is replicated, complicated and transformed in modern industrialized/pluralistic societies where there is no one defining culture and where different values, codes and rules exist side by side, and become integrated and transformed into new ideas of what is right or wrong.

Organizational values reflect the values of society but also the government of the time. The policy of government will influence the values of the organizations delivering services, which are reflected in policy statements, plans and mission statements. The managerialist and consumerist policies implemented since 1979 have greatly influenced the delivery of welfare services and have created a range of ethical conflicts for health and social care practitioners.

Societal and organizational values

Go to www.dh.gov.uk, browse the home page and have a look at some of the latest news and information from the government. You will find a wide range of government announcements and plans concerning the delivery of health and social care services. You may find the information overwhelming, so try to look at a current issue that you are interested in.

Try to identify the values and moral principles that seem to underpin the government's statements and proposals.

Can you identify statements that reflect a utilitarian or deontological approach to service delivery?

Do the statements reflect a service user perspective and to what extent are people in control?

(Continued)

(Continued)

To what extent does the government reflect a radical approach to service delivery? Is the government virtuous in its action?

Commentary

In looking at the government's statements you may have thought that the government is striving for the greater good in providing services to meet the needs of people who are in need. You may have noted the language of service user involvement, giving the impression that every one is treated with a degree of autonomy and that patients and service users are encouraged to have a say and be in control of the services they receive. You may have noted comments informed by ideas of care services being delivered equally yet quantified by statements reflecting ideas of distributed justice, where the market is mentioned. You may even have found statements that reflect the need for the workforce to have the virtue of compassion.

You may have found it interesting and fascinating to note how government rhetoric employs the language of values and moral principles. It is important to analyse these statements and policies with a critical approach and determine how statements that seem to reflect the language of equality may disguise policies and practice that disempower people.

Working in teams is an integral part of health and social care. A team is a group of people who are working together towards a common aim. The team has a shared task, and in terms of health and social care this shared task will be to provide a service to people who use that service. The team may also have a shared set of values influenced by the professional organization it works for and the people who use the service.

As health and social care services increasingly work collaboratively and in partnership with other agencies and organizations there may well be differences in professional values appearing. As services move towards integration with differing professional groups coming together, there may well be the formation of new integrated values. There may also be the possibility of a clash of values between different professional groups with differing professional ideologies.

Eby (1994, 2000b) points out that ethical problems arise when there is a conflict between competing values and principles, and this results in ethical distress or creates an ethical dilemma. Ethical distress is when a barrier prevents a course of action. In such situations the values of the organization may conflict with personal individual values. What you believe is right cannot be enacted because the organization has other priorities.

An ethical dilemma is when there is a choice to make between moral principles. In one instance there is a choice between equally right courses of action; the decision is which morally right decision to make between the two. The other instance is whatever decision you make will result in a compromise of values or principles. Ethical dilemmas can occur between competing values at the personal individual level and competing values held at different levels, such as the individual and organizational and within teams.

It is important to reflect on your role as a social and health care practitioner, to look at the wider social context of the work you are doing, the moral and ethical base of your work, and your guiding moral and ethical principles. Hopefully the discussion within the areas we have looked at so far in this chapter has helped you in reflecting on your moral position and determining what you believe to be morally right. As practitioners we need to act in a way that is morally and ethically right; for Husband (1995) this means we need to be morally active practitioners, and as Banks (2011) has suggested, have the moral courage to act in a morally right way.

To act as morally active practitioners with moral courage is to act as autonomous moral agents. This is about using internal values rather than externally imposed policies or guidelines, such as codes of conduct, to base ethical decision making on. For Husband the morally active practitioner would therefore recognize professional ethics as external guidelines backed by external pressures of professional bodies. This is not to say that ethical guidelines are not desirable, but Husband is suggesting that practitioners should not hide behind 'ethical anaesthesia' but keep responsibility for their own professional practice.

Exploring professional codes of conduct

Codes of practice become a method by which professional morality is formalized and codified. They often become rules as well as reinforcing professional obligations and values. For Eby and Gallagher (2008) they are there to not only serve the interests of professional groups, but also protect the public. Choose a professional area that is of interest to you and use an Internet search for the relevant code of professional conduct. For instance:

For social care in England: go to Skills for Care at www.skillsforcare.org.uk and search for 'codes of conduct'

For social work in England: go to the Health and Care Professions Council at www.hpc-uk.org and search for 'standards of conduct, performance and ethics'

For social care and social work in Scotland: go to the Scottish Social Services Council at www.sssc.uk.com and follow the link for 'Codes of Practice'

Wales: go to the Care Council for Wales at www.ccwales.org.uk and follow the links to 'Codes of Practice'

(Continued)

(Continued)

Northern Ireland: go to the Northern Ireland Social Care Council at www.niscc.info and follow the links for 'Conduct'

For social work in Britain go to the British Association of Social Work at www.basw.co.uk and follow the links for 'Codes of Ethics'

For health care (nursing): go to the Nursing Midwifery Council at www.nmc-uk.org and follow the links to 'The Code'

Consider the function of the codes and think about their role in providing guidance and information to professionals and the public. To what extent do you think they regulate professional activity and do they suggest any disciplinary measures? Do the codes offer any protection to the public?

Have a look at the language contained in the codes and consider if there is any room for negotiation, and consider if there are any conflicts within the codes themselves or with your own ethical or personal position.

Who do you think has produced these codes and has there been any input by professionals and service users?

Using the information you have read so far, explore to what extent professional codes of conduct can be regarded as moral principles. Is there any room to demonstrate moral autonomy or moral courage?

Commentary

From exploring the codes of conduct, you may have thought that they provide guidance to professionals on what is expected in terms of their duties and obligations. There may be statements about being up to date with relevant skills and knowledge and working in the best interests of service users and patients. There may be professional sanctions for breaking the codes which result in being taken off a professional register. Professionals may well have had an input in developing the codes, but it is unlikely that patients and service users have had any say.

You may have been able to recognize a range of ethical approaches within the codes. For instance, there may be statements relating to doing good and providing benefit to people which seem to have an overall utilitarian framework, where services are provided to the greatest number for the greatest good. There may be phrases reflecting duties such as respecting people, and refraining from harming people. You may have noted statements reflecting ideas around rights and self-determination. There may even be statements expecting virtues of honesty and integrity. In exploring these statements you may have come to the conclusion that some of them may even be in conflict with each other.

You may have considered the language in some of the codes leaves little room for negotiation as the codes contain statements clearly saying what a worker 'must do', which seems to place a set of duties on health and social care workers. Other codes, especially from BASW and the NMC, seem to be less restrictive. Some of the codes also place expectations on workers to behave in ways in their personal life and you may have thought that a worker's personal life should have no impact on their professional life. You may have noticed a difference between voluntary codes, such as the ones from BASW, and the required codes of conduct from the other bodies.

In exploring the codes you may have come to the conclusion that they seem to provide an aid to help in decision making and provide guidelines for practice, some of which we would not disagree with, but they fall short of being moral principles. You may have thought that keeping strictly to the codes themselves may restrict your ability to be morally active and demonstrate moral courage because of the consequences of acting outside the codes.

Empowerment: a core moral principle

Empowerment has become central to health and social care. It is a central moral premise to aid decision making, demonstrate moral courage and act as a morally autonomous agent. The problem is that it means different things to different people and has become diluted away from meaning a real shift in power from providers to users of services. As we explore empowerment we can see how as a central value it can encompass a range of moral principles to become a core moral principle.

Gillon (1994, 2003, in Dawson and Butler 2003; Open University 2010) sees autonomy as being present in the principles of non-maleficence, beneficence and justice, and particularly regards empowerment as the combination of the moral principles of beneficence and the respect for autonomy. In deontological terms it can be seen as a duty and reflects Kant's principle of respecting people as being able to make choices and decisions about their lives. From a utilitarian perspective it reflects the greater good, especially if the greater good is from a service user perspective. The moral virtue of courage seems to be a part of challenging oppression, which is clearly part of the radical and progressive approach to values.

An early definition of empowerment from Rappaport (1981) suggests that empowerment is about enabling people to be in control of their lives. This central premise of empowerment has been at the centre of service user initiatives calling for a greater service user involvement about the delivery of welfare services. This has ultimately led to current government policy where the language of empowerment has entered the everyday language of health and social care. There is now a different relationship between service users and providers, with more emphasis being placed on people being able to choose and commission their own services through access to a personal budget. The intention that people will be in control of the help they receive dominates government policy. The White Paper Caring for Our Future: Reforming Care and Support (Department of Health 2012b) is underpinned by the principle 'that people should be in control of their own care and support' through the 'new person centred system'.

The government and empowerment

Visit the Department of Health website at www.dh.gov.uk and search for a range of topics associated with the language of empowerment. For instance try searching for:

- Personalization
- In Control
- Person Centred

Read the information on the pages that come up and consider the language used and how the government hopes to empower people.

Commentary

You will have come across a wealth of information, policy statements, stories, news items and video links concerning how the government is implementing its care agenda. You may have noticed some interesting use of language, some of which may come across as contradictory. For instance you may have found statements suggesting that people 'will' be in control or 'should' be in control, and others about enabling people to 'feel' that they are in control. There seems to be language that resolves conflict between service users and providers where people will no longer have to fight against the system. You may have also noted a 'well-being agenda', where the aim is to help people feel they have more of a say and so are happier. There seems to be a distinction in the government rhetoric about actually 'being' in control and 'feeling' in control. It would seem that the focus on having a feeling of control detracts from having any real power.

It seems that the government's way to empower people, or to enable them to feel in control, is to give people an entitlement to a personal budget to enter the market place of care. The development of the social care market seems to be a significant part of the government agenda.

The problem is, as Gomm (1993) has pointed out, 'empowerment' has become something of a buzzword and can mean different things to different people and organizations. Payne (1997) defines empowerment as helping people gain power of decisions and actions over their own lives. Adams (2008) defines empowerment as the way 'the capacity of individuals, groups and/or communities to take control of their circumstances, exercise power and achieve their own goals and the process by which, individually and collectively, they are able to help themselves and others' (2008: 17). Aujoulat et al. (2007) see empowerment in terms of people being responsible for their choices and the consequences of their choices and as an alternative to compliance. In this sense empowerment becomes about moving away from a paternalistic and medical model of service provision to acknowledge that people can negotiate and participate to make decisions about their care needs. Piper (2010) suggests that empowerment is concerned with a levelling out of power between practitioners and service users. These views of empowerment suggest an equal distribution of power, which as Piper points out will depend on how much power service providers are willing to devolve. This process of empowerment is complicated by professional expertise, the drive towards evidence-based practice and by service users being comfortable with leaving decision making to professionals. With this in mind, Aujoulat et al. (2007) suggest that empowerment should be about self-determination, where people are able to determine the level of participation and decision making. It would seem, as Zimmerman (2000) suggests, that empowerment is context-specific in that it can take on different forms for different people in different situations.

Shardlow (2002) identifies empowerment as challenging oppression and is quite clearly linked to a radical approach in terms of values. Riger (1993) has pointed out that empowerment is both about having a sense of control and actually having power. Riger (1993) argues that a person's sense of having power is unrelated to having any real ability to influence and does not reflect an actual increase in power. Any confusion of actually having an ability to control resources with a sense of empowerment depoliticizes the process of empowerment. There is a danger that the language of empowerment can conceal the reality of professional power and dominance.

These definitions also reflect the process of empowerment as distinct from the outcome of empowerment. The process is how people are enabled to participate and make decisions while the outcome of empowerment is the consequence of being more in control (Zimmerman 2000).

Given this complexity around empowerment it is important that practitioners need to be clear about what it means. At the centre of the concept is power and control, so empowerment is about a struggle for power and exerting control at an individual level. It is also a political process, where an empowered person is someone who has power and can exert real control at a structural level. We will explore different models of empowering practice in an attempt to clarify its meaning and so enable you to use the ideas as a framework to develop an empowering value base.

Power and empowerment

To understand the concept of empowerment we need to explore the meaning of power, how it affects the people we work with and how we use power.

Davies (1981) pointed out nearly 35 years ago that social (care) workers are in a position of power and authority. His message continues to be applicable today: that practitioners need to be aware of their power and authority in relation to people who use social and health care services. The influence of authority has been famously demonstrated by Milgram (1963 in Banyard 2012) where he showed that people are willing to defer responsibility for their actions to those in authority. Power is a part of relationships between people, different groups and organizations. As they intervene in people's lives, practitioners need to be aware of their position in the web of power, which surrounds people who use services. Our value base needs to take into account this inferred authority as we make ethical decisions about and intervene in the lives of people who use health and social care services.

There are a range of sociological and social psychological approaches to exploring power. French and Raven (1959 in Orford 2008) describe authority in terms of coercive, reward, legitimate, expert, personal and informational. Wrong (1979, in Orford 2010) added persuasion, force and manipulation. Orford suggests the different forms of power can be used in combination or in sequence by those in a position of power. Thompson (2003) sees power as 'the ability to influence and control people, events processes or resources' and Smail (1995 in Orford 2008: 37) defines power as 'the means of obtaining security and advantage'. There is a positive side to power which enables things to be done, but there is also a flip side in which power can be destructive, exploitative, oppressive or abusive to dominate and constrain others. For Dahrendorf (1959) power and authority is complex and distributed amongst different organizations and people and because of this 'conflict' is an essential aspect of understanding power. It is important to understand issues concerning power if we are to work in an empowering way, both at a process and outcome level.

The use of power is not always overt; it is often hidden and this is apparent in Luke's ideas of power, where power is exercised by preventing issues being discussed, keeping information secret by controlling the agenda and by a subtle way of controlling attitudes and situations by the application of unchallenged assumptions (Luke 2005).

ACTIVITY

Thinking about power

Consider how these views of power relate to your role as a health and social care worker.

Think about your relationship with the people you work with and consider how the concept of power is apparent between you and others.

Think about what gives you power to make decisions, or even not make a decision, about the service provided to someone.

Do you have more knowledge about services that you are able to provide?

Consider your outward appearance, the clothes you are wearing and how you present yourself. Are these statements of your professional power?

Commentary

You may have thought that as a health and social care practitioner your position of power is in relation to the people you work with. Power may be inherent in the relationship itself, with you seen as an expert and a professional. You may have some influence over decisions that affect the service people will receive. You may be in a position to decide the resources that are available to provide the services that people say they need. You may have considered that having knowledge of which services are available or which to offer places you in a position of power in relation to the person requiring your service. Your choice to tell people about possible services could reflect a position of power. You may think that your theoretical understanding of issues and knowledge of research-based evidence places you in a position of power. You may have thought that your security comes from the organization you work for, which has a mandate to provide services as well as statutory duties to intervene in people's lives. If you wear a uniform, or work in a particular establishment, or for a particular organization, you may have considered that these give you security in your role as well as expectations of your role. As soon as you enter into the life of another person, you are the face and personal representative of a powerful organization and you may have thought that immediately creates an assumption about your position and the service you can offer. You may have thought that this places you in a clear position of advantage.

Allen (2000) and Thompson (2003) both refer to Weberian concepts and the ideas of Foucault to explain power.

In a Weberian sense welfare organizations such as health and social care agencies can be regarded as bureaucratic organizations, with clear hierarchical structures. There are people in definite positions of power. The structure of the organization resembles a pyramid and this hierarchy legitimizes and reinforces people's position and their power in relation to other people. There are lines of accountability and systems such as supervision and the allocation of tasks, roles and responsibilities also maintain everyone's position.

In contrast to this model of power Foucault sees power as something that is all around us and the idea of space becomes important in the way power is expressed, organized and exercised. Rather than being controlled by those above us in the hierarchy, power is seen as a guiding force that controls what we do and where we do it. We control ourselves due to the practices and systems of society, organizations and the actual space we are in. The space can be an office or waiting room where there are certain conventions and expectations of behaviour which are played out with implicit relationships of power. In this way power is felt directly and indirectly. Power is not simply from above but fully encompasses us in an interconnected complex web. Within this complex web of systems and processes we all know our place and we all tend to comply.

Looking at positions of power

(1) Consider your practice in terms of a Weberian framework.

Commentary

You can probably place yourself within a clear hierarchical structure with lines of accountability where power and authority are exercised through systems of supervision. You should be able to clearly identify who is in authority, and probably those people who have expert knowledge and are seen as an authority.

(Continued)

ACTIVITY

(Continued)

You should be able to recognize how your workload and tasks that you need to complete are delegated to you and how this infers a degree of power. You should not only be able to see how the mandate of having this power comes from above, but also from other people you work with and service users. The organization you are in will have a range of procedures and guidelines that you should be able to identify and locate.

(2) In the ideas of Foucault, power has a much more anonymous feel. Now consider your position in your organization using the idea that power is a guiding force and people regulate themselves.

You may have thought that there are various expectations of your role that you are expected to comply with. These expectations also influence how other people come to accept your position as a health and social care worker. You may have thought about how the layout of the office or establishment reflects positions of power and how the message that some people are in a more powerful position than others is transmitted through organizational practices. There may be separate rooms and spaces for people for different tasks. This would include how people who use services are treated and the restrictions placed on people in terms of the rooms that people can use and when.

You may have considered how your practice is observed and monitored feeling that you are under surveillance by others. This feeling of surveillance, being watched, and knowing your place by unseen powers may make you feel that you are in a web of power which influences your practice and your relationship with the people you work with.

An increasingly popular approach to understanding power has been to develop a framework of power from the work of Mary Parker Follett. In formulating her ideas Follet (1924) notes that power can be seen as psychological or personal power and in this sense comes from within. She also points out that power is seen as something that is transferable between people and groups, and can be allocated. She also identifies the idea of 'power over' where people have power and control over others and agues that the only way forward is to see power in terms of 'power with' where power is dependent on cooperation. This she sees as an integrative approach to power, where power is used in an integrated way between people and organizations to achieve desirable objectives.

Another way to look at power that combines individual and societal explanations is social dominance theory. Orford (2008) explains that it draws upon a range of psychological, social psychological and sociological ideas to address issues of unequal social power. Central to social dominance theory is the idea of social stratification, where society is stratified by age; where adults have power over children and young people; gender reflected in patriarchy, and an 'arbitrary-set system' where groups are hierarchically organized in terms such as ethnicity, class and belief, reflecting status and power. The hierarchy is maintained by individuals supporting the domination of 'inferior' groups by 'superior' groups. It is maintained at a societal level by the continuation of discrimination which can be overt or covert. It also maintained by those in higher status groups to a greater extent than it is opposed by those in lower status groups. The result of which is that those subordinate positions participate in and contribute towards their continual subordination. The hierarchy is also maintained by shared societal beliefs that reinforce the dominant ideology. This may result in sexism, racism and religious intolerance. Other beliefs may operate in more subtle ways such as placing responsibility for ill health and poverty onto individuals and communities. At the same time there are other influences that combat the maintaining forces such as service user groups, human rights movements and feminist organizations, and the result is a balance or equilibrium. The view of social dominance theory is a pessimistic one, as those with greater status and power continue to maintain their position.

An understanding of power may provide a framework for analysis, but putting into practice ideas of how power can be shifted, where people have a control and influence rather than just a sense of control and work in an empowering way is difficult and problematic. As health and social care workers we need to develop an understanding of structural barriers to empowerment and develop strategies of practice that can overcome these barriers. There exists a wide range of methods, practices and policies within health and social care where the intention is the empowerment of individuals, groups and communities and by exploring some of these we may be able to develop an understanding of empowering practice.

Normalization and social role valorization

The principle of normalization has been extremely influential in the development of community-based services in the UK since the 1980s and continues to be so. Different strands of the theoretical underpinnings of normalization developed in Scandinavia, the United States and also in the UK. It is seen as a model of empowerment because it called for people to be able to access everyday services in the community, such as housing, education, employment, transport and recreational facilities.

Normalization has its roots in the work of Erving Goffman and his concept of stigma. Goffman (1963) states that if a person is seen to be different and seen as a 'less desired kind' of person by others that person becomes 'tainted'.

The ideas around normalization are designed to counter stigma so that a person has a valued role and their 'undesired differences are reduced'. The principles underlying this concept have led to the ideas that people should be enabled to live ordinary lives, enjoy the benefits of living in the community and be regarded as part of the community and society with valued roles. Living an ordinary life is seen as a socially valued concept and something that should remove stigma and discrimination. Long-term institutions were closing in the 1980s and it was seen as right that people should live in the community rather than be excluded from the mainstream of society.

Wolfensberger and Tullman (1982) define the principle of normalization as 'the use of culturally valued means in order to enable, establish and/or maintain valued social roles for people'. Wolfensberger (1998) later elaborated on his concept and renamed his idea social role 'valorization'. He is very clear that:

> in order for people to be treated well by others, it is very important that they be seen as occupying valued roles ... [and that] ... the greater number of valued roles a person ... occupies, the more likely it is that [they] will be accorded those good things of life. (Wolfensberger 1998: 58)

He also goes on to suggest that it is a value judgement of the professional as to whether or not a person should be valued by others.

So, for Wolfensberger, service provision should be based on the creation and establishment of socially valued roles. If services promoted positive roles for people, the negative consequences of being labelled would diminish. Wolfensberger suggests some very specific examples of how devalued people should improve their chances of being socially valued. This includes for example the notion that people should wear appropriate clothing so as to fit in with social situations. Thus people become valued for fitting into the mainstream.

The concept was embraced by social work professionals to improve the lives of people leaving long-term institutions. Professional practice reflected the need to provide people with opportunities to experience valued social positions and these opportunities would deal with how people were treated as non-valued citizens.

Despite their influence on services the ideas of normalization and social role valorization have been criticized on a number of levels. Scott (1970) suggests that in responding to stigma professionals create their own conception of stigma, reflecting the 'social, cultural and economic environments' of which the professional is a part. In this sense normalization as a response to stigma can be seen as a professional construction of a person's identity based upon professional expectations of being a person who is stigmatized.

As Brown and Walmsley (1997) point out, service based on these principles may reject the need for services that are designed to meet individual need. The emphasis on normally valued roles and services could be at the expense of meeting specialized need and place the need for change with the individual rather than with the structures of society.

Normalization also has an emphasis on integration and relationships with people who are regarded as not being stigmatized rather than collective action. The condition responsible for the stigmatization of an individual is placed with the person rather than the organization of society and the ideas of what is regarded as positive are perpetuated by a dominant ideology. So the social dominance of people over people who are subject to normalization-based services is maintained.

Normalization has had a significant impact on empowering service users and has changed the face of service delivery from institutional care to community-based services. This should not be ignored, but as a basis for making value-based decisions and as a model of empowerment it needs to be questioned. People should be valued as people, not for the roles they have. It is a professional model devised and implemented by professionals with little or no input from the people who use services.

Advocacy

Despite the good intentions of service providers and professionals, some people who use services simply do not have their voices heard. A range of issues may be responsible for people's voices not being acknowledged, from a service that is not reciprocal or acknowledging that people have different methods of communication to implicit disempowerment of individuals by others in positions of power. Goodley and Ramcharan (2005) suggest that people's views, aspirations and ambitions are dismissed because of the view that some people have nothing important to say and that because of different cognitive abilities people lack the awareness to say anything of any worth. People's views are dismissed because they do not know what is best for them, or it is the professional who knows the most appropriate course of action. To enable people's voices to be heard the practice of advocacy has entered into health and social care practice. The central idea of advocacy is defined by Goodley and Ramcharan as that a 'person speaks for themselves or that an advocate speaks for that person as if that person's voice were their own' (2005: 152).

This raises a number of issues about enabling people to speak up for themselves and the position of the advocate. Systems need to be in place that enable people to voice their concerns and opinions concerning their services, and about being involved in the decisions that are made about them; people's voices need to be recognized as valuable and their views taken on board. This approach to advocacy presents challenges to social care workers and organizations as it is a challenge to professional and organizational power. Advocates also need to be able to voice the views of other people without any judgement of that view. To voice another's view as if it was his or her own, an advocate would need to represent that view regardless of his or her own views. The advocate's role is simply to represent the views of someone so that the view is heard and taken seriously.

A number of different models of advocacy (see Table 6.1) have developed over the past 20 years, with different characteristics and qualities. The different approaches to advocacy have a range of weaknesses yet it is a central theme of services, especially with people who use learning difficulty services.

In reviewing the evidence on advocacy for people with high support needs Lawton (2009) identifies five models for supporting self-advocacy: rights-based, person-centred, Watching Brief, witness–observer and 'best interest'. Each model attempts to deliver effective support for people with some focused on external issues, such as housing and practical support needs and others focusing on communication with the service user. Rights-based approaches focus on a person's civil, moral and legal rights, but can be limited to these areas. A person-centred approach recognizes that a way a person expresses their feelings is part of the decision making process. The Watching Brief is a framework for questioning service providers about the service provided, while the witness–observer model is where the advocate refrains from making assumptions but just reports facts based on observations. A best interest approach is about encouraging someone to be involved and to try to establish their views.

Table 6.1 Types of advocacy

Types of advocacy	Characteristics	Weaknesses
Citizen advocacy	Unpaid volunteers linked with a person offering one-to-one support	There can be a difficulty in the recruitment and training of volunteers
	Volunteers are trained in advocacy skills and are able to represent the views of the person they are working with	There can be a skills gap in the requirements of being an advocate
	The relationship can be mutual and significant for both the advocate and partner	The relationship between advocate and partner may create a relationship of dependency and still reflects relationships of power
	The independence from services can give the advocate a strong voice	Citizen advocacy schemes tend to be expensive to run and maintain
Peer advocacy	Advocates tend to have had similar experiences, especially of service provision	Advocates' experience may not always be relevant to the partner's experience
	Advocate and partner can have shared experience of surviving and using services	
	Advocate is independent of the service provider and can be supported by a service survivor/user group	Service providers may attempt to disempower peer advocacy as they disempower service users themselves
	Relationships between advocate and partner can be mutual and develop into meaningful friendships	
Professional advocacy	Trained, paid and qualified advocate acting with their partner	Advocates could be in danger of pushing their own agenda rather than the views of people they represent
	Independent from services or social care organizations	Professional advocates may reflect the needs of service providers to fund advocacy
	Funded from sources away from service providers so that their independence is not compromised	Professional advocates may move on to other employment and leave people in a vacuum

Types of advocacy	Characteristics	Weaknesses
	The professional advocate can be hosted within another community service such as Citizens Advice Bureau or within its own separate organization	Confirms positions of professional power and expert
	The professional advocate has the backing of an independent organization and is accountable to the organization as well as the person	
Parent/carer advocacy	Obligation, care and kinship define the relationship and parents and carers may have the best interest of people at heart	Parents' and carers' needs may override the needs of people who need to have their voices heard
		Possible conflict of interest between the needs of carers and the views of people
		Possible overprotection issues and denial of risk taking
Self-advocacy	People voicing their own views either collectively in groups or individually	May require support from other people
	Challenges professional power and expertise	Requires support from professionals and agencies who may limit the impact of self-advocacy

Source: Based on Goodley and Ramcharan (2005)

Goodley and Ramcharan (2005) also suggest that advocacy has shifted from being led by professionals to being supported by professionals and the Social Care Institute for Excellence (SCIE 2009) suggest that as services develop this advocacy support should also change from enabling people to challenge decisions to focusing on enabling people to be in control. In this way supporting people through a process of advocacy can be seen as a model of 'power with'.

In the move towards being more in control, there has been a rise in self-advocacy as a model of empowering people. Workers at People First (Open University 1996) define self-advocacy as speaking up for yourself, being able to stand up for your rights and making choices. For self-advocacy to be a successful empowering process professionals and organizations need to support fully the ethos of self-advocacy and be prepared to have their power challenged and to relinquish the power they have. As Aspis (1999) points out, people in self-advocacy groups should have more power than those advising them and challenge the imbalances of power between disabled and non-disabled people. This moves away from a 'power with' model to a 'power to', where power becomes transferred.

People also need to develop the skills required to advocate for themselves and others, and yet there are problems in who defines what these skills are. Agencies and professionals tend to define what is an accepted method of communication rather than accept that different people have different methods of speaking up for themselves.

Aspis (1997, 1999) is critical of how organizations and society have reacted to the self-advocacy movement. She comments that self-advocacy groups have successfully campaigned for moral rights, that is, what people should have. Moral rights are different from legal rights. Legal rights are enforceable while the granting of moral rights is dependent on the goodwill of those in power. As a consequence, there is no sanction against those that fail to uphold the moral rights requested by self-advocacy groups.

Aspis (1997) also suggests that self-advocacy groups are in danger of becoming mechanisms for service user consultation rather than challenging the provision of services. Such a method of empowering people reflects a managerial approach rather than a democratic approach. Beresford and Croft (2003) point out that a democratic approach would lead to user-controlled services and a redistribution of power from service providers and professionals to service users. A managerial approach on the other hand maintains a provider-led approach to service delivery.

Despite these concerns service carer and user groups have been increasingly involved in local policy decisions about service delivery. This may reflect the idea of organizations transferring power to service user groups, but some groups may still lack personal power to challenge more powerful professionals who still maintain their influence over people. Service providers can also set the agenda for the scope and influence of self-advocacy. Advocates can speak up, tell their social care worker what they want, tell the Social Services Department how services should look, but those who have influence and control over resources and decisions with the power can control the agenda and choose to ignore or dismiss the requests of groups and individuals as being inappropriate or unrealistic and maintain their socially dominant position. Any concessions made to self-advocacy groups or individuals could be limited and as a result do not challenge the power of organizations or professionals. For advocacy to work real concessions of power are needed.

Participation and shared decision making

The idea of participation has a long standing in health and social care. Martin and Henderson (2001) presented a four-stage continuum of participation which can be used to locate a service's commitment to empowerment. At one end is the idea that people have information about the services that they receive. The next point on the continuum is consultation, where people and service user groups can be asked about the services being provided. Consultations with people can be acted upon or ignored by those doing the consulting. Working in partnership involves service users being part of the decision-making process and being members of relevant policy-making bodies. Partnerships tend to contain a relationship of power, and service users may find themselves in unequal partnerships. Delegated control implies giving authority and resources to service user groups to plan and develop user-run services. Delegated services are still accountable to the funding authority. We would add a fifth stage where service users are in total control of services and able to plan and develop services and employ staff to meet their needs (Figure 6.3).

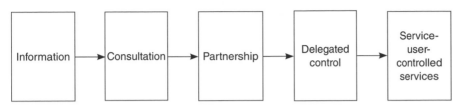

Figure 6.3   The five stage continuum of participation (adapted from Martin and Henderson 2001)

Tritter and McCallum (2006) criticize continuums of participation as they do not support the idea that simply being able to participate is enough for some people. They suggest that in such models the measure of participation is the power to make decisions and the seizing of control becomes the aim of service user involvement. With its focus on outcomes rather than the process of participation they suggest that the process of service user involvement is devalued.

Participation, rather than having control, is central to the idea of shared decision making. Bryant (2012: 38) sees shared decision making as a process where service users/patients and practitioners have access to information and time to discuss 'each other's views so that they can come to a shared understanding of the best plan of action for that particular individual'. Bryant (2012: 41) suggests that the ability to share decision making with patients is a central role of health professionals, who must change 'from experts who care for patients to enablers who support patients to make decisions'.

Coulter and Collins (2011: vii) define shared decision making as the 'process in which clinicians and patients work together to select tests, treatments, management or support packages, based on clinical evidence and the patient's informed preferences'. This mutual discussion process should only take place if the patient wants it to and it should focus on combining the evidence-based knowledge of professionals with the preferences of patients. Coulter and Collins point out that shared decision making is an 'ethical imperative by the professional regulatory bodies' (p. vii). They also highlight that there is 'compelling evidence that patients who are active participants in managing their health and health care have better outcomes than patients who are passive recipients of care'. There is also an assumption that the relationship is mutual and has a sense of equality.

Cribb and Entwistle (2011) see shared decision making as working with the autonomy and responsibility of practitioners and patients and as a middle way between paternalistic and informed choice/consumerist models of decision making. They critique the idea of shared decision making in that it is simplistic, and that it could undermine good decision making because of the limitations it places on professional decision making. They argue that to have a beneficial outcome it is ethically legitimate for health professionals to question, challenge and influence the preferences of patients.

Shared decision making seems to ignore the idea that power, in all its complexity, is at the centre of the relationship between patients and professionals. Participation models clearly illustrate the powerful position of professionals and the unwillingness to shift power from themselves to service users. The idea that participation is enough, and that it is legitimate for professionals to influence the decisions of service users and patients, illustrates that in participation models of empowerment, the goal of empowerment, of being in control, is a myth. Dismissing conflict ignores the complexity of power. As Dahrendorf (1959) points out, conflict is an essential process of justice and freedom. To deny conflict is to deny justice.

Social model of disability – a rights model of empowerment

The social model of disability reflects a democratic approach to empowerment with its aim being user control of services.

An individual or medical model of disability regards an individual's impairment as being responsible for the limitations the individual faces in the world.

Oliver (1981) suggests that it is the physical and social environment that imposes limitations upon people. It is the failure of the social and physical environment to recognize the needs and rights of disabled people.

For Swain et al. (1993, 1998, 2004) people encounter barriers that disable them. The barriers are not just the physical ones associated with access to buildings or transport. They are within the organizations and institutions of society, the language and culture we experience that reflects society's attitude towards people and the organization and delivery of services. These disabling barriers are seen as barriers that oppress people and deny them their rights to be full members of society. Disabling barriers affect people's civil, social, political and moral rights. Underlying this is Swain et al.'s (1998) SEAwall of institutional discrimination (see Figure 6.4) which prevents disabled people from fully participating in society as full and active citizens.

The underpinning of the SEAwall is the structural level. The structures of society reflect hierarchical structures of power and dominant ideologies. A view of normality is sustained by the structures of society and organizations that marginalize disabled people and exclude people from society and is linked to poverty and wider inequalities such as access to employment and services. These structural barriers result in people being denied political, social and human rights.

The environmental level is about the interface between individuals and the physical and social environment. So these are not only the barriers faced by disabled people in terms of physical access to buildings and public transport, but also the barriers to information through a lack of Braille, appropriate signs and symbols, or interpreters.

The attitudinal level is characterized by the personal prejudices of individuals who may hold stereotypical views of disabled people. This becomes an issue when professionals in positions of power hold prejudicial attitudes towards disabled people, which results in discriminatory and oppressive practice.

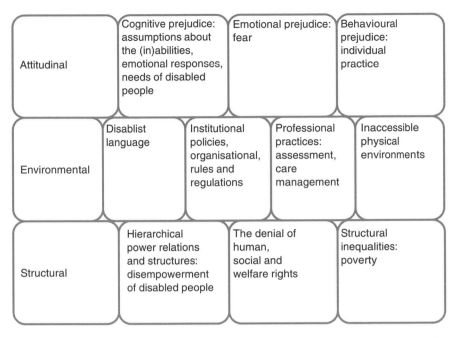

Attitudinal	Cognitive prejudice: assumptions about the (in)abilities, emotional responses, needs of disabled people	Emotional prejudice: fear	Behavioural prejudice: individual practice	
Environmental	Disablist language	Institutional policies, organisational, rules and regulations	Professional practices: assessment, care management	Inaccessible physical environments
Structural	Hierarchical power relations and structures: disempowerment of disabled people	The denial of human, social and welfare rights	Structural inequalities: poverty	

Figure 6.4 The SEAwall of disabling barriers (from Swain et al. 1998; reproduced by kind permission of the British Association of Social Workers)

The oppression of disabled people is maintained through what sociologists term the dominant ideology. Ideology can be regarded as the values and beliefs of a specific social group. The dominant ideology is the ideas, values and beliefs of the most powerful groups in society. It is these ideas that are transmitted through our cultural heritage, through the media, our newspapers, television and other forms of mass communication, and are taken as common-sense ideas or what is seen as normal and what is seen as abnormal. It is through this transmission of ideas of what is normal that people, who do not fit into the normal, experience disabling barriers. The disabling barriers locate a person's impairment within the individual rather than society, and so the cure for being abnormal is located within the person rather than society.

The social model of disability has been challenged in some of its central ideas. Shakespeare and Watson (2001) point out that the social model of disability excludes the issue of impairment, and that the experience of impairment is an important part of people's lives and the distinction between impairment (as a bodily difference) and disability (as a social creation) is unsustainable. They also point out that not all barriers can be removed, especially if there are aspects of impairment that are not created by the environment. This is especially so if someone has an impairment that causes pain and medical intervention may be needed. Shakespeare and Watson also raise issues around identity, where identity derives from a range of experiences, not just an experience of disability or impairment. In light of their analysis, Shakespeare and Watson argue for a more sophisticated approach to disability. They point out that everyone is limited or impaired and society is able to minimize most problems but has failed to deal effectively with the problems of a minority of people with impairment and has 'excluded, disempowered and oppressed ("disabled")' the minority. So for Shakespeare and Watson, 'everyone is impaired' (p. 25).

The social model of disability is important in that it encourages us to consider how people with impairments are marginalized by the way services are delivered and designed. A model of empowerment based upon the social model of disability is concerned with the breaking down of disabling barriers and the promotion of people's rights. Service users are seen as experts on their own situation and people are regarded as equal and in control of the services that are delivered.

In taking account of the social model of disability Swain et al. (1998) suggest that practitioners need to be aware of disability issues and the factors that create institutional discrimination. This means being aware of the attitudes and behaviour of others and ourselves and the wider structural reasons for the exclusion and marginalization of disabled people. So as practitioners we need to be aware of how our practice may reinforce disabling barriers.

Personalization: person-centred care

Personalization is the government's model of empowering people who use social care services. There is a wealth of information explaining the personalization agenda easily accessible through the Internet on both the Department of Health website and the Social Care Institute for Excellence (SCIE) website, where there are interactive learning modules and guides. As this is a new area of policy development you should keep up to date with the latest initiatives from these sites.

The Department of Health (2012b) defines personalization as enabling a person to have 'real choice and control over the care and support they need to achieve their goals, to live a fulfilling life, and to be connected with society'. To achieve this goal the government intends to reform the provision of social care. It is part of a wider agenda of improving well-being and independence, developing communities and supporting economic growth. The government claims that people will have control over their own budget and their own care and support plan and that they will be empowered to choose the care and support that best enables them to meet their goals and aspirations. This is to be achieved by implementing a new person-centred system. There are also proposals for councils to outsource assessments to multiple providers in each area, giving service users choice over who assesses their social care needs (Cooper 2012).

Carr (2010) suggests that personalization reflects the values of respect for the individual and self-determination and points out that service user movement and the social model of disability have been driving forces behind the idea. She also points out that personalization policy has been influenced by the work of 'In Control', which has pioneered the use of self-directed support and personal budgets as a way to reform the current social care system, reflecting the ideas of a consumerist empowerment model. The personalization agenda is underpinned by a model of citizenship. Duffy (2002 in Open University 2010) identifies six keys to citizenship

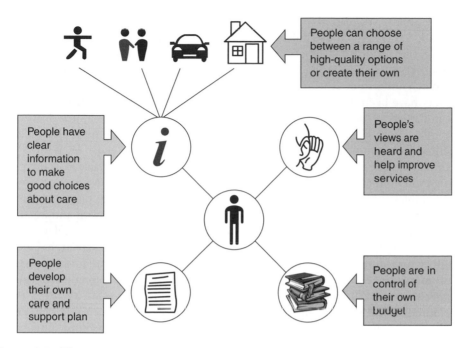

Figure 6.5   The new person-centred system (Department of Health 2012b)

of self-determination, direction, money, home, support and community life, and it would seem that these have been influential.

Needham (2011: 65) points out that the supporters of personalization have put together a range of supporting arguments around 'the dignity and autonomy of the individual, the power of consumer choice and the failure of bureau-professional welfare states'. She points out that this promise of user empowerment may cause problems in terms of what is and is not permitted within personalized approaches to care, especially in times of financial cutbacks. The six keys to citizenship seem to reflect what is valued by society. The personalization agenda, like the model of normalization before it, may be about requiring people to fit in with the norms of society rather than enabling people to express their unique identity and have real choice.

Leece and Leece (2011) highlight an apparent contradiction to the personalization agenda, with its focus on increased power and autonomy for disabled adults as other government proposals are intended to give social work a stronger collective voice and to raise levels of competence in the workforce which will elevate social work to a new level of professionalism, with a possible extension of professional power.

The ethic of care is seen by a number of writers (Barnes 2011; Lloyd 2010; Rummery 2011) as providing a relevant and useful framework through which to analyse the current personalization agenda. Tronto (1993, in Tronto 2010) developed the ethic of care principles of attentiveness, responsibility, competence and responsiveness to provide an ethical content to the four phases of care: caring about; taking care of; care giving; and care receiving.

Lloyd (2010) suggests that Carr's comments overlook debates concerning individualistic values which are linked to consumerist agendas of choice and independence, creating enforced independence for those who have little choice. There is also the assumption that an individual is expected to take greater responsibility for their care, which undermines the aims of choice and control. For some people, the choices they may have been used to could be removed, as they are not regarded as legitimate choices to make. Lloyd (2010) uses the example that a positive choice decision to move into a care home would be reduced. People with learning difficulties may be prevented from choosing day services not seen as socially valued. The White Paper and the personalization agenda has an emphasis on maintaining people in their own homes and Lloyd (2010) has pointed out this has driven the development of telecare, which enables the surveillance of older people at home, triggering responses to unusual activities or alarms. This has the potential to exacerbate isolation and loneliness and misses the point about the fundamental human need for social relationships. Rummery (2011) also points out that ideas of independence are patriarchal and do not allow for the reality of interdependence and reciprocity of care and support.

Rummery (2011) suggests there are legitimate concerns that personalization allows the state to step back from its moral responsibilities under an ethic of care. Central to personalization is a consumerist model of empowerment which will change the relationship between individuals, families, communities and the welfare state, which Rummery (2011) suggests may result in the development of an unregulated and unprotected employment market for paid carers where cost-containment results in low pay and possible long hours.

Barnes (2011) suggests that in such a market there is a possibility that workers are not trained or supported to care, and that the skills that are valued are those of brokerage rather than the morals, practices and principles of care. For Barnes (2011) this devaluing of care risks devaluing those in need of care, and personalization reinforces the marginalization of those who are most vulnerable. One objective of personalization is to shift the emphasis from professional assessments to self-assessment, resulting in individuals commissioning their services. This reflects the individualism of the responsibility for care and from an ethic of care perspective, responsibility for care needs to be shared. Barnes (2011) suggests that there are implications for strategies that undermine both the public provision of services and opportunities for people to come together. For Barnes this reflects patriarchal values that prioritize the individual over more collective values and an understanding of what constitutes quality of life. People may wish for communal services offering support and social interaction, which could be denied them.

In her analysis Rummery (2011) suggests that personalization offers a reconciliation between a feminist demand for an ethic of care on the one hand, and a disability rights demand for empowerment on the other. She suggests that personalization should include a role for the state in terms of governance to ensure that both an ethic of care and the empowerment of disabled and older people can be protected: 'It is not necessarily the commodification of care that is of concern, it is the unchecked, under-governed commodification of care that leaves both carers and the cared-for vulnerable, disempowered and exploited' (p.151). But Barnes is more critical as she points out (2011: 166) that 'substantial claims have been made for personalization in social care on the basis of very limited evidence and experience in practice'.

Although through personalization it is clear that people will be given a sense of control, it is unlikely that people will have real control, which involves a fundamental shift in power. There is a focus on the process of empowerment rather than the outcomes. There is also a denial of conflict, in that people will be working together and will not have to 'fight' the system. There is also an assumption of what a fulfilling life is and the choice to make decisions based on collective notions of care will be reduced. There is a clear economic driver, which clouds the purpose of providing empowering services. It would seem that despite the rhetoric behind the social care reforms and personalization, power, in all its complexity through a process of social dominance, will remain in the hands of those already in power.

A practice model for working with values

As we have seen, working with values in our practice is a complex yet fundamental part of health and social care practice. For students embarking on their career in health and social care this may create more confusion and dilemmas rather than clarify what is the right way to practise.

Rather than having a prescriptive set of values and moral principles or codes of ethics it is important to take the moral responsibility for your practice. This may seem daunting, even scary, but recognizing this is part of the process.

Drawing on Husband's (1995) idea of the morally active practitioner, both Dawson and Butler (2003) and Hugman (2003) have proposed a framework to guide ethical decision making. Using these suggestions as a background and a central value of empowerment it is possible to outline a framework of ethical ideas that you will need to guide your practice. Such a framework can help you as a health and social care practitioner work in the complex area of making ethical decisions that affect people's lives.

To guide your ethical decision making there are things you need to do:

- **Values:** You need to be aware of your values and moral principles and what you believe in. How do your moral principles fit in with the moral principles that have been explored in this chapter? Can you stay true to your values or do you need to alter your moral perspective and how? Do your beliefs and values reflect the dominant ideology?
- **Ethical conflicts:** You need to be aware of the ethical issues that arise in your practice. This means being explicit about the ethical dilemmas and moral conflicts that you may face when making decisions that affect the people you work with. You need to be aware of and identify the values that exist at different levels and that people have different and diverse ethical principles. Once you have recognized the contradictions and conflicts that exist, you can use this to inform your decision making.
- **Ethic of care:** Your actions should be guided by the need to care for other people. It is about looking after our world and the people in it and also ourselves.
- **Power and empowerment and rights:** Develop an awareness of power in your relationship with people who use services and question where the power is and try to work in an empowering way. Be careful not to be part of the social dominance of others and having 'power over' rather than 'power with'. Enable people to have a say, make decisions about their lives and really be in control.

- **Being reflective:** It is important to reflect upon your practice and decision making process. This chapter has covered some complex areas; try to use them in a reflective way. This process not only enables you to identify values and the ethical issues that you face, but also enables you to learn and develop your practice.
- **Develop a cultural awareness:** Be culturally aware and develop your cultural competence and an awareness of other people's belief and faith. It is also important to recognize and engage in debates concerning multi- and inter-culturalism.
- **Taking risks:** As a practitioner making ethical decisions you need to be prepared to take risks. Taking risks based on your ethical judgement may bring with it feelings of apprehension. It is important to recognize this as the responsibility for your decision making is yours.
- **Have moral courage and be morally active:** As a practitioner in health and social care you are intervening in people's lives; your caring practice is both a practical and moral activity. Be aware of the constraints upon your practice but do not let these restrain your practice. Make ethical decisions based upon your moral principles, take responsibility for them and do what you believe is the right thing.

To act without an understanding or regard of values and ethics is to be 'drained of morality, volition, of responsibility, like dead leaves in the wind' (Lawrence 1940: 27).

Summary

This chapter has explored the values and moral principles that should underpin and inform practice. It is important to understand these issues as social care is a practical and moral activity and when we intervene in people's lives we need to do the right thing. There should be a central value of empowerment based on the ethic of care and rights, with people being in control of their services and the decisions that affect their lives. We have also presented a practice model for working with values, stressing the importance of empowering practice and working as a morally active practitioner with moral courage.

Further reading

Beckett, C. and Maynard, A. (2012) *Values and Ethics in Social Work: An Introduction, 2nd edn*. London: Sage. This is a readable text which introduces students to values and ethics and manages to bridge the gap between theory and practice.

Cuthbert, S. and Quallington, J. (2008) *Values for Care Practice*. Newton Abbot: Reflect Press. This book applies values to practice in health and social care and enables students to analyse their own value base.

Parrott, L. (2010) *Values and Ethics in Social Work Practice: Transforming Social Work Practice*, 2nd edn. Exeter: Learning Matters.

7

The Political and Organizational Context of Health and Social Care

Graham Brotherton

Summary Chapter Contents

- Government in the UK
- The history of health and care services
- The current legal and organizational structures of health and social care services
- The broader debate around the 'mixed economy of welfare' and the role of markets in providing health and social care services
- The changing roles of workers and the move towards new models of regulation

Learning outcomes

By the end of this chapter, you should be able to:

- Understand the broad structures and systems of government in the UK.
- Appreciate the history of services and how this has influenced current practice.
- Develop your understanding of the centrality of the mixed economy of care.
- Understand how the regulatory structures of health and social care are changing and the importance of this.

The structure of government in the UK

In this chapter we will be looking at the broader political and organizational context of health and social care. In order to do this it is first necessary to look at how government is structured and the implications this has for all governments in terms of how legislation and policy are developed, both generally and in the context of health and social care.

One of the key features of the UK government is that it is very centralized, even allowing for the recent impact of devolution (see later section). This means that the government in general and the prime minister in particular has considerable power and the ability to exert considerable influence on policy. There are a number of overlapping reasons for this. In part this stems from the way in which the government is elected. The 'first past the post' system in which Members of Parliament (MPs) are elected on the basis of who gets the greatest number of votes in a geographical constituency means that effectively government will almost always come from one of two parties, Labour or Conservative. Whilst this is not the case at present, it must be borne in mind that this is the first elected coalition for about a hundred years and even in the current coalition one party has much greater power and influence than the other. This gives the leaders of the 'main' parties considerable power within the party, as effectively political careers are dependent upon being successful within party hierarchies. This is reinforced especially in government by the fact that the leader/prime minister (with close colleagues/advisers) has considerable power of patronage: that is, the ability to appoint people to positions both within government and in 'Quangos' (see text later in chapter), which play an increasingly significant role in health and social care.

There are three main elements to central government: the executive, the legislature and the judiciary. The *executive* consists of those who have decision making power, namely the prime minister, cabinet ministers and those who advise them. In policy terms this is where policy tends to be initiated, i.e. where 'ideas' about new policy tend to come from.

The *legislature* consists of the two Houses of Parliament, the Commons and the Lords. This is where policy – especially that which requires changes in the law – is discussed or 'debated' and sometimes amended. All potential legislation has to go through a series of readings in the two Houses and also through a series of committee stages where it is scrutinized in more detail by a committees of MPs. Whilst this process does lead to some changes, it is important to note the government can still exert considerable influence because it chooses the timetable for the readings and the composition of the committees that scrutinize the legislation.

The *judiciary* contains the senior judges, who play a role in terms of defining the way in which legislation 'works' in practice; through the process of hearing 'test' cases, hearings that clarify the scope and nature of legislation. It is important to note that to a very considerable extent a government's ability to initiate and push through legislation is dependent upon the size of its majority in Parliament. The larger the majority, the easier it is to maintain control of the process outlined above. Over the past 25 years or so governments have for most of the time enjoyed sizeable majorities and have therefore been able to push through radical change if they wished.

The 'traditional' view of the policy process is that governments start the process by putting out a consultation document in the form of a Green Paper which organizations such as local authorities, charities, private companies or 'think-tanks' are then able to respond to. Green Papers often include a range of options that are then either proceeded with or dropped on the basis of the response from interested parties. This is followed by a White Paper that tends to set out more definite proposals. The extent to which governments take account of the advice they receive is subject to some debate. After the consultation on the White Paper the government will produce draft legislation, a 'Bill' that then enters the process described previously. At the end of this process the Bill becomes a new piece of legislation or Act. It is, though, important to highlight that not all new policy follows this route: some changes do not require changes in the law and are brought about by government changing the advice/'instructions' it gives to local or NHS authorities in the form of policy guidance. A change in the way funding is provided or targeted can also be used to change the direction of policy.

This process of utilizing the mixed economy as a basis for policy and using non-governmental agencies as a key element of policy implementation has been described as a shift away from government to a broader framework of governance. In other words the state regulates services provided by a range of organizations rather than providing services itself, this can be seen across health and social care, e.g. through the private provision of most care at home or in related areas such as education in the move to Free Schools. The current Health and Social Care Act 2012, which is the subject of much debate at the point of revising this chapter, is an important example of this shift in action.

There is a good summary of how the process of introducing legislation works as well as useful information on many other aspects of government at www.parliament.uk/about.

Devolution

One of the key changes of the past few years has been the introduction of devolution, which has led to the creation of a Scottish Parliament and Welsh Assembly and the transfer of powers to this 'new' tier of government. In the case of the Scottish Parliament this includes full responsibility for health and social care issues. In the case of the Welsh Assembly there is a greater overlap with the UK Parliament but policy in Wales is clearly diverging in some areas.

From a policy point of view, one of the most interesting implications of devolution is the emergence of different emphases and approaches to health and social care policy within the different parts of the UK as illustrated in relation to charging policies for both prescriptions and social care services.

Local government

In Scotland and Wales, the structure of local authorities is quite straightforward, with a system of 'unitary' authorities, a single layer of local government where all have the same roles and responsibilities. In the case of England the system (largely for historical reasons as reform has been incremental) is more complex; some areas of England (mainly the large urban areas) have unitary authorities, whereas other areas have a two-tier system of district and county councils. In this case responsibility for health and social care lies with the county authority. The role of local authorities in the provision of social care has changed significantly, with a move away from direct provision towards a purchasing and coordination role, though there are still considerable variations in the amount of direct provision between local authorities.

Current consultation documents can be found on the relevant government departments' websites (Department of Health, Department for Education, Scottish Executive, Welsh Assembly). Have a look at any relevant consultation documents.

If there are any that are particularly relevant to your area of interest, think about whether you might want to respond individually, as a student group or as a group of work colleagues.

Quangos

'Quasi Non-Governmental Organizations' is a term used to refer to a range of organizations that are linked to government (often by funding) but are not technically part of government. There are a number of significant ones in health and social care, for example the Care Quality Commission or the General Social Care Council. Governments of all political persuasions have been accused of appointing people whose views support the government's to significant roles on 'quangos', though in the last few years there has been a move to a more open selection process, through advertising for suitable applicants.

Find out about the role of the above organizations (the website addresses can be found using a search engine). How do they contribute to setting and evaluating the health and social care agenda?

The use of quangos to implement policy is not without its critics, who highlight the fact that they are not directly accountable to either local or national electorates in the way that governments or local authorities are. From the point of view of government, however, quangos provide a useful way of distancing themselves from difficult or controversial decisions. One high-profile example of this in recent years has been the role of the National Institute for Health and Clinical Excellence (NICE) in the regulation of medicines.

Implementing policy

In implementing policy, governments have a number of 'levers' in terms of ensuring that policy 'works' in the way that was intended. The first is finance. Central government provides the bulk of the money the local authorities use to provide services, and often this is given as targeted funds so that it has to be used for specific purposes. A second way in which central government is able to control policy is through using legislation to create 'statutory duties', which are things that local authorities must do, e.g. providing a child protection service.

A third option open to central government is to give local authorities 'powers', which are the ability to undertake particular functions. Much of the Community Care legislation works in this way and it gives local authorities greater discretion. However, in many cases the use of 'powers' is clarified by the production of guidance, which may in itself create a fairly tight framework within which agencies have to operate. The final major 'tool' available to government is the use of inspectorates such as the Care Quality Commission or Ofsted to scrutinize services; this is discussed in more detail in a later section.

The historical development of health and social care services

In order to understand the current structure of health and social care services, it is helpful to give a brief history of the development of services. This is inevitably a brief overview and for more detail you might want to look at the history chapters in the recommended texts at the end of the chapter. A more detailed account can be found in Fraser's fascinating history of the development of welfare in the UK.

The nineteenth century

The government started to become significantly involved in welfare in the nineteenth century through the Poor Law Reform Act of 1834. This is best remembered now as the piece of legislation that introduced the 'workhouse' system under which the only form of assistance available to people in poverty was to enter the workhouse, an institution systematically designed to be as unpleasant as possible in order to deter all but the 'genuinely' destitute. The legacy of this system has had a major influence on the development of health and care services in several ways. Firstly, one of the consequences of the poor law system as it developed was the recognition of the need for some form of (fairly rudimentary) health care system. This led to the development of the 'Poor Law Infirmaries' which grew up in the latter part of the nineteenth century. The Poor Law Infirmaries tended to be poorly staffed – often with virtually no medical presence – and were often overcrowded. Reports from the time suggest that the quality of care was also very variable. However the Poor Law Infirmaries were later to become a central part of the NHS at its inception (of which more later).

A second way in which the workhouse had an impact was that the population of the workhouses tended to consist predominantly of those with few other options: older people, those with disabilities, those who might now be perceived as having acute mental health conditions and women who had become pregnant outside of marriage. As a consequence, in many cases the workhouses soon reached capacity. There were two responses to this. One was an attempt to categorize the workhouse population and develop other institutions to provide for those that 'needed' it. This was a key factor in the growth of the mental health and learning disability institutions in particular and the placement in those institutions of large numbers of women under the catch-all category of 'moral defective'. A 'flavour' of life in the workhouse can be found on the National Trust website in respect of the workhouse at Southwell.

The second response was quite different: this was the emergence of charitable organizations. Many of the big charities that still exist today, such as Barnardo's, the National Society for the Prevention of Cruelty to Children (NSPCC) and its Scottish equivalent, the SSPCC, have their 'roots' in this period as did 'Cottage Hospitals'. They emerged partly because the workhouses, especially in urban areas, were unable to respond adequately to the prevalence of poverty, but crucially in many cases because of the moral or ethical beliefs of those who set them up. These were predominantly associated with particular non-conformist Christian groups such as Methodists or Quakers. By the latter part of the nineteenth century these many and varied charitable organizations were providing more 'poor relief', as most welfare was at this time categorized, than the 'state' system based on the workhouse. There are very useful sections on some of the charities' websites which give a clear picture of their development; see for example the history section on the Barnardo's website.

As much of the charity was based on a moral perspective, there was a perceived need to ensure that assistance was given to the deserving poor. A group emerged that tried to give charitable giving a clearer structure to ensure that the above aim was met, namely the Charity Organization Society or COS founded in 1869. The COS pioneered a way of working based on 'casework', the systematic collection of facts about an individual's or family's circumstances to ensure that resources were given to the most needy and deserving. This model of casework has remained a central underpinning of approaches to care work, especially social work, ever since, right through to current models of care management.

A further consequence of this model was to ensure that those who were not seen as deserving, namely unmarried mothers, those characterized as feckless, etc., found it even more difficult to access help, thus tying them to the workhouse and its successor institutions.

The creation of the 'welfare state'

By the end of the nineteenth century there was increasing pressure for reform, partly from elements within the charitable movement but also from organizations such as the growing trade union movement and the political party that this produced – the Labour Party. In addition, elements within the Liberal Party, at this stage a much more significant party than Labour, also recognized the need for change. In 1906 this combination of factors led to the election of a Liberal government with support from the Labour Party. Over the next few years this government introduced a series of measures that are still recognizable as the basis of our existing system: old age pensions, school meals, legislation against child neglect and the introduction of National Insurance to fund a limited benefit system and the first attempt at systematic health care (at least for male workers), the 'panel doctor' system. These were all introduced between 1906 and 1912. By 1912 the focus shifted to international issues with the impending First World War and whilst the post-war Liberal government did introduce some reform, notably by giving local authorities extended powers to build houses, the system remained fundamentally similar until the start of the Second World War.

During the Second World War the government commissioned a senior civil servant, William Beveridge, to look at the technical workings of the benefit system. Beveridge's report somewhat exceeded his brief and called for wholesale reform of the whole welfare system, arguing that the interconnected nature of the problems associated with poverty, unemployment, etc., required an interconnected response. The Beveridge Report, 'Social Insurance and Allied Services', published in 1942, was effectively a blueprint for a welfare state and formed the basis for the general election at the end of the Second World War with the Labour Party promising to implement Beveridge in full and the Conservatives largely opposed. The only aspect of Beveridge that was implemented before the election were the proposals for education, which formed the basis for the 1944 Education Act with its introduction of a unified system of grammar and secondary modern schools that have shaped all subsequent education policy.

The post-war election resulted in a landslide victory for Labour, the first time the party had enjoyed an overall majority in Parliament, and the Beveridge proposals now became the basis of far-reaching social reform in health, benefits and the personal social services. In part the NHS had already come into existence as the Wartime Health Service, a co-ordinated system set up to meet the demands of war. It was not popular with many within the medical profession for a number of reasons, both financial and professional, and the concessions offered by the Health Secretary, Anuerin Bevan, to persuade the medical profession to join the NHS, in which doctors remained independent contractors within the NHS rather than employees, have had long-lasting consequences (see the section on NHS reform). When the NHS was formally set up in 1948 it marked a decisive shift, giving women and children full access to health care for the first time, setting up a proper primary care system through the General Practitioner system and integrating the various strands of hospital provision, the teaching hospitals, the cottage hospitals, the municipal hospitals (which the Poor Law Infirmaries had become), into a coherent whole. The NHS was a hugely popular innovation, a status it was to maintain for the next 30 years or so. However, it also proved much more expensive than had been anticipated: costs doubled in the first two years and there was no 'peak' as some had anticipated (that costs would be high at first but would fall as people became healthier as a result of the NHS and consequently costs would fall). Managing the cost of the NHS rapidly became a political issue that has endured right through to the present.

In the social care area the government set up both Welfare Departments for adults and Children's Departments, marking the first time that the state had become significantly involved in provision in this area – many of the services that now form the mainstream of social care provision such as residential care and child protection were introduced at this time. The Children's and Welfare Departments were merged into generic Social Services Departments in 1970.

Perhaps the most significant of the Beveridge proposals were those for the restructuring of the benefit system, which proved to have ramifications that have influenced the whole of subsequent policy development. Beveridge proposed a contributory system based on National Insurance in which workers would pay in while in work and receive while not working (providing that they had paid sufficient contributions). Women would pay contributions while working, but as they left the workforce upon marriage they would then receive access to benefits through their husband. Beveridge anticipated that as there was a return to near full employment after the war, the system would become largely self-funding.

For those who were unable to access the contributory scheme, a safety net scheme called National Assistance was introduced. This was intended to be a minor part of the system, but for a complex variety of reasons, e.g. the fact that there was no return to full employment and later that this was the only benefit women not living with their husband could claim, this soon became the larger element of the benefit system. Efforts to control National Assistance and its successors, Supplementary Benefit and Income Support, have been a major feature of social policy right through to New Labour and 'Welfare to Work'.

A central element of the Beveridge plan in the years immediately after the war was housing provision. In the decade immediately after the war two-thirds of all house building was undertaken by local authorities and social housing became a significant part of provision. While there were some significant attempts at reform and reorganization over the next 20 years, the basis of the Beveridge system remained in place until the late 1970s, though after the recession of the early 1970s spending in some areas, e.g. house building, fell markedly.

The Neo-Liberal reforms

The period after 1979 saw a process of radical reform in a number of areas. In housing, there was an end to local authority house building and the introduction of the opportunity for local authority tenants to buy the house they lived in. The consequence of this has been the effective removal of housing from the welfare policy area.

In benefits, the period saw the introduction of the Income Support System based around fixed levels of payment for people who fall into specific categories, which still exists in amended form. For health and social care, though, the significant change was the implementation in 1990 of the National Health Service and Community

Care Act. In order to explore this fully it is important to place this in the context of the debate about the ideological context of health and social care.

The ideological context of health and social care

Health and social care, as with other areas of welfare, takes place in an ideological context: that is, they are heavily influenced by the political views of the government of the day. The expansion of 'Welfare' between 1945 and 1951 took place in the context of a government committed to social democracy whereas the reforms of the 1980s and early 1990s took place in the context of a Neo-Liberal (sometimes referred to as 'Thatcherite' after the prime minister for the bulk of this period) approach.

The basis of social democracy is that the state has a positive role to play in the provision of services. This is because in a 'market' context (see next section) services (in our case health, education, etc.) will be allocated on the basis of ability to pay rather than need. This is what social democrats refer to as 'market failure' – in order to ensure fairness the state needs to get involved to ensure all citizens receive adequate support. This is sometimes called 'positive freedom', the idea being that people need positive support from the state in order to be able to take advantage of the opportunities that might be available to them. The money needed to provide for these services is raised through taxation. Taxation is also related to income and the ability to pay, so higher earners pay tax at a higher rate. This is referred to as progressive taxation and is linked to a belief that the system should be redistributive, giving on the basis of need.

Neo-Liberal thinking emerged as a reaction to this. It argued that the inevitable consequence of social democracy was bureaucracy and inefficiency and that the welfare system had a tendency to trap people in dependency on the state. The solution was to reduce the role of the state by reducing its role as a service provider, through the privatization of services. This would also introduce competition between service providers, leading to greater choice and efficiency, and free up money that could be used to reduce taxes, giving people the opportunity to take greater responsibility for themselves. Of particular significance to the Neo-Liberal critique has been the way in which public services, it is argued, tend to be inflexible and unresponsive and to deliver a 'one size fits all' service, rather than one tailored to the specific needs of patients and service users. While in practice even most Neo-Liberal governments have retained some limited element of progressive taxation, most are critical of the principle, arguing for a move towards a 'flatter' tax system in which everyone pays the same rate on all income.

(Continued)

(Continued)

Central to Neo-Liberal thinking is a belief in a 'free market' system, which in this context is a belief that market principles of supply and demand apply even to welfare services, i.e. that if someone 'supplies' a good or service at an appropriate price there will be 'demand' for it: the better the price and quality, the greater the demand. If a good or service is of poor quality or priced too high for its market 'demand' will fall and the supplier will need to adjust price, quality or both in order to become competitive. This leads to the best goods or services being available at the most competitive prices – so-called 'market discipline'. It also leads to flexibility and choice, as there are likely to be a range of providers competing to provide appropriate services. In this model the NHS and social care services could and should be provided in the same way as any other good or service.

There are, however, two key problems in the area of welfare. One is how to introduce market forces into areas where the state is the only or most dominant provider of services. This is dealt with in the next section. The second is the 'problem' of free services, as, from a market perspective, providing a service free is likely to lead to an excess of demand – of which more later.

New Labour emerged in the 1990s as an attempt to reconcile a commitment to social justice with a belief in markets. Its adherents claimed that it encompassed key features of both social democracy and the Neo-Liberal critique, hence the claim to be a new approach – the 'Third Way'. New Labour in government retained in a modified way most of the market reforms of the 1980s and 1990s but also developed some distinctively new elements which are explored later in this chapter.

The ideological position of the present Coalition government is disputed, not least as the economic context it has inherited as a result of the global banking crisis is a complex one. However, there are clearly significant elements of Neo-Liberal thinking in the way in which the role of the public sector is being reduced and the emphasis on market solutions, and it can be argued that the way in which the crisis has been constructed as a crisis of the state and public services rather than as a crisis of the financial system locates the Coalition securely with a Neo-Liberal context.

The NHS and Community Care Act 1990, which still provides the broad framework for health and social care services, is best seen as an attempt to introduce this market approach into health and social care services. There were a number of parallels between the health reforms and the social care reforms, but there were also significant differences, therefore each is dealt with separately.

NHS reform

The NHS prior to reform was a large and monolithic organization. Reforms in the 1980s had attempted to introduce more 'effective' management but the 1990 changes took things much further. At the heart of the reforms was the so-called 'internal market', an attempt to create market-like structures in the NHS. In order to facilitate this, the NHS needed to be broken up structurally into units that could compete with each other. In addition, in order for the principles of supply and demand to apply there needed to be parts of the NHS that supplied services (providers) and parts that demanded/bought services (purchasers or commissioners). For this reason the reforms were often referred to as introducing the purchaser/provider split.

The purchaser 'organizations' were firstly health authorities, the part of the NHS that had previously dealt with local planning; their role in the new system was to identify likely local demand and to buy services to meet this demand. The second purchasing organizations were 'GP fundholders', GP practices which had opted to take the sum of money that would have been allocated to the health authority to buy services for the practice's patients and to spend it directly on the patients' behalf. Over time the government felt that the role of the health authorities would diminish (and eventually disappear) as more and more GP practices would become fundholding.

In order to have a range of possible 'providers' the remainder of the NHS, primarily hospitals and associated services, was broken up into a series of competing 'trusts'. These were of variable size and composition as they emerged from a bidding process, but have become increasingly similar in the intervening period through a process of mergers. NHS trusts were independent organizations with their own management structure of chief executive and board which in their original form were intended to compete with other trusts for the 'business' provided by health authorities and GP fundholders (e.g. common surgical procedures) on the grounds of both price and quality. This was referred to as the internal market.

When the Labour Party was elected in 1997 the system was reorganized again. The NHS trusts were maintained with similar management structures but given a new role as local service providers. The purchaser role was given to a new type of organization – the primary care trust (PCT) – which over a period of time took over the role of purchasing (now referred to as commissioning) local health services. The Coalition has recently announced another phase of NHS reform which creates yet another purchasing structure – Clinical Commissioning Groups who will 'buy' services from hospitals, GPs, etc. In many senses this can be seen as a return to the market model of the early 1990s. However, the proposals are controversial and at the time of writing it is not entirely clear what the new structures will finally look like and there are other significant complications. Firstly, the NHS budget is being reduced in real terms so savings of around £20 billion will have to be made by those providing health services by 2015; secondly, there is a greater emphasis in involving private companies in providing health services (though this has been happening to some extent for about 20 years anyway).

A useful guide to the complex structure of the NHS and the at times confusing terminology can be found on the NHS website.

Social care reform

Social care reform has in many senses paralleled NHS reform. The NHS and Community Care Act 1990 also applied to social care, but the reforms took a slightly different form. The 'purchaser' role here was given to Social Services Departments who were to be responsible for a new system of assessment and care management in which individuals who might require assistance were assessed, firstly to see whether they were eligible for services and then to see what their needs were. A financial assessment also took place at the same time to identify whether the person should pay part or all of the cost of the services they require. It is important to highlight that need alone is not a sufficient basis for providing services, local authorities are required to also make judgments about what services they are 'able' to afford. In the current economic context this has led in many cases to a reduction in the support being provided and to a potential crisis in terms of providing care for older people (Kings Fund 2010).

The services that people need were to be provided largely in the private and voluntary sectors. The financial regime that introduced this version of community care forced local authorities into spending money buying services from private and voluntary organizations and they were also encouraged to divest themselves of the residential and related provision that they had. In most cases these were separated from the local authority and set up as independent not-for-profit companies.

Unlike in health care the general structures have remained largely unchanged though in some specific areas there have been changes. These have sought to introduce slightly more standardization of both financial and needs assessments though there remain variations between different local authority areas.

Direct payments and personalization

A current priority is the expansion of the direct payments approach. While direct payments have been around since the Community Care (Direct Payments) Act 1996, the number of people utilizing them has been small. The principle of direct payments is that following assessment the person who needs support is given a sum of money to purchase the support that they need. In recent years this process has been called personalization and was promoted by the previous Government. This remains Coalition policy though there are very wide local variations in the uptake of personalization in differing local authority areas.

Managerialism and surveillance

One way in which the changes of the past 20 years or so have been explained is through the emergence of managerial approaches to health and social care. Managerialism is a set of ideas that emerged from the Neo-Liberal critique of welfare services and is based on the idea that public services need to be managed in the same way as commercial organizations. There are tensions in managerialism as an approach in that it has tended to highlight both the need for flexibility in service delivery and the need for targets to assess performance/service delivery, with critics suggesting the latter approach has proved dominant. Linked to managerialism has been a distrust of professional autonomy, which has led to increased surveillance through the various inspection bodies.

What does the future hold?

Overall the changes of the past twenty years can be characterized as an increase in marketization across health and social care, though this was linked to an emphasis on collaborative and multi-agency working and increased spending during the New Labour era. Whilst health has featured heavily in the coalition agenda, the future of social care is less clear. With the increased emphasis on public sector reform in the context of significant overall reductions in spending, this suggests that the future in organizational terms for both health and social care agencies is uncertain. Perhaps the clearest statement of general principles can be found in 'A vision for adult social care: Capable communities and active citizens' (Department of Health 2010), which the government describes as a vision for the future of social care. The following quote highlights this:

The Vision for a modern system of social care is built on seven principles:

- **Personalization:** individuals not institutions take control of their care. Personal budgets, preferably as direct payments, are provided to all eligible people. Information about care and support is available for all local people, regardless of whether or not they fund their own care.
- **Partnership:** care and support delivered in a partnership between individuals, communities, the voluntary and private sectors, the NHS and councils – including wider support services, such as housing.
- **Plurality:** the variety of people's needs is matched by diverse service provision, with a broad market of high-quality service providers.
- **Protection:** there are sensible safeguards against the risk of abuse or neglect. Risk is no longer an excuse to limit people's freedom.
- **Productivity:** greater local accountability will drive improvements and innovation to deliver higher productivity and high-quality care and support services. A focus on publishing information about agreed quality outcomes will support transparency and accountability.
- **People:** we can draw on a workforce who can provide care and support with skill, compassion and imagination, and who are given the freedom and support to do so. We need the whole workforce, including care workers, nurses, occupational therapists, physiotherapists and social workers, alongside carers and the people who use services, to lead the changes set out here.

Though there has been little concrete change, the principles are stated in language that fits with the broader approach to public sector reform but the promised White Paper on the future of care services has not, at the time of writing, appeared and certain key points such as how any amended system will be funded remain uncertain.

Review questions

As you finish this chapter you might want to think about the following questions:

- To what extent are current patterns of health and care services the product of the historical development of services?
- What role does ideology play in the development of services?
- How likely is the Coalition agenda to deliver better health and care services? Why? What are the strengths and limitations of the current model?

Further reading

Many of the sources identified in Chapter 3 would be useful here, especially the various government websites and the 'trade press'.

One of the main difficulties with policy is that its rapidly changing context means that books tend to date quickly; using journals is therefore important in maintaining a clear view of the current position. The following journals are likely to be particularly helpful:

Journal of Social Policy

Social Policy and Administration

Social Policy and Society

For a historical perspective in clear and highly readable accounts, see:

Fraser, D. (2002) *The Evolution of the British Welfare State*. London: Palgrave Macmillan.

Timmins, N. (2001) *The Five Giants: A Biography of the Welfare State*. London: Harper Collins.

For a fuller exploration of ideological perspectives and how they link to policy, see:

Lavallette, M. and Pratt, A. (2006) *Social Policy: Theories, Concepts and Issues*. London: Sage.

For a clear overview of policy on a more general level, see:

Blakemore, K. (2003) *Social Policy: An Introduction*. Maidenhead: Open University Press.

Bochel, C. et al. (2005) *Social Policy: Issues and Developments*. London: Prentice Hall.

Robert Gordon University provides an excellent social policy website with lots of useful content at: www2.rgu.ac.uk/publicpolicy/introduction/contents.htm.

Kings Fund (2010) *Securing Good Care for More People; Options for Reform*. London: Kings Fund.

8

Psychology for Health and Social Care

Nadine Pearce

Summary Chapter Contents

- The components of behaviour
- Psychological theories
- Lifespan development
- Psychology and working in health and social care

Learning objectives

By the end of this chapter, you should be able to:

- Provide a brief explanation of the major psychological perspectives.
- Give examples of how emotions, cognitive processes and social interactions influence observable behaviour.
- Identify the changes associated with significant life stages and suggest reasons for possible responses (developmental outcomes).
- Discuss how selected psychological theory and concepts can be applied to enhance practice in health and social care settings.

This chapter was published in Brotherton, G. and Parker, S. (eds) (2008) *Your Foundation in Health and Social Care*. London: Sage.

Introduction

As you have chosen to study subjects related to working in the field of health and social care you are inevitably going to be interested in people. Working in this area means that you will be involved in helping people manage their lives, meet their needs and support changing behaviours. By understanding psychological processes you will be able to increase your insight into both your own and your clients' behaviours, which will allow greater reflection and enhance the care that you provide.

Psychology and components of behaviour

Psychology is defined as the study of human behaviour. It is concerned with how people behave and the influences that are responsible for that behaviour.

When psychologists use the word 'behaviour' they recognize different elements that include:

- Physiological changes
- Emotional responses
- Cognitive (thinking) processes
- Social interactions
- Actions (observable behaviours).

ACTIVITY

Think of a behaviour involving stress, and suggest how each of the above elements of your behaviour could be affected. As an example, you could use an important hospital appointment or interview.

Examples of changes you may have considered are as follows.

Physiological changes

If you are feeling anxious or hurried then you may feel that your heart is beating faster or that you have 'butterflies in your stomach'. You may notice that you are either pale or flushed and may even find your hands shaking.

Emotional responses

You could feel frightened or worried and either become more likely to cry or get angry.

Cognitive processes

If you are very worried it may be difficult for you to concentrate so that you need to keep checking the information about time or how to get to the appointment.

Drawing on memories and knowledge, you may find yourself trying to predict what will happen in the consultation and rehearsing explanations and questions.

Social

From previous experiences of your own or others you will be able to make assumptions of how both you as a patient and the doctor are expected to behave. This will influence the clothes that you wear and how you speak to the hospital staff.

You may find it reassuring to take a friend or relative with you so that you have the opportunity to share the experience.

Actions

How you act as a result of these processes will vary with the individual. Some may become so anxious that they do not even go to the appointment, while others will be sufficiently familiar with the situation to feel quite calm and be able to give information clearly and ask appropriate questions. You may find yourself being disorganized and arriving late, or having a high need to be in control so that you get to the appointment very early.

Now think of an example of a client's behaviour that seems unusual or is causing a problem for the client, family or staff.

Under each of the same headings try to suggest alternative influences that could be causing this behaviour. For example:

- What stresses might be causing unusually angry behaviour in a client?
- In what ways could they be showing this anger?
- What could be the effects on their physical health or social relationships?

ACTIVITY

By recognizing the complexity of influences on behaviours, the health and social care worker is able to remain open to alternative contributory factors and be able to help plan effective interventions and strategies. The study of psychology introduces you to how different theorists can explain the causes of behaviour. In the next section you are encouraged to consider how you can apply this knowledge to individual situations and service users with whom you work.

Psychological theories

Psychologists have different approaches to the way that they attempt to explain the causes of behaviour. Some of these are known as 'schools' or theoretical perspectives. Early psychologists believed that it would be possible to develop a single theory that could explain all aspects of behaviour, but we now realize that human behaviour is so complex, and there are so many different influences, that this may never be possible. However, the different approaches have all contributed to our understanding of how people behave and why. The major theoretical approaches include:

- Physiological approaches
- Learning theories
- Developmental cognitive theory
- Psychodynamic psychology
- Humanistic theories
- Ecological theory.

Physiological approaches

This approach examines how behaviour is determined by heredity and the body's structure and functioning. You are probably aware of how your physical state can also affect your mood, ability to manage your life and your susceptibility to illness.

Some of these influences on development and personality will originate from before birth:

- Genes and chromosomes are inherited from both parents. This will determine whether you are male or female, the colour of your eyes and skin, and whether you will be susceptible to some diseases, e.g. sickle cell anaemia and cystic fibrosis. It sometimes happens that following fertilization there can be faulty cell division which may lead to genetic disorders such as Down syndrome.

- During prenatal development the fetus may be exposed to substances that can harm it, including drugs, infections or lack of important nutrients or oxygen.
- Birth experiences, including premature or difficult births, may also affect later development.

Other influences appear after birth, and relate to the speed and nature of maturation. For example, sometimes a baby is born with teeth while others will not start to get any until they are over a year old. Equally some families have a tendency towards greying hair, early or late onset of puberty or menopause.

Developmental charts are based on the recognition that there is a 'normal' or average time when maturational stages occur. These are used to check that milestones in a child's development are consistent to the expected range. There will be considerable variation in rates of development but if a child does not seem to be following the anticipated pattern the child would be monitored more closely or have investigations made. If developmental problems, such as restricted growth syndrome or deafness, are noticed early, interventions can be started that will help improve the chances of the child reaching his or her potential.

Nature or nurture?

The extent to which people are influenced by their inherited characteristics formed part of a major issue for developmental psychologists known as the Nature *v.* Nurture debate. This was an attempt to try to identify the effect of genetic inheritance compared with the experiences that children are exposed to as they grow up.

The genetic inheritance that you are born with is known as the genotype, and how this is actually realized is the phenotype. A child may be born with a gene for height, but detrimental effects of disease or diet might result in the child not growing very tall. Similarly, if you are born with the ability to learn to talk but never hear anyone speaking you are unlikely to be able to speak a language fluently. However, it is more difficult to separate genetic inheritance and environmental influence in other behaviours such as intelligence, obesity or special skills such as music.

Some psychologists are particularly interested in how genes contribute to the development of personality, suggesting that inborn temperaments will affect how we interact with others, including carers. Being born either shy or emotionally reactive, placid or restless, could affect how others respond to us, which could impact on the way that we are accepted or 'fit in' with others' expectations of how we 'should' behave.

The key issue for this debate is the recognition of how inherited characteristics interact with environmental experiences in contributing to development and behaviours.

Case study

Elsa's parents both describe themselves as shy. They moved to this country before she was born but have not made many new friends.

Elsa has always been content to stay at home and play but her parents are anxious that she should learn to mix and not be shy with other children. They took her to a toddler group and now at 3 years old she has started playgroup. However, Elsa seems unhappy and rather frightened of the more boisterous children. In discussion with the playgroup supervisor it has been agreed that Elsa would get to the hall early so that she had chance to settle in before the others arrive. An allocated play leader would spend time with Elsa starting with quiet activities and then gradually moving further into the centre of the room. After a few weeks Elsa seems much more settled and although she still does not take part in some of the noisier activities, she is at times willing to play without the presence of 'her special play leader'. It is hoped that through these experiences she will continue to gain in confidence and develop friendships to help with her transition to school in two years' time.

Learning theories

Behaviourist approaches

Learning theorists focus on how behaviour is changed as a result of environmental experience, with the concentration on observable behaviour rather than mental processes. This has led to the development of two explanations of learning:

- Classical conditioning
- Operant conditioning.

Classical conditioning is based on the work of Ivan Pavlov, who identified that biological responses could become associated with a previously neutral stimulus. Food brings about salivation but learning makes you salivate to familiar ice cream jingles. Likewise, feelings of nausea can result from the smell of a food that has previously caused severe sickness.

Theory box

'Learning to be Frightened'

Classical conditioning theorists such as Pavlov believed that phobias (a form of extreme and irrational anxiety about a situation or object) can be acquired by conditioning. This type of learning can be very resistant to change and can form an important part of apparently illogical or habitual behaviours.

Children who have learnt to associate doctors or dentists with pain may still experience a fear of visiting them in adulthood even when they know that no pain will be involved.

Operant conditioning focuses on how behaviour is shaped by its outcome. If there is a pleasurable outcome then it is more likely to be repeated in the future. These good outcomes, described as reinforcers, may be either when something pleasant happens such as praise, attention, money or 'brownie points' or where something unpleasant stops happening, e.g. when a headache improves after taking a tablet.

Conditioning is widely used in both social and educational settings. Examples of how it can be used include developing a programme to help someone recover their mobility or for a child to alter his or her disruptive behaviour.

It is necessary to be very clear about:

- What is the existing behaviour, i.e. the starting point.
- The hoped-for change or goal.
- The steps needed to reach that goal.
- The reinforcer.

The reinforcer must be significant for that person and the steps towards the goal achievable so that they can be rewarded (Figure 8.1).

In everyday life it can be difficult to be clear about what behaviours are being reinforced and it may not be the ones that are expected; it is also very common to try to be too general and aim at modifying too many behaviours at the same time.

Six-year-old John is considered a difficult pupil. In his class, children work in small groups and are expected to remain in their seats when working at activities but John is always getting up and wandering around other tables interfering with their work or chatting. When he approaches the other children they can get cross at him and may shout or cry. The teacher may also tell him off, and will usually take him back to his table and talk to him about his work, therefore trying to get him to focus on the activity.

What do you think the teacher is hoping will be the reinforcement for John?

What might the teacher actually be reinforcing which will increase the likelihood that he will continue with his disruptive behaviour?

ACTIVITY

In this situation it is possible that attention is the important reinforcer for John, so it is his disruptive behaviours rather than quiet activities that are being reinforced.

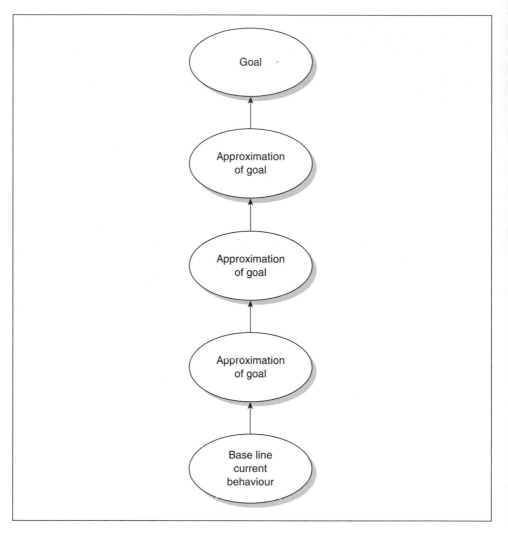

Figure 8.1   Reinforcers given on successfully achieving each approximation of the goal

Learned helplessness

According to Seligman (1975), another consequence of conditioning can be that we learn what we cannot do. In situations when people believe that they have little or no control they may initially react by increasing effort to find ways of managing the situation, described as a stage of *reactance*. However, if despite all their efforts they still feel powerless, then they have learnt that it is not possible to succeed and they give up trying.

Learned helplessness has also been associated with depression, as both are characterized by apathy and a low belief in the ability to control situations.

Case study

Rita had been successfully managing at home but has recently had a few falls, causing a fracture of her wrist. This made it difficult for her to take care of herself so she agreed to move into a residential care setting. Rita settled in well apart from a worry that due to urgency incontinence she needed to be able to get to the toilet quickly.

Due to concerns about the risk of falling, Rita was advised to ring for help when she wanted to go to the toilet. However, it was not always possible for Rita to get help immediately, so to avoid problems she would try to walk to the toilet on her own.

As this behaviour was seen as a risk, Rita's room was reorganized making it difficult for her to get out of her chair without help. After a few times when she was incontinent, because she was not able to get help quickly enough, it was recommended that she wore an incontinence pad to avoid getting distressed.

Within a few weeks Rita had become incontinent and made no effort to use the toilet.

Practice tips

When developing a client's care plans consider:

- How the programme is designed to be specific to that individual rather than a group of individuals or diagnoses.
- The need to empower people by consulting and involving them in decisions about their own welfare and management.
- Recognizing the validity of their perceptions about their ability to control their situation.

Social learning theory (observational learning)

Bandura et al. (1961) drew on the earlier learning theorists but examined how people can learn through observation of others to imitate some behaviours. This theory was later renamed as social cognitive theory.

Obviously we do not copy everyone all the time and it appears that some characteristics of models (people whom we may copy) make them more likely to be imitated. This includes people who we can see are:

- Similar to ourselves in some ways
- Behave in role- or gender-appropriate ways

- Have personal warmth
- Are rewarded for their behaviour
- Have power over resources.

When you are new to a job you may find that you are inclined to follow the example of a co-worker whom you have identified as showing good practice. Consider whether the co-worker may have some of these characteristics.

The knowledge that people have the ability to learn from others is used by parents, schools and workplaces where others are held up as good examples of desired behaviour. Examples include the public acknowledgement of achievements, introduction of student ambassadors and deliberate recruitment of people from under-represented groups into high-profile jobs. However, the role models that are copied may not necessarily be the ones that the organization would choose. The class clown may well prove a more powerful model than the studious form captain.

Cases such as the murder of James Bulger, where it was suggested that the older boys were copying actors on violent videos, highlight some concerns about the extent that television and the media influence the way people act. This is far from clear cut, and is an important ongoing debate, but evidence suggests that it is unlikely to be a sole reason for extreme violent behaviour.

Developmental cognitive theory

Everyone is aware that children develop in their understanding and ability to solve problems. This is shown in the kind of tasks given to children, the way that they play and the expectation of how they explain events. You would not be surprised by a 5-year-old talking about the toys coming alive and playing at night but you would not usually expect a 15-year-old to hold the same beliefs.

Jean Piaget made a major contribution in stimulating studies on how children developed the ability to reason, understand and problem-solve. He suggested that this was related to their age and that learning opportunities needed to be appropriate for their stage of cognitive maturation. He emphasized that play and the opportunity to explore their environment were crucial in the development of children's cognitive ability.

Piaget identified that children pass through stages that typify their cognitive development, shown in Figure 8.2.

Piaget used the term 'schema' to explain how we adapt to our world through the way that we organize and build up knowledge. As we find out more about an object or event we take in or assimilate information. However, if the new information does not fit with our existing understanding it is necessary to alter our schema – a process

Sensori motor	0–2 years	Learning and understanding mainly through physical actions
Pre-operational	2–6 years	Using symbols such as words to represent objects Playing alongside other children
Concrete	7–12 years	A rather limited ability to understand other's position Capable of more complex thinking Beginning to understand rules of games and becoming capable of logical reasoning
Formal operations	12 onward	Able to use abstract thinking, including thinking about themselves in more complex ways and identifying their personal morality

Figure 8.2   Piaget's stages of cognitive development

called 'accommodation'. Driving this is the idea that we strive to be in *balance* or 'equilibrium', where new information becomes integrated into our schema, but *imbalance* stimulates us to seek more information. The ideal learning opportunities are considered to be when the imbalance is sufficiently stimulating and interests us in finding out more rather than being too familiar or over-challenging.

Think about a time when you were given a task that really interested you and made you want to get on with it. Now try to recall times when the task just seemed too difficult so that you avoided it. Have you ever been bored at work because the job is not giving you sufficient challenge or interest?

   Think of an example of how an understanding of the balance between 'known' and 'not known' could help you to devise learning activities for staff or clients.

ACTIVITY

Psychodynamic psychology

Sigmund Freud was the originator of this school but there have been other psycho-analytical psychologists after him who have adapted and developed these ideas.

   Key points in Freud's ideas are that behaviour is assumed to be the result of unconscious process and previous experiences. The main drives or sources of motivation that govern human behaviour are described as the libido, associated with the sex drive and need to continue the species, and thanotos, the destructive force that is shown by aggression. He believed that the personality was formed from three parts: the id, ego and superego. Babies when they are born are domi-nated by their id (the pleasure principle). According to Freud they can only seek gratification to maintain their comfort, e.g. by crying when they are hungry or uncomfortable. As they get older they then start to develop the ego (the reality principle). This happens as they come to realize that they need to interact with people and the real world in order to get what they want. The final stage of personality development is through the acquisition of the superego. This acts as a conscience, which dictates what it is acceptable to want, with an accompanying sense of guilt if this is ignored.

The way that we view ourselves is so important to our well-being that Freud believed that we develop 'ego protective mechanisms'. Events or ideas that are potentially destructive to a positive view of the self are repressed from consciousness but remain within the unconscious and can affect behaviour many years later. Examples of ego defence mechanisms include denial: by suppressing awareness we can ignore painful or disturbing thoughts. When meeting clients you may be surprised that they did not seek advice and help about their symptoms, even where they could indicate severe illness. Similarly those who are experiencing bereavement may not accept that someone has a terminal illness or has died.

According to early psychoanalytical theory, suppressing information was always harmful and therapy was needed to help people to recognize why they had suppressed these thoughts into their unconscious. However, it is now recognized that, at least in the short term, mechanisms such as denial can help in coming to terms with a severe and distressing problem.

Freud also believed that development went through a number of stages which were associated with areas of the body that provided a source of pleasure. If a child was not able to pass successfully through each stage then the child would be considered to be fixated and continue with typical behaviour into adulthood. For example, a person who drinks excessive alcohol could be assumed to have fixated at the oral stage or someone who is compulsively tidy fixated at the anal stage.

Erikson (1963) developed the psychoanalytical approach but suggested that development was characterized by conflict between the person's unconscious drives and their social world. Development of self-identity came as a result of resolving conflicts associated with eight life stages. These ranged from the first stage for the young baby of trust versus mistrust to the final stage of integrity versus despair.

Humanistic theories

These assume that individual development is through personal growth. Maslow (1970) proposed that everyone has an innate drive to achieve 'self actualization', which is a similar concept to that of realizing our full potential. He suggested that this could only come about through essential needs being met and organized this into a 'hierarchy of needs' (Figure 8.3).

You may feel that the idea of a hierarchy is too restrictive and there can be times when the need for that love or a need for respect can become more important than food or personal safety. However, it does emphasize that everyone has needs and that general well-being and development will be enhanced by their fulfilment.

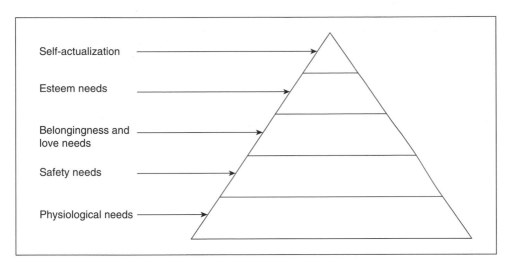

Figure 8.3   Maslow's 'hierarchy of needs'

The humanistic tradition underlies person-centred counselling based on the work of Carl Rogers, which is further explored in Chapter 9.

Ecological theory

This theory is characterized by recognizing the importance of individuals' whole environment (their ecosystem) when identifying influences on their development. Bronfenbrenner (1979) identified this as being composed of:

- The microsystem – the immediate world of the individual, e.g. home, school and social activities.
- The mesosystem – the relationship between the various microsystems, e.g. home and school.
- The exosystem – the effect of wider influences, e.g. parents' working conditions and social activities.
- The macrosystem – the more indirect effects such as social institutions and ide-ologies, e.g. political decisions and the wider culture.

Associated with this theory is interest in how a child's personality and environment interact to lead the child to being 'at risk' of behavioural and developmental prob-lems. Not all children seem to be equally vulnerable and Terrisse (2000) reviewed studies that identify factors that appear to be associated with risk or protection. These are seen as being significant at each level of the ecosystem, so can include birth experience, socio-economic status, parental education and employment, school and recreational opportunities, government funding in supportive organizations and measures for providing equality of opportunities. Children who seem able to cope, despite experiencing some of these difficulties, are described as 'resilient'. It is through understanding what contributes to their ability to resist apparently adverse conditions that intervention programmes have been devised. These aim both to support and to modify the environmental stresses as well as promoting the development of the individual's own resources in coping. These approaches have been applied with a range of groups, including aggression or drug taking in adolescence, children with disabilities, families in poor socio-economic conditions or those who have moved through immigration.

Although none of these theories is able to provide a complete explanation, together they help to build up our knowledge and gain understanding of the processes and influences on human behaviour. This is shown in the next section, which looks at developmental psychology.

Lifespan development

Psychology is interested in not only recognizing the changes that take place in people, but also identifying factors that might influence these changes.

Before reading further it would be helpful for you to reflect on your own life experiences and the factors that have influenced them.

ACTIVITY

The River of Life (how you came to be you)

Beginning with conception, identify important landmarks in your life. This could include:

- Major life events: starting work, changes to relationships, illness, etc.
- Transitional life stages: adolescence, becoming a parent, ageing, etc.
- Transient life events: these could be very minor such as a conversation with someone at a crucial point in your life or seeing a television programme that affected your understanding of a social issue.

You might want to draw your own river of life and highlight key events/transitions. Try to think about what may have caused or influenced these changes.

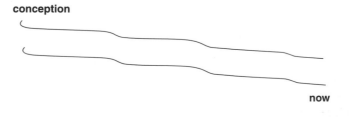

conception

now

In reflecting on your 'River of Life' you will have identified events that have personal significance as well as those that have similarities to others' experiences.

The areas of development that are being discussed in this section are:

- Two developmental processes:

  a The development of early social emotional relationships
  b The development of a self-concept.

- Two significant life periods:

  a Adolescence
  b Ageing.

Socio-emotional development of relationships

Relationships form a significant part in our lives and are important to development. You will be able to identify a number of your own significant relationships, which could include parents, children, siblings, partners, work colleagues, friendship groups, care worker, clients and many others. Relationships may be important for different reasons and can be seen as essential to supporting and promoting development, as a source of satisfying our needs and for moderating stressful experiences. Those who are isolated and do not have close relationships can be some of the most vulnerable people in society.

It is assumed that there are behaviours that support or challenge the successful development of relationships and part of the explanation of how we acquire these skills is provided by studies of early social emotional development.

Video studies of new-born babies and their carers show how they engage in 'conversation' from soon after the baby is born and so start to establish their relationship. Babies are not passive dolls but participate and start to show their own needs, initiate and respond to the other person and communicate through sounds and eye gaze. Even very young babies show preferences for familiar people and can recognize smells and voices; they will look at faces with their complex shapes and movement rather than simpler patterns.

Shared time provides the opportunity for attachment between children and their carers. Bowlby (1969) described this as 'bonding' and proposed that the opportunity to develop specific attachments to others is an essential foundation for forming later relationships, including the ability to be sensitive and respond to the needs of others.

A child who has formed this attachment bond is assumed to show his or her attachment through behaviours including:

- Preference for the main carer.
- Greater willingness to be comforted by that carer.
- Using that carer as a safe base for exploring or returning to when feeling anxious.

What helps the development of these early relationships?

Clearly this must include some form of contact, but beyond this there are various parenting practices throughout the world with differences in attachment experiences and outcomes. Ainsworth et al. (1971) studied the responses of a child during a brief separation from the mother and suggested that the sensitivity and responsiveness of the parents would affect the child's security and confidence in forming later relationships. Some parenting classes will include sessions on facilitating new parents' understanding and responsiveness to their babies. However, while developing these interactional skills is important, it is necessary to recognize that individual differences in temperament, cultural practices and disabilities will also have an impact on early communication and its consequences.

Theory box

Working just after the Second World War, John Bowlby studied the effect of separation between the mother and young child, mainly within institutions. He described the consequences of separation from the mother as contributing to permanent long-term harm to the child's ability to develop relationships and integrate into society. From observations he described a child's responses to separation from the carer including:

- Protest: The child cries and shows anxiety about being separated.
- Despair: When this fails to bring about the return of the child's attachment figure, the child seems to be depressed, and becomes apathetic shown by reduced communication and play with others.
- Detachment: Following prolonged separation the child starts to form new attachments although these are mainly superficial and may be characterized by demonstrations of the child's uncertainty and loss of security in the predictability of new relationships.

However, Rutter (1972), while acknowledging potential harmful effects, also highlighted that the consequences would be affected by factors such as age, previous experience and how relationships were maintained during separation.

The demonstration of attachment behaviour between carer and child is considered one of the markers of a healthy relationship and is used by social workers and health professionals to inform their observations of quality of attachment experiences and responses to disruption and separation.

An important debate within our culture is the extent to which child and carer need to spend time together and the effect of separation through alternative care arrangements either as day care or longer periods. Some detrimental effects have been shown by group care of very young children; however, evidence also identifies the value of programmes that can enhance the different levels of the child's environment.

Any decision about the most appropriate child care arrangements needs to consider:

- How the alternative care options can contribute to the child's development.
- Characteristics of the child, including personal history, age and temperament.
- Sensitivity and quality of the day care provision.
- Relevance and support for the child's overall environment.

Applications of attachment theory are not limited to children. The consequences of disruption can be seen throughout life in experiences of grief and loss. This may occur through dissolution of peer or adult relationships or bereavement, loss of role from redundancy, or children leaving home. All have consequences for health and well-being.

This can help in understanding the way that people respond to problems such as a young child starting nursery school, the breakdown of a relationship or an older person entering a residential care setting. Attachment experiences influence how others respond to you which will affect the development of your self-concept.

Self-concept

The self-concept is defined as the way that we organize information into an understanding of what we think we are like. Psychologists often try to divide this understanding into different sections as it makes it easier to comprehend and study. This can include:

- An ideal self
- Body image
- Self-esteem.

The development of self-perception depends on increasing cognitive maturation in order to recognize, describe and eventually be able to reflect on the person that we have become. Learning about ourselves comes through the responses of others, their expectations, and the extent to which we meet them, as well as gaining self-knowledge through testing our own abilities.

During our development we incorporate the ideas of others into what we believe we should be like and so construct a self-ideal that may differ from our perception of what we are actually like. The bigger the difference between our ideal and our perceived reality, the more discontented and uncertain we may become. This personal evaluation is a measure of self-esteem.

This may involve self-questioning about:

- What we think we are worth.
- What we value about ourselves.
- What we tolerate as acceptable.
- What we like or despise about ourselves.

One of the aspects of ourselves that we can be particularly sensitive about is body image. The way that we think that we look can have an important effect on our behaviour and mood. If we believe that we look good, and fit somewhere near our ideal image, then we are more likely to feel comfortable and interact positively. Discontent with our image may severely affect our willingness to engage with others.

Body image includes the body size and shape, features, hair, smell, blemishes, colour and texture of skin. As part of ageing the body continues to change and there are particular points in people's lives when they have to come to terms with differences in their appearance. The onset of secondary sexual characteristics at adolescence coincides with an important stage in cognitive maturation. This stage allows individuals to think of themselves in more abstract terms so that they may be more self-conscious of their appearance and aware of how others might perceive them. It is also a period where there can be changes in social expectations as they look increasingly adult and sexually mature.

Other changes, such as pregnancy, the early onset of baldness, changes in weight, disfigurement and ageing, can all bring their own demands with a risk of negative re-evaluations and lowering of self-esteem. Increased self-awareness can lead to a fear of negative evaluation by others, causing emotions such as embarrassment and shame.

Intervention programmes, aimed at helping people overcome their unhappiness or difficulties in fitting in with their social world, target self-esteem and use strategies to raise an individual's sense of self-worth and perception that others value the individual.

Practice tip

If we are to help clients cope with situations that may lead to embarrassment and shame it is essential to:

- Treat them as individuals and take time to understand their concerns and perceptions.
- Act in a professional and non-judgemental manner to help reassure them that otherwise socially taboo activities are acceptable in that therapeutic environment.
- Not show your own embarrassment or how the situation may be making you feel uncomfortable.

During development some periods assume particular significance. Some of the influences on development in childhood have already been discussed and the next section will consider the changes that are associated with adolescence and ageing.

Adolescence

Essentially this is the transitional period between childhood and adulthood and a time of considerable change that can make demands on the individual to adapt. Erikson (1963) considered this as a time of conflict between dependence and the need for autonomy progressing onto the stage of increasing need to develop a sense of self-identity.

Jot down the changes that you associate with adolescence and try to organize these into categories.

ACTIVITY

Some of the changes that you may have identified are:

- Physical changes, including the adolescent growth spurt and the development of secondary sexual characteristics.
- Socio-emotional relationships, with the increasing importance of peer groups and the development of adult sexual relationships.
- Increasing cognitive maturation increasing the ability to think in more abstract ways. This usually brings a greater capability for problem solving, reflection and independent decision making. It also often means more challenges to the self-concept and increasing self-consciousness.
- Social expectations and roles alter with age and increasing physical maturity. It is also a time when age or activities increase the likelihood of being stereotyped.

These changes are not necessarily going to develop at the same pace and can show wide variation between different people that may cause problems for the individual. Early sexual or physical maturity may occur before the cognitive development. Boys who experience late maturation tend to find themselves more isolated during their adolescence but more inclined to sensitivity and understanding in adulthood.

Despite general assumptions that adolescence is a difficult time, or that teenagers have problems, for many this is a period of development with successful adaptation to the changes. However, for others this will be a time of real concern, with problems coming to the fore that may have long-term consequences.

At this point there is an increase in behavioural difficulties including conflicts at home and at school as well as a susceptibility to crime and antisocial activities. What is less clear is whether this is due to changes within the individual or social expectations. It is also a time often associated with the start of health-risk behaviours. Peer groups increase in significance in influencing behaviour as the teenager looks outside the family for a source of identity. When looking at the onset of adolescent smoking, Kobus (2003) pointed out that by behaving like others, adolescents increase their acceptability to their peers. Belonging to a group provides a sense of belonging with opportunities for sharing social activities and the development of independence.

Another important time of transition comes with increasing age.

Ageing

Who is old?

There are many different ways of trying to decide when someone is old. Social policies will define retirement and pension age, cultural stereotypes vary over time and between societies, yet individuals have their personal understanding which may certainly change as they get older. People's perceptions will be influenced by their changing roles in society, health and fitness, comparison with others and personal expectations. Chronological age assumes less importance as people get older; this will be shown by widening differences in the ageing processes and emphasizes the need to be aware of individuals' own view of their age.

Age a time of inevitable decline?

There is a common perception that old age is a time of inevitable decline and this is often reflected in the language that we use. However, for many older people there arc positive benefits and it can be a very fulfilling period of their life.

ACTIVITY

Make a thought shower of the changes that you associate with ages. Try to group them under:

- Physical
- Cognitive
- Emotional
- Social.

You may find that you need to add some other categories or that some things fit in more than one. Underline all the ones that seem to show the negative parts of growing older. If they are mostly negative, try to add others that may reflect more positive elements, such as greater confidence, acceptance of abilities or attributes, more leisure time and less demands being made on you.

Cognitive changes

Cognitive changes such as loss of memory, impaired problem solving or ability to undertake new learning are often a source of concern for people as they get older.

Some changes do take place, but this is more complex than assumptions that these can be measured by simply a loss of brain cells or is inevitable for a particular age group. These changes are not just about loss of function but also about the use of previously acquired skills, current situation and opportunities for mental activity and personal perceptions. It may be necessary to use different strategies to learn new information and activities can take more planning, but older people will be able to use their life experiences to help them achieve their objectives in spite of any reduction in speed of information processing. When working with older people it is essential to recognize that development varies in individuals and not to make assumptions based on ageist stereotypes.

Keeping physically and socially active does seem to contribute to successful ageing and maintaining health. This has been associated with the personality characteristic of hardiness, which was identified by Kobasa (1979) and appears to aid in resisting stress and is linked to engaging in health protective behaviours (Magnani 1990). Hardiness is characterized by a personal sense of control over their lives and events, commitment, which implies involvement, and interest and challenge, suggesting a willingness to engage and adapt to new experiences.

Bereavement and loss

These can occur at any age but will become increasingly likely with increasing age.

Bereavement can lead to a sense of loss regardless of the cause; it can arise from loss of a significant person, health, a home, even a lifestyle or pet. People can also suffer anticipatory grief, e.g. when someone is given a diagnosis of a fatal disease.

Russell (2000) identified the four main emotions associated with actual or anticipated loss as:

- Fear
- Anger
- Guilt
- Sadness.

Theorists such as Kübler-Ross (1969) suggest that there is a normal grieving process which requires the person to pass through specific stages of bereavement which may include periods of denial and depression, among others, before achieving acceptance.

For many people, bereavement is certainly associated with both physical and emotional consequences, which can increase mortality and the need for medical treatment. However, some help can contribute to moderating these harmful affects including:

- Social support
- Self-help groups
- Quality of care
- Being consulted and making decisions concerning the place of death.

Lifespan development

Identify how lifespan development theories and ideas can help in understanding behaviour associated with:

- Childhood obesity
- Adolescent smoking
- An older person adjusting to moving into residential care.

The next section will consider further applications of psychology to working in the health and social care sector.

Psychology and working in health and social care

Stress

Stress usually results from a need to adapt to a changed situation and usually leads to an increase in physical arousal level.

Theory box

The Yerkes–Dodson law (1908) explains the relationship between levels of arousal and when you are most effective in coping with the demands being made on you. It suggests that everyone has their individual optimal level of arousal where they perform best (Figure 8.4).

Too low a level of arousal leads to boredom and not using skills, but too high a demand brings about reduced ability to cope with the situation, increased inefficiency and potential for developing illness associated with stress.

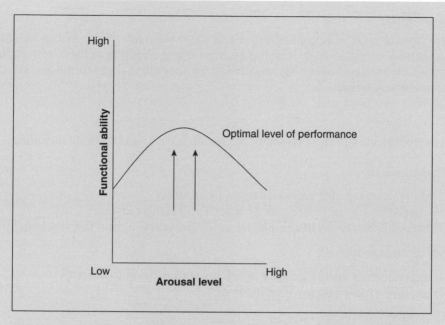

Figure 8.4 The Yerkes–Dodson law – functional ability against arousal level
Source: Yerkes, R. M. and Dodson, J. D. (1908) 'The relation of strength of stimulus to rapidity of habit-formation', *Journal of Comparative Neurology and Psychology*, 18: 459–82.

Functional ability is how well you carry out your activities.

Arousal level is when there is an increase in physical and psychological responses to demands (how stressed you are).

Optimal level of performance is the level of arousal that allows you to work at your most efficient. Too low and you are probably bored; too high and you are unable to cope with the demands effectively.

Case study

Jason has been working as a supervisor on day duty within a supported housing setting for a number of years. Recently his partner left him and he is having difficulty arranging suitable access to his 7-year-old son. He is also finding himself in financial difficulties so has arranged to move to night duty for extra pay. Unfortunately he is having difficulties in sleeping. Managers are concerned that while he was previously very conscientious and meticulous they

(Continued)

(Continued)

are finding work is being neglected and mistakes made. Some of the service users have complained that he has become angry, shouting at them with little provocation. A co-worker has mentioned his suspicions that Jason has started to drink very heavily.

As is demonstrated in the case study, stress can have harmful effects including:

- Physiological:
  - short term, e.g. disruption, changes to appetite;
  - long term, e.g. increased risk of heart and vascular disease;
  - harmful changes to health behaviours, e.g. excessive drinking, smoking.

- Social and emotional:
  - aggression or apathy causing problems with relating to others;
  - unemployment and lowered income.

- Cognitive:
  - problem-solving abilities.

The transactional model of stress (Lazarus and Folkman 1984)

This suggests that stress results from:

- A perception of the situation as threatening to our well-being.
- The perception of personal resources to be able to cope with the challenge.

A sense of stress may result from:

- The number of different and possibly competing challenges needing to be dealt with at the same time.
- A situation where previous methods of coping are either inappropriate or ineffective.
- There is insufficient social support.

It is important to recognize that a person's anxieties and responses are due to their interpretation of events and assumptions of their ability to cope, although these may appear trivial or unrealistic to others. Individuals will all respond differently to a breakdown in a relationship, moving schools, entering into a care home or adjusting to their own or someone else's illness.

Work within the health and social care field requires developing skills that help in managing personal and clients' stressful experiences. This can include:

- Helping to develop more effective coping strategies, including looking at alternative ways of dealing with the problem or trying to change the negative emotions that have become linked to the situation.
- Using 'social support' from others through being given information or practical help, having someone show their belief in your ability to manage or just being part of a social network.
- Regaining a sense of control over the situation by facing the issues or starting to take actions that will eventually lead to possible solutions.

Changing health behaviour

It is now recognized that many of the modern illnesses and causes of death are related to people's lifestyle and behaviours. Diseases such as cardiovascular disorders resulting in coronary artery disease, high blood pressure and strokes may be associated with diet, stress and lack of exercise. We are all familiar with health promotion campaigns that point out the health risks of cigarette smoking, drug taking or excessive drinking of alcohol. Other effects of behaviour on health come through whether we take part in screening programmes or to what extent we follow recommended treatments.

There are many situations in the health and social care field where help is needed to support people in changing or adopting behaviours to enhance the quality of their lives. This will include:

- Prompting or encouraging someone to seek advice from a health professional.
- Through an understanding of possible influences of changing behaviour, help in planning how to carry out changes.
- Providing support and understanding especially when they are having difficulties.
- Being ready to discuss treatment and rehabilitation programmes to make sure they understand the advice and can make informed choices.

Influences on health behaviours

Most people are aware that they could live a healthier lifestyle but for many an inability to change will lead to very real risks to their health. Influences involved in supporting and maintaining changes to health behaviours have been incorporated into theoretical models such as the health belief model (Becker and Rosenstock 1984).

Theory box

The health belief model suggests that whether we take action, i.e. change our behaviour, is influenced by:

- Individual variables: This includes things like our age, sex, religious beliefs, knowledge and experiences of ourselves or friends and family.
- Perceived vulnerability: These variables can affect how seriously we consider the consequences of not taking action as well as to what extent we consider ourselves to be at risk.
- Cost and benefits: Part of deciding whether to take action will be based on an assessment of perceived benefits compared with anticipated costs. Costs can include financial costs, such as joining a gym, but would also include time, increased anxiety or embarrassment.
- Cues to action: Check-up reminders, media articles or contact with someone who has become ill can all act as prompts to take action.

Other influences on whether we act more healthily include:

- **Attitudes:** The theory of reasoned action suggests that forming an intention to change health behaviours will be determined both by our own attitudes towards a particular behaviour and by an awareness of other people's attitudes. This can be seen when children or adolescents start to smoke, because that is considered to be the right way to behave by other members of their group, or in decisions about breast feeding being influenced by partners' or parents' attitudes.
- **Reinforcement:** Operant conditioning identified how we are more likely to carry out behaviour that is reinforced. A behavioural change plan should be designed to have clear achievable steps that can be reinforced by acknowledgement of success, such as praise or treats, provided either by others or ourselves.
- **Self-efficacy beliefs:** Self-efficacy refers to our belief about whether we can succeed in making changes. If we have a high self-efficacy we will have greater expectations and confidence in our ability to change. Working with service users can involve both assessing their self-efficacy beliefs and introducing strategies to increase them.

A related idea is outcome expectancies. Again you are more likely to attempt to change your behaviour if you believe the effort will bring about the outcome that you actually want.

Decide on a behaviour that you believe would make you healthier. Examples might be drinking more water, giving up chocolate, reorganizing your life/work balance or changing your diet to include more vegetables.

Try to change this behaviour for a week and keep a diary of the type of things that helped or made it more difficult. Find examples from the influences that have been discussed in this section.

Carrying out this activity can help highlight the problems people encounter when changing health behaviours.

Observation and report writing

Observation and making reports is an integral part of most care work, yet as everyone is aware it is possible to make mistakes through not noticing all the relevant information, forgetting or misinterpreting what we have seen.

Part of this is due to our attempts to make sense of the world. Information about our environment comes through the senses: sight, smell, sound, taste and touch. However, our ability to take notice of these stimuli is selective. Perception is the way that we select, process, interpret and draw inferences about the meaning of the information that we have received. This will be influenced by previous experiences, learning and personal significance.

Through experience we develop our personal schemas and understanding of the world which influence what we notice and can predict how we respond. Schema represents our reality rather than a true reflection of the actual world and is unique to the individual.

Our schemas lead us to take more notice of the familiar and information that supports our existing ideas. The result is that we can miss unexpected symptoms or behaviours that do not fit in with our expectations.

Since working on and studying psychological aspects relevant to health and social care issues, consider how you have become more aware of related topics in the media.

Reflect upon your developing awareness of the psychological needs of service users.

How do you think you have become more aware of people's emotional and social needs?

Stereotyping

Through our perceptions we simplify and organize information that contributes to the formation of stereotypes. This tendency to over-generalize from very limited information is a characteristic of human behaviour. It does have important implications when working in the health and care sector. Challenging the tendency to use stereotypes and generalizations helps the care professional to focus on the needs of the individual rather than provide care that is based on the assumed needs of 'the elderly, nursery-age children or people with learning difficulties'.

Some terms are particularly powerful, especially where they have negative connotations. A report on a new service user that included words such as 'difficult, demanding, aggressive or manipulative' could affect how staff approach the person and influence perceptions of their behaviour.

Attribution theory

We not only observe people, but also make judgements about the causes of their behaviour. Actions are often attributed to being the result of either personality characteristics of the person or recognition of how they have been influenced by the situation. These cognitive biases make us more ready to see our own behaviours resulting from the situation that we are in, while seeing others' behaviour as mainly determined by their personality characteristics. An example would be:

> I failed the exam because I was so busy at work; they failed the exam because they are too lazy to study.

The following tips will be helpful when writing reports or passing on information.

Practice tips

Be aware of the need to:

- Be objective rather than subjective. When reporting on an individual talk about your actual observations not assumptions about the individual's character.
- Avoid stereotypical and judgemental language.
- Make use of care plans to identify how to meet the needs of an individual rather than assumptions based on group membership.
- Keep an open mind. If someone has a specific condition, still take notice of other symptoms or behaviours.
- Make judgements about the reasons for behaviour. Think about how the situation could contribute to people's actions.
- Use the organizational records to make sure that you are not ignoring relevant information.
- Write down information as soon as possible to make sure that you are accurate.

Summary

Psychology seeks to understand and explain the causes and consequences of behaviour.

The different psychological theories all contribute to an understanding of the influences on human behaviour.

It is necessary to recognize the complexity of behaviour and that observed behaviour is affected by cognitions, emotions, physiological status and social interactions.

The study of psychology can enhance delivery of care through greater understanding of service users' behaviour, how to support them in meeting their needs and promoting their well-being. It will also help in reaffirming the importance of treating people as individuals and increasing awareness of potential factors that can challenge our objectivity in planning and delivering care.

Awareness of psychological processes contributes to personal and professional development including management of issues such as stress and health protective behaviour.

Further reading

This chapter has introduced a range of psychological issues that are relevant to your work in health and social care. In order to develop your studies further, aim to find additional readings and books that fit with your existing knowledge level but provide additional detail, different perspectives or applications.

There are many very good psychology texts; some will provide a general approach while others will cover a specific area, subdivision of psychology or practice focus. This list includes a few to help direct your further reading.

Russell, G. (2000) *Essential Psychology for Nurses and Other Health Professionals*. London: Routledge. A very readable text; although some of the examples are based in clinical settings most are applicable to the wider health and care sector.

Crawford, K. and Walker, J. (2003) *Social Work and Human Development*. Exeter: Learning Matters. Provides an overview with useful case studies and learning activities to reinforce your understanding. Although directed at social work, the emphasis on practice can be applied to a wider area of health and social care work.

Smith, P., Cowie, H. and Blades, M. (2002) *Understanding Children's Development*, 4th edn. Oxford: Blackwell. A comprehensive text that will provide the opportunity for further study of development in children.

Walker, J., Payne, S., Smith, P. and Jarrett, N. (2004) *Psychology for Nurses and the Caring Professions*, 2nd edn. Maidenhead: Open University Press. Case studies and questions make this a useful book for exploring some of the issues raised in this chapter in more detail.

Albery, I., Chandler, C., Field, A., Jones, D., Messer, D., Moore, S., Stirling, C. and Davey, G. (2004) *Complete Psychology*. London: Hodder and Stoughton. An extensive introduction into general psychology which could serve as a valuable resource for developing further reading and understanding.

9

Interpersonal Communication

Judith Mann

Summary Chapter Contents

- Your role as a care worker
- Communication skills
- The structure of interaction
- Working in groups
- Barriers to communication
- Managing conflict situations
- Summary

Learning objectives

By the end of this chapter, you should be able to:

- Understand the importance of effective communication.
- Recognize a range of communication skills.
- Monitor and evaluate your use of communication skills.
- Gain knowledge about groups and group behaviour.
- Reflect on 'difference' within the communication process.
- Recognize barriers to communication.
- Learn how to manage conflict situations.

Introduction

You have made a choice to pursue a career in health and social care, working with people who, at the particular time at which you are involved with them, will be feeling 'vulnerable'. The skills that you will need will primarily be those that many of us take for granted, but which you will need to develop in order to enhance work with the service user, and if appropriate the carer.

Effective communication skills underpin all the values which you, as a health and social care worker, need in your work with people. These are the skills by which people judge you. Your development of these skills and the way that you interact with people will be reflected in the work that you do. The skills are important in your day-to-day contact with people who may require your help and support. They are important when you meet prospective service users for the first time, in maintaining an ongoing relationship or in the assessment and review process.

Your values and moral principles (which are explored in Chapter 6), and how you convey them, are what help to make you a professional care worker. They ensure that you consider the needs of the service user and keep them central to your interactions with people. A failure to achieve this can result in the service user losing confidence in you as a worker, a factor that can greatly impede and disadvantage ongoing work.

This chapter will provide you with relevant knowledge that will enable you to reflect on your communication skills and appreciate their importance when working with people.

Your role as a care worker

Partnership working

The Department of Health (2012b) in the White Paper 'Caring for our Future: Reforming Care and Support' emphasizes the importance of working with service users and carers in a way that ensures that their views are listened to and that their choices are considered. The care worker's role in health and social care is centred on the needs of a vulnerable person – child or adult. This involves the worker being able to be aware of that person as an individual with whom they are 'in partnership' in their care.

> A vulnerable person is someone who is in need of community care services by reason of mental, age or any other disability and 'who may be unable to take care of him or herself' (Department of Health 2000: 8–9).

For the current government (Department of Health 2012b), integration across the National Health Service, public health and social care is key to improving the quality of services and people's experiences of the services they receive. There is an emphasis on a joined-up approach to improve the health and wellbeing of the population.

To deliver this, the government recognizes that this involves health and social care workers working in partnership not only with each other, but also with families, communities, a range of service provider organizations, and most importantly with people who use the services.One way in which you approach this notion of partnership will be evidenced by your use of effective communication skills. Your use of these skills will convey to the service users your attitude towards them and how you intend to work with them. For example, a community care assistant will often be required to assist an older person in the task of dressing. In taking the service user's views into consideration, the community care assistant would ask the person what they would like to wear that day and how much assistance they require with dressing. This action demonstrates making decisions with people, not for people.

The following activity will help you to consider further requirements of an effective helping role.

Professional approach

Think of a situation in which you need to go to someone for help: for example, an interview with your GP about a problem or symptom that has been worrying you for some time; a discussion with a health visitor about the feeding pattern of your newly born baby; a discussion with a tutor at college about writing an essay on a subject you are studying.

- What did you expect from the professional?
- How did the professional respond to you?

ACTIVITY

You would most likely want the professional to take your concerns seriously by listening to you. You would also want something from the professional: advice, reassurance or acceptance of your concerns. What would be most important would be that you were listened to and that you felt valued as a person.

We all appreciate being treated as individuals; none of us likes to be treated as a category, e.g. 'old person', 'youth', 'disabled', 'resident'. In care work the way we address people, and the way that we speak about them and to them, are significant in demonstrating our respect for the people that we care for and work with.

> The professional worker should respond to you as a 'person', not to you as a 'category', i.e. *patient, new mother, parent, student.* The 'Valuing People' White Paper (Department of Health 2001), although specifically directed at people with learning disabilities, sets the standard for services to respond to individual need.

In the activity above, the professional that you saw needed to demonstrate a range of qualities and characteristics in order to give you that sense of being attended to as a *person.* What do you think these qualities were able to do?

- Did they make you feel that you mattered?
- Do you think the professional responded to you with interest?
- Was the professional attentive to your needs?
- Was the focus of the interaction on you?

Such characteristics and qualities could be described as empathy, having a non-judgemental approach and demonstrating respect for you as an individual.

Person-centred care

Putting the person at the centre of the interaction is not a new concept. Carl Rogers, the distinguished American counsellor and psychotherapist, spent most of his life refining an approach he called the person-centred approach. He emphasized that it was the attitude of the worker, in his case, the counsellor towards the client, that gave it its *person-centredness* or *client-centredness.* The helper should demonstrate *empathy, genuineness* and *respect* as the *core conditions* of the helping relationship. If the counsellor offered these and used effective communication skills, then a feeling of helping would follow.

Rogers' core conditions can be applied to all helping roles and in particular to care work. Consider what is meant by the word 'empathy'. You may be more familiar with the notion of sympathy. Sympathy is when someone is sorry for you. This can be helpful in the first instance, but it does not necessarily help you to resolve your problem. However, empathy is when someone demonstrates an understanding of your situation as you are experiencing it, is respectful of your point of view – not judging you or discriminating against you and giving you the feeling that they were genuinely there to help you. Their words match their feelings (Rogers 1951). Empathy is to feel *with*, sympathy is to feel *like* (Stewart 1992).

To demonstrate that you have empathy with service users is to understand their position, recognize their condition and respect their point of view. Rogers (1951) described empathy as the ability to 'sense the client's world as if it were your own'.

Characteristics of a helper

Your role as a care worker is different from that of a counsellor, but there are many similarities in the characteristics of all helping roles. To be an effective helper it is generally recognized that these qualities should be demonstrated, qualities and characteristics such as:

- Empathy and being non-judgemental
- Being genuine
- Showing respect for the person
- Being non-discriminatory and honest
- Having good listening skills
- Demonstrating warmth towards the person
- Being likable
- Adopting a professional approach
- Being a good communicator
- Being aware of the need for confidentiality.

These characteristics are skills that can also be learned; they are characteristics that your service users will want you to evidence. Taken together, they will enable you to demonstrate effective communication skills that become essential for your relationship with the people you work with.

Self-management and self-presentation

Care work involves your 'self' more than some other forms of work. As a care worker you need to consider how you relate to the other people you meet during your working day, most especially service users and carers. This involves how much information you may reveal about yourself and how you present your self to others.

This information you reveal about yourself to others is referred to as 'self-disclosure'. It becomes important in helping relationships as Myers and Myers (cited in Burton and Dimbleby 1988) state:

> A relationship develops only when you and the other person are willing to go through the mutual process of revealing yourself to each other. If you can't reveal yourself, you cannot be close. To be silent about yourself is to be a stranger. (Burton and Dimbleby 1988: 33)

Johari's window (Luft and Ingham 1969, cited in Hartley 1993) illustrates different types of information about the 'self' and shows how the 'self' changes through interaction.

The window has four 'panes' (Figure 9.1). Each 'pane' represents information about the 'self'. You can experiment by putting your own information into the different 'panes'. Consider how you feel about the different information, how readily you might reveal it and to whom:

- **Public pane:** This is information most people would willingly share: what job they do, how they would describe themselves, which town they live in; the answer to the question 'Who am I?'
- **Private pane:** This is information that is personal and private to yourself which you would not so easily share with others: your medical history, your family background, the contents of your bank account.
- **Hidden pane:** Information known to other people that is not known to you. How others see you, your bad habits or the special qualities that you are unaware of.
- **Unknown pane:** This represents your potential: what you might be capable of through personal and professional development; where you might be when you finish your course of study.

Johari's window is a useful way to consider how you relate to other people. The key way to make successful relationships within or outside work is to reveal information *appropriately* about yourself. It is important to think about this when developing a professional approach with service users. They will want to tell you about themselves as well as listen to you. The 'window' demonstrates a useful model for when information is shared appropriately; the person's 'private pane' decreases as they extend their 'public pane' (see the dashed line in Figure 9.1). In sharing yourself with others you will discover more about both them and yourself. In order to do this you need to communicate effectively.

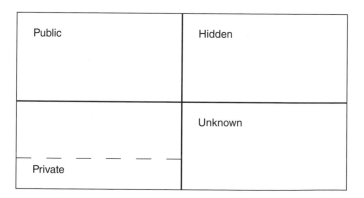

Figure 9.1   Johari's window

Self-presentation

As well as being aware of how much you reveal to service users, as a care worker you need to give consideration as to how you present yourself in the working environment and to service users and the impact this may have. This will be particularly important in the work-based learning element of your Foundation Degree.

Self-presentation consists of the manner and attitude which you put forward, and also aspects of your appearance. Self-presentation becomes an aspect of non-verbal communication – you are communicating something about yourself. Your dress, hair, make-up, jewellery, any piercings and visible tattoos all say something about who you are and about yourself.

Some employers will have strong views on how you should present yourselves for work; some of these will be based on health and safety. They will not want you to put yourself or the service users at unnecessary risk. You may be required to wear a uniform and may want you to remove jewellery and piercings while at work. Most importantly they will want you to be neat, clean and tidy. These aspects will also be important to consider when you attend for interview.

When you give consideration to the above components of non-verbal communication, you are conveying a professional approach to your work.

Communication skills

Communication skills can be divided into written, verbal and non-verbal communication. Written communication is vital for accurate record keeping and is likely to involve information about the care needs of service users, such as care plans, handovers, assessments and other reports. Information that is written down in this way should contain factual information that is objective, valid and reliable. It should inform rather than direct action.

This chapter is mainly concerned with 'interpersonal communication': that is, communication between persons which is verbal and non-verbal. Non-verbal communication is communication that does not involve words, such as facial expression, but which conveys much meaning.

The skills of interpersonal communication

An interpersonal skill is *any skill which is part of interpersonal communication and which can be learned, practised and improved upon.* The person sending the message and the person receiving the message are subject to a number of social, environmental and psychological influences.

There are a range of interpersonal skills that you will need to be aware of. These include:

- Empathy
- Self-presentation
- Being aware of and using non-verbal communication
- Listening
- Questioning
- Establishing rapport
- Attending
- Using touch and personal space
- Observing
- Clarifying
- Reflecting
- Summarizing
- Being able to conclude and end an interaction.

Listening

Until you think about it carefully many people would not regard listening as a skill. Listening is something that they do (or do not do) without thinking about it!

Consider what is involved in listening. When you are next with a friend, or with a child, make a point of paying closer attention to what they are communicating, not just the words they use but their facial expressions. This should involve your full attention. To give your full attention to someone else is hard work because you have to concentrate.

Think about how you listen to people most of the time. Most people only really listen to a percentage of what they hear. They are selective listeners and tune in and out of the conversation unless it is something in which they are particularly interested.

Being a good listener is about:

- Giving your full attention.
- Maintaining eye contact.
- Following the story.
- Sitting or standing near to the speaker at a reasonable distance.
- Looking interested in what people have to say.
- Interrupting them as little as possible.
- Making appropriate comments to them, indicating that you are responding to what they have to say.

One of the key skills you will be demonstrating is that of *attending*, demonstrating by your *non-verbal communication* that you are interested in what they have to say.

Attending

Attending involves:

- Sitting squarely and facing the person at a slight angle.   (S)
- Having an open posture.   (O)
- Leaning slightly to show interest.   (L)
- Giving eye contact.   (E)
- Having a relaxed posture.   (R)

The acronym SOLER should help you to remember the skill of *attending*.

Practise this skill the next time you are required to listen to what someone has to say and see what difference it makes to them. If possible ask them if it made a difference. If you use this skill effectively you will have demonstrated that you were an active listener and the speaker will know by your non-verbal communication that you have heard and understood what they had to say.

The structure of interaction

An interaction describes action between persons. This is generally referred to as face-to-face communication. It is only one aspect of communication as communication can take other forms, namely written, verbal, non-verbal, electronic.

Interaction is interpersonal, literally between people, and can be one-to-one or in a group with two or more people.

Structure refers to the process of interaction. An interaction can be formal, such as an interview, or informal, such as a casual chat, but still has a beginning, a middle and an end. Nelson-Jones (1997) refers to the first part of this process as 'meeting, greeting and seating'. It may or may not have a purpose, such as a job interview, it may simply be social, but this also has an outcome.

As a health and social care worker your interactions can influence the other person's sense of well-being. This requires you to think more carefully about how you communicate with your service users.

Just ask yourself when you are next in a working or college environment:

- How often do you plan what you want to say?
- Do you think about how you should say things?
- How often do you get distracted in the middle of a conversation?
- Have you ever been so distracted that you leave the person you have been talking to without finishing the conversation, perhaps leaving the other person feeling uncared for and not listened to?

Think about the structure of an interaction.

Thinking about the structure of an interaction

Watch a couple of interviews on television and observe the interaction:

- Did the interview have a structure?
- Could you recognize:

  o A beginning
  o A middle
  o An ending?

- What actions or activities did the interviewer demonstrate to give the interview its structure in each section?
- What skills of interpersonal communication did the interviewer demonstrate?
- Can you identify any other skills the interviewer used?

The beginning should have a greeting, preferably using the person's preferred form of address. This should have helped put the person at their ease.

The middle should show that the interviewer was able to demonstrate good listening skills, perhaps adopting 'SOLER'. The interviewer may have shown empathy and listened to any concerns of the interviewee.

At the end the conversation should be concluded and closed, perhaps with a thank you and goodbye.

Now that you have thought about the structure of an interaction, think back to the examples you were asked to think about in the first activity, when you wanted to be treated as an individual, and relate this to a health and social care environment.

Non-verbal communication

Non-verbal communication (NVCs) is that type of communication which happens *without* words. In the second activity, it was suggested that you watch interviews on television to study the structure of an interaction. This activity can also be useful in studying non-verbal communication.

Watch an interview on television by turning down the sound and only watching the movements that people make.

Write down what you notice about the two people and the way they interact. This will encourage you to focus on non-verbal communication. You will notice that you become a much better observer of behaviour.

Did you manage to observe some of the following components of non-verbal communication? They are sometimes referred to as *paralanguage*:

- **Spatial distance and personal space** – how far apart each person sits and how they use the space between them.
- **Touch** – whether or not there is any physical contact between them.
- **Head movements** – nods, shakes and inclinations of the head.
- **Body movements** – movements of the whole body.
- **Leg and foot movements** – crossed/uncrossed legs.
- **Gestures** – movements of the hands and arms.
- **Facial expressions** – smiles and other movements of the face.
- **Dress, jewellery, hair, make-up** – adornments of the body, which are part of self-presentation.
- **Posture and orientation** – the way a person is standing/sitting and the way one person is angled towards another person.
- **Voice** – volume (how much they speak), tone, pitch, intonation (the ups and downs of speech), rate (how fast they speak). These components of NVCs are to do with voice or speech rather than words and are therefore also part of non-verbal communication. By turning up the television and listening to the voices of the interviewer and interviewee, you will be able to hear some of the emotion conveyed in what they are saying.

It is worth considering a couple of areas of non-verbal communication a bit further as they seem to be particularly relevant in health and social care.

Spatial distance and personal space are important areas because, when working with people, you may be entering their own personal space at home. Personal space (proximity or territory) refers to that space around a person which feels part of themselves.

Next time you are in a classroom at college, note how you and your fellow students manage your personal space:

- Do you sit in your usual place in the classroom and then regard it as your chair?
- Experiment with moving around the room yourself and sitting in different places.
- How does it feel to sit in a different place?

ACTIVITY

Personal space for service users may be apparent in that they may have their favourite chair to sit in. People may want their possessions kept in a particular place. You will need to respect their personal space and talk to them about what you need to do to help them. You will need to ask permission to provide the care they need and perhaps be entering into the different zones of a person's space.

Hall (1966) identified that individuals have different zones around them which suit different situations:

- Your 'intimate' zone is a distance around you of up to 18 inches (45 cm). Your intimate zone is normally entered only by family, friends, children, partner, close friends and pets.
- Your 'personal' zone is a distance of 1½–4 feet (0.5–1.2 m) and is normally entered by acquaintances and people that you know fairly well.
- The 'social' zone is a distance of 4–12 feet (1.2–3.7 m) and entered by other friends and acquaintances, work colleagues.
- A 'business' zone, which is regarded as a distance of 12–20 feet (3.7–6 m), would be for those people you know less well at formal meetings and through business.
- A person's public' zone of about 20 feet (6 m) or more would be for strangers or people you know less well.

Observation of these zones is very important in a social interaction.

It is also important when thinking about 'personal space' or 'territory' that you recognize cultural and individual differences. Some people that you work with – both work colleagues and service users – may represent this variation. Some will 'invade' your territory, and some will feel 'invaded' by your approaching them at what you consider to be a 'safe' distance. This is especially true when working with people with an impairment – hearing, or learning disability, or dementia – where there may be a difficulty in 'reading' non-verbal communication.

Practice tips

- Develop your own sensitivity to NVCs.
- Be observant to the needs of others.
- Make sure that you get to know the people/service users you are working with.
- Communicate with people as you approach them.
- Approach people from a face-to-face orientation, rather than from where they cannot see you.
- Take advice from other care workers.

Your skills of observation will be very important in recognizing NVCs. Observation may not just involve 'seeing' but also involve using other 'senses' of smell, hearing, touch if appropriate and perhaps what might be called a 'sixth sense', one of intuition, where you sense all is not well with the other person.

Touch

As a care worker whose role may be to provide personal care to a vulnerable person, you may assume that it is appropriate for you to 'invade someone's space' in order to provide this care. However, you will now recognize from considering the zones associated with personal space that this has to be managed very carefully. It is important that boundaries of touch are carefully observed. Communication skills can help you achieve your working goals in the most person-centred way, by maintaining respect and dignity towards those for whom you provide care.

Think of three ways in which you can use communication skills to maintain the dignity of a disabled person when giving assistance with personal care.

ACTIVITY

As a community care worker, these might involve:

1 When assisting someone with bathing, using a towel as much as possible to maintain dignity and privacy.
2 Finding out how much assistance they might need with dressing.
3 Promoting choice in decisions about what to wear.

Questioning skills

Most people would not think of 'questioning' as a skill of interpersonal communication. However, questions are the way that we find out about people and are fundamental to how we make relationships. A question is the first greeting when people meet each other: How are you?

Questions can be divided into two main types – 'open' questions and 'closed' questions. 'How are you?' is an open question, because it can be answered in many different ways. A closed question is one that allows only a one-word or yes/no response. For example:

- 'What day is it today?'
- 'Would you like to wear these black trousers?'
- 'Shall I make you some toast?'

Many questions begin with one of the following: what, where, which, when, why and how? A quick way of referring to these is as the 5WH. This is not the only way a sentence may be made into a question, but it is a frequent method.

Closed questions are frequently used to find out facts. They can be useful in quickly making an assessment of a situation and obtaining a history or the person's background.

Think how you might change the following questions into more 'open' questions:

'Have you eaten breakfast today?'………………...……… 'Yes'

'Would you like a bath?'……………………………...……… 'No'

'Which socks would you like to wear?'………...……… 'The blue ones'

Open questions give a person the opportunity to respond in a variety of ways:

'What would you like for breakfast?' ……………….'I'd like some porridge
                                                    followed by some
                                                    toast'

What would you like to wear today?' ………….......… 'I'd like to wear my white
                                                    shirt, black trousers and
                                                    my blue socks'

Generally you will find out more about someone, or their situation, by asking open questions.

Questions can also be framed by altering your tone of voice, by raising it at the end of a sentence:

'You'd like to wear your blue socks?'

or responding in what is called a 'reflective' way:

'Did you say you wanted to wear your blue socks?'

This tells the person that you have listened to them and that what you heard was correct. This is called *clarifying*.

Not all questions are helpful. The use of the word 'why' at the beginning of a sentence can be rather intimidating:

'Why are you wearing your blue socks?'………...……….'Oh dear, my others are dirty!'

Try getting someone to ask you some 'why' questions about what you are wearing and see how it feels.

Questions, when well used, can be a great way of developing good working relationships.

Reflecting and paraphrasing

These are skills of interpersonal communication which assist with the listening and clarifying aspects of an interaction.

Reflecting can be used to ask a question as mentioned above, or it can be used to demonstrate your attention to what someone has said. Reflecting can have two aspects: reflection of content or reflection of feeling.

Reflection of content

Reflection of content can also be called paraphrasing, but there is a slight difference between the two. Reflection of content is when it is primarily the speaker's words that are reflected back to the speaker. Paraphrasing is when the content of the speech is reflected back in the listener's words but in a way that captures the meaning. It can be a useful way of summarizing what the person has said.

Hartley (1993: 46) refers to the use of key words as a way of encouraging the speaker to say more about a particular subject. This is helpful when a counsellor or other helper wants to encourage someone to 'elaborate'. For example:

Statement: I have always wanted to travel to Kenya.

Question: *To Kenya?*

Response: Yes, ever since I watched 'Born Free' as a child.

Reflection of feeling

As has been mentioned above, non-verbal communication often conveys what people feel about a subject they are talking about. This can be conveyed by tone of voice, facial expression or body movement or gesture. A skilled observer will notice that there is feeling behind the words spoken.

The following is a variation on the conversation above:

Statement: I had a plane ticket booked and then my mother became ill and I had to cancel it. It was all right, though, because I knew I would go later on.

Response: You sound a bit regretful that you got as far as booking your flight and then were unable to make the journey.

Statement: Well, yes, it did feel like a missed opportunity.

Using reflection enables one person to discover much more about the other person's underlying emotion.

The above skills are important in demonstrating empathy in communication.

Concluding and ending

This section began by looking at the structure of interactions. There are friendly ways of greeting people – for example, smiling, saying 'hello', and using their name. These are very good ways of 'getting off on the right foot'. It is also important to end your interaction in a positive way. This might involve saying when you will see the person again, confirming any future arrangements and saying 'goodbye'. This is the skill of concluding/ending.

Any interaction will have a conclusion or an ending, which should leave both parties feeling satisfied with what has taken place and that a reasonable outcome has been achieved. The conclusion might involve one person summarizing what has taken place. It might involve arrangements for the next meeting with a clarification of the time and place. It will most certainly involve social factors such as saying goodbye, and some sort of pleasantries about what has taken place – if that is appropriate.

Working in groups

Communication within groups is more complicated than communication on a one-to-one basis. Most health and social care workers will work in teams, even if they interact with service users on a one-to-one basis. They will need effectively to pass on information and learn to work with different co-workers.

When thinking about working in a group it is important to think about membership of the group. Most people will want to feel that they are a part of that group or team to which they belong.

Think of social groups to which you belong.
    What makes you feel part of that group? Is the group composed of like-minded people? What do you have in common?

A working group usually has a goal or purpose in common, but it might not work effectively. Working effectively usually requires more than a common goal.

Groups have different sets of needs, which are referred to as:

- Task
- Maintenance
- Individual needs

as in Figure 9.2.

Task needs are those to do with the task or purpose for which the group has been set up. This might be the aim of the group or mission statement of the company. It is the reason why the group or team has been brought together. The task needs of a group would be to do with 'getting the job done'. This is the more formal aspect of group life.

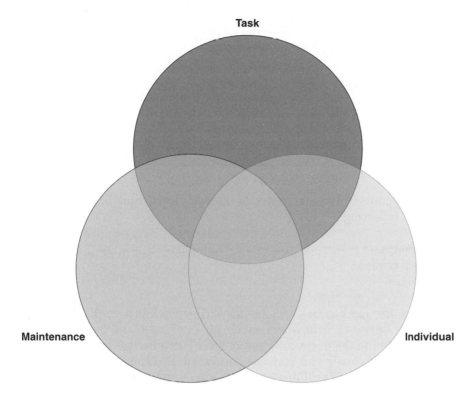

Figure 9.2 Task, maintenance and individual needs in groups

Maintenance or social needs of a group are to do with what makes being part of a group enjoyable – it is the fun side of group life. It is getting together at a Christmas party or going out for a drink after work. It is having a chat over a cup of coffee or finding out that your children are at the same school.

Individual needs are the needs of each individual group member. They are the personal aspects we bring to the group – our own attitudes, skills and values – our own individual 'agenda'. To some extent these are superseded by the needs of the group as a whole, but they cannot be ignored.

There is an overlap between these sets of needs which makes every group unique.

If a group were concerned solely with the task needs it would be a very formal group. If the group were concerned only with the social or maintenance aspect, it would never get any work done! If each individual were concerned only with their own needs, the group would not work towards its common goal. So what, therefore, makes for an effective group?

An effective group is likely to have the following characteristics:

- A common goal
- Two-way communication

- Leadership that is democratic
- A sense of group cohesion
- Conflict that is seen as positive
- High-problem-solving capacity.
  (Johnson and Johnson 1998)

ACTIVITY

Consider which of the groups you belong to are 'effective' groups.

There are, of course, different types of groups. Tajfel and Fraser (1978) have suggested the following:

- Family groups
- Friendship groups
- Work groups.

Each of these groups has been set up for a different purpose. Each will have a different set of *norms* or behaviours which are associated with being a member of that group. Knowing the norms of a group gives you a better chance of acceptance into that group. Of course you may not always want to conform to the norms of a particular group, but that will depend on your own value base.

The 'life' of a group

Some groups are set up for a specific purpose and only last for a particular period of time. One aspect of groups is that they change over time – they go through a process of evolution. Tuckman's model (cited in Inskipp 1996) provides a framework for tracking the changes in a group over time. His stages are:

- **Forming:** This stage is when a group first meets together. The task may be set, but the way to achieve it may be unclear. Group members are uncertain of each other and their own roles. They worry about belonging to the new group and whether other members will accept them.
- **Storming:** This next stage is when the group members are more familiar with each other and may jockey for position within the group. There may be conflict between group members as they negotiate the task and there may be competition for leadership.
- **Norming:** The group members begin to settle down with each other. Group roles begin to be established. There is an open exchange of views and a friendly atmosphere develops.
- **Performing:** This is the most productive stage of group life. There is a good sense of group cohesion. Members pull together and they work together to carry out the task.

- **Mourning:** The natural span of the group has come to an end. The task will have been achieved or the reason fulfilled its purpose. The group members begin to disband. There is talk of a reunion and an ending has been achieved.

Not all groups will go through all of these stages and they may get 'stuck' at one stage and not move beyond it. This will depend upon how effective the group is and on the group's problem-solving capacity. You may not always be aware of the stages a group has gone through, because it depends when you joined that group. Unless you were there at the beginning it will have a history that preceded your membership.

Roles in groups

This relates to the different individuals in a group and the roles they play. As Shakespeare wrote in *As You Like It*:

> All the world's a stage,
> And all the men and women merely players.

We perform roles in a variety of situations: we do not just have work roles such as care workers, but we have social roles, professional roles, family roles, e.g. as daughter, mother, wife, or partner. In a group we will 'perform' a role in the way we have learned for a given situation, or in a way that is familiar to us, and according to our own given need or 'agenda'.

What role do you play within your class group?
    Are you active as a leader or are you a team player? This could determine what role you are comfortable with as a member of a group.

ACTIVITY

Barriers to communication

Communication with other people is not always straightforward. There are factors that can be called *barriers to communication*, because they get in the way of our effective communication with others. The barriers may be to do with ourselves, the other person, or the interaction between us.

When we communicate and transmit a message to another person there are things that get in the way as illustrated in Shannon and Weaver's model:

Figure 9.3   The transmission of a message (Shannon and Weaver 1949)

In the model in Figure 9.3 the communication is not just one way (from sender to receiver) but forwarded on. In the course of transmission 'the message' may become confused or distorted.

ACTIVITY

Think of some examples of barriers to interpersonal communication.
   What gets in the way of your being able to communicate with another person?

There are a range of factors that you may have thought of such as:

- Not always immediately liking those people with whom we have to work.
- Having prejudices.
- Difficulty in understanding others.
- Someone may have a speech impediment.
- Someone has a hearing problem.

In addition there may be some problem with the environment in which the communication takes place:

- It is noisy
- There is no privacy
- There are distractions.

In some of these examples specialist skills may be required. You might be required as a care worker to gain some additional training and learn other forms of communication, such as MAKATON or British Sign Language. You may need extra training to understand better the need of the service user, e.g. dementia care, knowledge of autism, deaf awareness.

   In all of these situations you may need to be aware that your service user's experience is different from that of your own, especially if you have not come across the situation before. The person may have a range of different needs. The person may have English as a second language or may not speak English at all. In each of these cases you may need to use your own initiative to get the help or training that you need. You should not be afraid to discuss your needs with someone at work, such as your supervisor, who will be pleased that you have identified this training need yourself.

Managing conflict situations

As you develop the work-related part of your Foundation Degree, you will increasingly come into contact with service users. It is likely that one of your main motivations for undertaking this particular course of study will be to help people or to work with a particular service user group. Working with others is not always 'plain sailing'. There may be times when the job is frustrating and when tensions creep into the work. Care work is in the top 10 of most stressful jobs, along with the police, the armed services, nursing and teaching. When people are stressed, they sometimes say and do things they wish they had not. Equally for the service users, their vulnerability means that they are also in stressful situations. The two factors combined can lead to potential conflict situations.

Being aware of the degree of stress you are under as either a student or a worker is important in monitoring your own stress levels. We all need a certain degree of stress in order to motivate ourselves in everyday situations. If we have too much stress we fall into 'eustress' or 'distress' – a level of stress, which, for us, is unhelpful. Everyone is different and not everyone experiences stress in the same way. When we are feeling like this and we are at work, we may be liable to 'fall out with' either the people we are working with, or maybe more likely the service users momentarily in an unhelpful way.

It is important therefore to be aware of the factors that can avert conflict and also how to manage conflict situations if they arise.

One way of looking at our behaviour is to consider our own individual conflict style. How do we approach situations? Are we aggressive, non-assertive or assertive? What do these words mean in relation to our behaviour?

How would you recognize a person who was being aggressive? They may be:

- Looking angry
- Shouting
- Tense
- Flushed in the face
- Glaring at somebody
- Clenching their fist
- Sarcastic
- Unkind towards somebody.

It is most likely that when someone is behaving aggressively they want to be in control of a situation and feel they have to 'win' at all costs, whether it is the argument or another outcome. If this happens it will leave the other person in a 'lose' situation. In other words, there will be a positive outcome for the aggressor but a negative outcome for the 'loser'. This is not the best outcome for either party.

What about someone who was being non-assertive? They may:

- Be very tentative as they approach new situations
- Speak quietly and apologetically

- Find it difficult to stand up for themselves
- Be unable to speak from their own point of view.

If a person behaves like this in a given situation, they will leave it feeling dissatisfied, confused and that no one has listened to them. They will certainly be unlikely to have gained what they wanted. A good example of the above would be getting served in a busy shop, complaining about a meal, being asked to change shift when it is not convenient. Many people, particularly women, find it hard to stand up for themselves and say 'no' when they think they might hurt people's feelings.

Assertiveness is the third 'conflict management' style. To assume this style is to be calm and confident in your approach, to be prepared to state your point of view, but prepared to negotiate. If you adopted this approach because you were not happy about your meal, you would be polite, ask for the waiter to give you a moment and then clearly state what you felt was wrong with your meal without apologizing for it. It would go something like this:

Excuse me. Could I have a word with you for a moment, please?

[Voice level] This soup is cold.

The response should be:

I'm very sorry; I'll replace it for you.

If you said:

[Apologetically] I'm afraid the soup is cold.

it sounds as if you do not feel that you have the right to complain when your food is not the correct temperature.

Equally if you said aggressively:

[Sarcastically] This soup is cold. Can't you get the temperature right?

it would not help the waiter to continue to give you good service, because it would make him nervous and annoyed.

> To summarize:
>   The best way to communicate in order to gain a satisfactory outcome for both parties and to avoid escalating a conflict is to:
>
> - Remain calm.
> - State your point of view.
> - Listen to the other person's point of view.
> - Maintain eye contact.

- Have an open body posture.
- Be prepared to negotiate

Use assertive behaviour to create a 'win–win' situation for both parties.

Here is an example in a care situation:

Elsie is an older service user in a residential home and has dementia. She becomes confused when dressing in the morning and requires assistance. The care worker is in a hurry because she has other residents to assist, and becomes impatient. The resident reacts by snatching away her skirt. The tension builds.

What should the care worker have done differently?

Be aware of the special requirements of Elsie as a woman with particular needs. That is:

- Allow her more time.
- Be patient.
- Promote her independence.
- Communicate with her supportively.
- Treat her with respect.

Elsie, like any older person, will be sensitive to the way her care is delivered and to the person who delivers it.

Summary

Working with individuals and groups with effective communication skills is essential when working in health and social care. You need to be able to overcome the barriers of communication with the people you will be working with to provide an effective service to people. Interpersonal communication skills are the essential tool that you must have when working with people who may require your help and support. By reflecting on your use of communication skills you can continue with your personal and professional development by learning how to use effectively the core skills of empathy, listening and attending using SOLER and adopting a person-centred way of working. These essential skills will not only benefit the people you will be providing services to, but also benefit your other personal and professional relationships.

Further reading

Hargie, O. and Dickson, D. (2004) *Social Skills in Interpersonal Communication: Research and Practice*, 4th edn. London: Routledge. This is a good book because it provides a detailed overview of interpersonal communication covering many of the essential areas. You will be able to use it to develop further your interpersonal communication skills.

Johnson, D. and Johnson, F. (1998) *Joining Together: Group Theory and Group Skills*. London: Prentice Hall. If you are interested in working with groups of people this is a key text for understanding communication in groups.

10

The Future of Health and Social Care Services

Graham Brotherton

As we reach the end of this second edition it is important to take stock of the current picture with regard to health and social care in general, but also to look at work-force issues and the implications that this might have as you reach the end of your course. As suggested earlier in the book, the current picture is complex with a process of rapid change meaning that the health and social care sector in 10 years' time is likely to be very different from the one of 10 years ago. In order to look at this, three major themes will be considered:

- The changing policy and practice context.
- The role of technology in shaping the future development of services.
- The changing health and social care workforce.

Inevitably a chapter on where things are going has to be a little speculative, though as highlighted in previous chapters there are a range of very clear 'clues' as to the future direction of services.

Using the three themes above, what seem to you to be the main 'issues'?

How has the way you work changed over the past few years in response to these issues?

How do you think it will change over the next few years?

(Continued)

ACTIVITY

(Continued)

What are the main implications for workers in health and social care services?
You might want to look at your answers again when you have finished reading the chapter and compare your thoughts with ours.

Policy and practice issues

Before returning in more detail to the changing policy and practice context, it is worth looking a little more broadly at the way in which society itself has changed and the implications that this might have for the future of welfare services. The start point for this has to be that we live in an ageing society and that older people are the main users of health and social care services. Life expectancy in the UK has risen significantly in the last half century and the birth rate has fallen. As a result the balance of the population has significantly altered, though it is worth pointing out that these changes are not happening as quickly or dramatically in the UK as in many other European countries. This has very significant implications, in that the welfare system has to a considerable extent worked on the assumption that the generation currently working will pay through taxes and National Insurance for the services required by the generation who have retired. As retirement has become longer and the number of people working as a proportion of the total population has fallen, this has led to a perceived crisis of funding. This is most obvious in terms of the current debate about the future of pensions, but it applies equally to health and care services. In addition we are now told that as a result of the banking crisis and its knock-on effects on social policy we are living in the 'age of austerity' with several more years of proposed cuts in overall public spending.

In effect, in recent years the way in which this has been addressed is through the increased targeting and means testing of services, which has a number of key policy consequences; firstly, the increasing number of older people who are reliant on means-tested benefits to 'top-up' the state pension, secondly the number of older people who have to sell their home in order to pay for the costs of residential care, thirdly the targeting of services on those in 'greatest need' means a reduction in services to some groups and hence a greater reliance on informal care. We are also about to see a major reform of the social security system with uncertain consequences for a range of health and social care users.

In addition, as referred to in Chapter 7, there has been an increased debate on the future of the NHS and health care funding more generally, with the call from a number of sources for the introduction of a social insurance model.

ACTIVITY

Would the introduction of 'up front' charging and social insurance be a good way forward? What are the principal arguments for and against?

Social insurance, which is widely used in mainland Europe, is a system in which there is a more explicit link between contributions and access to services. For example, in France, which has often been used as a 'model' for good health services in recent years, both employer and employee pay a contribution to an independent insurance scheme run by a board on which both employers and trade unions have significant representation. As an example, people seeing a doctor pay up front and then claim back a proportion of the cost (around 75 per cent). There is also a facility for people to make extra contributions and claim a higher level of benefits/services and around 90 per cent of the population do this. The majority of European countries have systems based on variants of this model and supporters suggest that it has two very significant advantages. Firstly it can enable greater direct contributions from service users or potential service users, perhaps creating a greater sense of ownership of services. Secondly it is sometimes argued that the use of 'up front' charges would encourage people to think more carefully about using services thus reducing inappropriate use of services (e.g. GP appointments).

The main complications or arguments against are around how you build in a 'safety net' for those who are unable to make contributions or whose contributions are insufficient to meet the costs of care, especially care in later life once someone has retired and is no longer making contributions. One solution used in Germany is to use the contributions of members of the wider family to meet the costs of the care of older people.

Globalization, neo-liberal politics and the repositioning of welfare

The idea that health and social care services take place in a social, political and ideological context was introduced in Chapters 4 and 7. As you reach the end of this book it is important to look at how this context is currently evolving. Central to this is a belief that the world we live in has changed fundamentally as a result of globalization. While globalization is a complex and multi-faceted set of issues, it can be summarized as greater interconnectedness between nation-states in a variety of ways:

- Economic – the rapid movement of jobs and financial resources.
- Social – increased movement of people through both migration and tourism.
- Technologically – through the use of communication technology, computers, mobile phones, etc.

Globalization also acknowledges that there is a changing balance between large global corporations and nation-states, in that some of the largest corporations now have a turnover gross domestic product (the amount of money produced by a country) which is greater than most of the countries in the world.

However, this debate around the impact of globalization has increasingly taken place within the context of the dominance of the neo-liberal world view, with its emphasis on the centrality of the free market, the limited state and individual responsibility; hence the emphasis in policy solutions on making individuals more responsible for themselves and on private sector involvement in public services.

How might each of these issues influence the development of health and social care services over the next few years?

Some examples might include:

- Economic – as welfare services are largely tax funded is it possible to maintain the 'flow' of resources as companies (and perhaps individuals) can move their financial resources rapidly around the globe?
- Social – this might include providing appropriate services in an increasingly multicultural society and issues about the recruitment and training of staff both from the diverse communities of the UK and from those who might have come from a variety of places to work in the British health and social care system. Some of the issues that arise from this are discussed more fully later in this chapter.
- Technology – using cameras to provide remote surveillance of vulnerable people; some nurseries already provide 'web-cams' so that parents can watch their children during the day. It has been suggested that this sort of technology could be used to support vulnerable older people. What do you think?

As a result of globalization and other factors it is argued that people's lives in the West have become less predictable. The certainty that characterized the lives of most people, especially in the period after the Second World War when people's lives were 'mapped out' by social context, has largely disappeared. For most men in the post-war era this meant working in the same occupation for most of their lives; for women it meant being primarily perceived as a wife and mother. For most people it also meant living in the same geographical area for all of their lives. While for individuals this was clearly very constraining in terms of the organization of welfare, it made planning of services easier in the sense that it was possible to make certain assumptions, especially about women's availability to provide informal care both for children and for older relatives. This was a central premise of the post-war Beveridge system.

The massive social changes of the past 40 years have had a profound influence on the assumptions made here. Changes in women's patterns of employment and changing family structures have combined with the decline of the large-scale manufacturing economy on which the Beveridge model was premised to create a world very different from the one the system was designed for. The idea of a 'job for life' for example now seems a very dated one with most people expecting to change not just jobs but also quite probably careers several times during their working lives.

However, these changes have not impacted upon everyone evenly. According to Giddens (2000), the 'risks' associated with these changes (e.g. the risk of long-term unemployment) have fallen disproportionately on particular groups of people who often feel that they have little ability to resist change. An example might be people living in a town dependent on a single large employer who find that their jobs have been moved to another part of the world leaving them with very limited employment prospects. This process can lead to people feeling passive and perceiving themselves to be unable to deal with the circumstances they find themselves in. This is taking place in the context of significant demographic changes as described in the last section. It means that there is in practice an increased demand for people of working age to be working. A central purpose of the welfare system needs therefore to contribute to maximizing the available supply of workers.

The welfare 'system' therefore needs to be able to create the circumstances in which people will be able to take some measure of control of their own lives through a combination of training and benefits designed either to 'encourage' or 'coerce' people into looking for work depending upon your viewpoint. This includes an emphasis on 'encouraging' people who have been historically excluded from work into work, such as many people with disabilities and a number of initiatives from New Labour's 'Welfare to Work' through to the Coalition's 'Get Britain Working' have sought to address this with somewhat variable results.

Moving to a social model for health and social care?

Another significant trend that links to the issues discussed in the previous section has been a move towards thinking about both disability and illness in different ways. As outlined in Chapter 4, there are tensions in the way in which both disease and disability are conceptualized by differing groups. A useful way of exploring this is through the social and medical models.

The medical model focuses on abnormalities or limitations within the person, which require expert diagnosis and either 'cure' or management by those with expert knowledge, in this context usually doctors. The focus is the 'disease' or 'condition' and on the specialist knowledge and services required to manage this. This often requires the use of specialized services, which may be segregated and require the 'approval' of a professional gatekeeper in order to gain access. The responsibility for adjustment lies with the individual, who is expected to adapt to 'fit in' with existing social structures.

The social model focuses on the way in which social situations or structures contribute to excluding those with either a disability or a limiting illness. In this model disability is a combination of individual impairment and social attitudes. An obvious example of this process is the way in which physical environments have often been designed to meet the needs of younger, physically fit people and can inhibit many others, be they older people, people with disabilities or parents attempting to push young children in buggies. Supporters of the social model highlight the fact that professional power has been a significant factor in defining the way in which disability is thought about or 'constructed', and argue that progress can only be made through the changing of attitudes and the creation of inclusive services open to all, for example, through a genuinely 'inclusive' education system.

A useful insight into this process is provided by the ideas of Michel Foucault, who argued (though it is important to acknowledge that this is oversimplifying the argument somewhat; see, for example, Turner 1995) that as religion had declined as a way of providing a moral framework for living during the Enlightenment, this role was picked up by science and the emerging medical profession. An example of this can be found in the notion of classification, which underpinned both the workhouse system and the subsequent emergence of the institutions. One of the major classifications was that of 'moral defective', a catch-all category that included women who became pregnant outside marriage and those who committed crimes such as theft. Many writers, especially from the disability movements, have highlighted the way in which the legacy of this approach continues both attitudes and services; again the debate around 'inclusive' versus 'specialist' education can be seen as an illustration of this.

Surveillance versus empowerment

A further dimension of this debate concerns one of the central tensions of health and social care practice. Care services are expected both to support those 'in need' and to regulate those who are perceived to have behaved in ways that are seen as 'wrong' or unacceptable. This balance plays out in different ways in different parts of the health and social care sector, so for example in child protection the emphasis is very much on the latter, in some (but by no means all) adult social care services the emphasis is on the former and in other areas, e.g. mental health services, both aspects are explicitly present. This places front-line workers in often difficult positions in that they can be simultaneously expected to act in both supportive and coercive ways. This can be seen as a continuation of the moral surveillance described by Foucault whereby practitioners can be seen as policing acceptability in terms of particular aspects of behaviour, e.g. attitudes to seeking work or parenting practice.

There is, though, a further dimension to the surveillance debate: some commentators have argued that one of the defining features of health and social care practice in general but perhaps of social care practice in particular has been 'deprofessionalization', which can be defined as a reduction of the amount of discretion given to practitioners to make professional judgements and the introduction of greater levels of scrutiny of day-to-day practice. This has its roots both in the various inquiries that have criticized the quality of social care practice, of which perhaps the most significant are the Laming Report into the death of Victoria Climbié (Department of

Health 2003) and the more recent Munro Review of Social Work (DfE 2011) with its rather different message about encouraging professional autonomy as a counterpoint to managerialist approaches that emphasize the achievement of externally defined targets.

For younger or newer practitioners it is perhaps worth pointing out that the idea of independent inspectorates is a relatively new one and not a model that is widely used internationally. In many other countries ideas about professional discretion and peer review of practice remain the dominant models, though it has to be acknowledged that the debate about how best to ensure good practice and professional accountability is an ongoing one in most welfare systems.

How far should practitioners be involved in the process of 'surveillance'? Are there occasions when this is important? What do you perceive as the dangers and how can workers and organizations set boundaries on their role?

In contrast to this, how far should we go in monitoring the actions of practitioners: do you think inspection promotes or hinders good practice?

ACTIVITY

One of the major problems that can be associated with the rise of inspection and accountability is the tendency to develop defensive models of practice. This means a model of working which involves 'playing safe' in terms of the way we work with people and an emphasis on formal record keeping as a basis for the justification of a particular approach or intervention. While there are clearly some important benefits to this model and we would all wish, for example, for our GP to practise safely when prescribing medication, there may be drawbacks in some situations. Much health and social care work has an explicitly developmental function, which involves the managed taking of risks. In the context of defensive practice it may be that we find ourselves taking an overly cautious approach because of concerns about accountability, which may not be in the service users' best interests. This is obviously a difficult area but one to which practitioners need to give considerable thought.

As outlined in the previous chapter, one of the key apparent drivers of health and social care policy at the moment has been an explicit commitment to the empowerment of service users; that is, the process of giving service users greater choice and control over the services they receive. This can be seen as a countervailing pressure to the issues of accountability described above. However, it is important to consider the mechanism of this process of empowerment and the implications that this might have. Empowerment is perceived as being largely achieved through the application of market mechanisms.

There is an ongoing tension here between the philosophical position being taken, which is very supportive of the values associated with good practice as outlined in Chapter 6, and the possibility of defensive practice as outlined earlier in this chapter. This is likely to remain a key issue for the foreseeable future.

Diversity, ethnicity, and health and social care

There is a long history of people coming to the UK to work in welfare services at all levels, from doctors and qualified nurses through to front-line care staff and those who support care. Initially migration was from the Caribbean, later from South Asia and most recently from the former 'Soviet bloc' countries of Eastern Europe. This has major implications for those recruiting health and social care workers, for training, for the workers themselves and those receiving care. In general terms and with the exception of doctors, the care workforce tends to be ethnically diverse at the level of front-line practitioners and support staff but increasingly less diverse as we move up through the professional and managerial 'ranks'. Ensuring that there are genuine equal opportunities for all workers is another ongoing challenge.

Historically there is also considerable evidence that health and social care services have not been aware of the needs of the whole community and that assumptions have been made on the basis of cultural stereotypes with regard to both care needs and the capacity to provide care. To give one example, assumptions are being made as part of the assessment process about the existence of the extended family that are willing and able to provide care within the Asian community, without this being checked out. Furthermore some groups face particular and ongoing difficulty in gaining any access to services, e.g. the traveller community or some sections of the homeless population.

The reasons for this are many but include direct racism, or other forms of discrimination, the application of stereotypes that influence assessment and what the Macpherson Report (the report into the Metropolitan Police's failed investigation of the killing of Stephen Lawrence) called 'institutional racism':

> ... the collective failure of an organization to provide an appropriate and professional service to people because of their colour, culture or ethnic origin. It can be seen or detected in processes, attitudes and behaviour which amount to discrimination through unwitting prejudice, ignorance, thoughtlessness and racist stereotyping which disadvantages ethnic minority people.

> [Racism] persists because of the failure of the organization openly and adequately to recognize and address its existence and cause by policy, example and leadership. Without recognition and action to eliminate, such racism can prevail as part of the ethos or culture of the organization. It is a corrosive disease. (Home Office 1999: 28, para. 6.34)

The concept of institutional racism has been applied to health and social care services in recent years, highlighting the impact both on service users in the ways outlined above and in terms of the career progression of workers from minority groups. It remains, though, a difficult and contentious area. Perhaps the most high-profile example in recent years was the case of David 'Rocky' Bennett, an Afro-Caribbean man who was an inpatient at a mental health unit in Norwich and who died after being restrained by staff. The inquiry concluded that institutional racism played a significant part in his death. It is still the case that African and Afro-Caribbean people, especially men, are significantly over-represented in the mental health system, as the 2006 'Count Me In' Census has identified:

> admission rates were lower than average among the White British, Indian and Chinese groups, and three or more times higher than average in Black and White/ Black Mixed groups. In the Other Black group, patients were overall 14 times more likely average to be admitted (amongst men this was almost 18 times – the same as in 2005) (National Institute for Mental Health 2006).

A number of commentators have identified institutional racism as a key factor in this (see for example Pilgrim and Rogers 2005).

Some writers have suggested that the way forward is to develop specialized services to meet the needs of particular communities or groups, while others have suggested that the only long-term solution is to ensure that 'mainstream' services are able to meet the needs of the whole community.

- What do you think are the advantages and disadvantages of each approach?
- What is the best way forward: is it one or other or both?

ACTIVITY

Brokerage and markets – choice and consumer culture

In Chapter 6 the possible introduction of a form of service brokerage was discussed. This represents a way of empowering within the context of a 'mixed economy' approach to the development and delivery of services. It highlights the role of service users as consumers of care services and makes assumptions about both people's willingness and capacity to 'choose' services. There are, though, some very considerable limitations of the model, which need to be considered. Hirschman (1970) suggests that there are two fundamental models of empowerment: 'exit' and 'voice'. Exit models work on the assumption that if users do not like a service they will 'exit' this service and use another one. Voice models highlight the limitations of this: that there may not be effective alternatives especially for those who need specialized support, for example. In this model it is not the ability to choose between services but the ability to influence the way in which existing services are delivered that is important. As we move more fully into the mixed economy in both health and social care it becomes increasingly important to think carefully about whether the market/ consumer model can provide adequate guarantees in terms of ensuring and protecting the best interests of service users. In this context Hirschman also identifies the significance of a third factor, 'loyalty', which is the tendency of people to accept rather passively whatever is familiar, which again may impact on the consumer model of empowerment. As an example of this we need to think very carefully about whether measured 'satisfaction' of service users through surveys etc. (see Chapter 3) is 'real' or influenced by the factors illustrated above and by the power differentials discussed earlier.

Technology for both workers and users

A further significant issue for the future is the changing role of technology. To give one perhaps controversial example, there are advertisements in the United States from companies that install Web cameras and closed-circuit television in the homes of older people so that family members can ensure the safety of 'loved ones'. Once again this raises issues of individual rights versus surveillance and control. While we might wish to accept scrutiny from family members, would it be acceptable if this scrutiny came from the control centre of a care organization?

Another range of issues stems from the increasing use of IT systems for the storage and transmission of information. Some of the issues are technical ones: to what extent can systems be relied upon to do what they are intended to do? There have been a number of examples in recent years of large-scale IT projects in both the NHS and the wider public sector which have had significant implementation problems. The range of activity for which IT-based systems are expected to be utilized is increasing rapidly, with a range of assessment, recording and control functions being undertaken not just using IT but in an online form. Examples include the Single Assessment Process for Adults, the Common Assessment Framework for Children and Families and the online Criminal Records Checking System. While there are clearly advantages in terms of facilitating multi-agency working etc. of online and integrated systems, they also raise a number of issues about:

- what information is to be shared and under what circumstances;
- who should have access and how;
- ensuring accuracy and consistency of recording, especially if the same framework is being used by people from different professional backgrounds.

There is therefore a clear need for a range of protocols, which are currently being developed by government. Nonetheless, for many with an interest in this area concerns remain about the difficult balance between civil liberties and the need for the effective monitoring of practice.

In the same way as technology is impacting on the lives of those who work in health and social care, a parallel set of issues is emerging for those who use these services. Technology can in some circumstances be liberating, e.g. through the use of more sophisticated equipment to support people with daily living, or it can be controlling by creating opportunities for increased surveillance and control.

As we reach the end of the book (and as you reach the end of your course) what is the health and social care workforce within which you will be developing your career going to look like? In this book we have already identified a number of key trends:

- The move to a mixed economy of welfare.
- The move to greater emphasis on multi/interprofessional working.
- An increased emphasis on accountability.
- The emergence of a new range of contexts and approaches for working.
- A greater emphasis on supporting service users' rights and choices.

Looking at this range of issues, what do you see as the main implications for you in terms of your own career development?

ACTIVITY

Concluding remarks

Crystal ball gazing is of course a slightly dangerous activity; however, there do seem to be a number of ways in which the factors outlined above might influence the future direction of services. In terms of the mixed economy this obviously creates a greater range of potential employers, though there is also some evidence that it has had a negative impact on salaries because of the pressures of competition. The move to greater multi/interprofessional models of working is a more complicated and difficult area to explore, though what is certain is that there will be a need for those working within health and social care to be aware of the changing context and to operate comfortably with a range of other professionals.

Linked to this is the issue of 'deprofessionalization', the way in which roles formerly carried out by 'professionals' such as nurses, social workers, etc., have increasingly been carried out by other workers, namely health care assistants, social work assistants, etc., leaving professionals to focus on more complex elements of their role. This has been accompanied as discussed previously by an increased element of monitoring of the work of all by external inspectorates. This creates a further set of uncertainties around the boundaries of roles which can be perceived depending upon your viewpoint, such as creating a new, more flexible and possibly creative workforce, or an attempt to devalue professional skills and knowledge. This is a particularly pertinent and positive issue in respect of Foundation Degrees as graduates may well find themselves at the 'cutting edge' with the sorts of skills the new roles are likely to demand, as this debate is played out in the future development of services. Recent developments such as the case of the substandard care being provided to adults with learning disabilities at Winterbourne View in Bristol and the inadequacies in training identified in the Serious Case Review highlight the need for a cohort of well-trained staff for supervisory and managerial roles.

Undeniably the most important set of issues concerns the areas of user empowerment and accountability. As explored previously, there has been a much greater
emphasis in recent government policy on the importance of user empowerment,
e.g. through the slow introduction of brokerage models or the greater choice being
offered to patients around hospital treatment. While it is possible to argue both that
progress has been slow and that the model of empowerment has considerable limitations, finding realistic ways of working in genuine partnership with service users is
going to be at the heart of the emerging health and social care role. As you develop
your career, responding in positive and creative ways to this challenge will be a central element of your effective professional development.

Glossary

This is a glossary of commonly used health and social care terms which relate to the content of this book.

Abuse – actions that lead to harm to others. This can include physical harm, emotional harm, financial harm or sexual harm. Abuse is usually taken to mean deliberate acts or failures to act; inadvertent harm resulting from a failure to act appropriately is usually referred to as neglect.

Accountability – being responsible for your own actions; this can include accountability to managers, stakeholders and professional bodies (e.g. through codes of conduct).

Acute care – the short-term medical care provided in hospitals (e.g. surgery).

Advocacy – ensuring that those who use care services have a voice. In this context this includes both self-advocacy, which is supporting people in speaking for themselves, and professional advocacy, which is 'speaking up' to ensure users' voices are heard.

Agency – a body providing health and care services; this can be a statutory body (e.g. NHS trust), a private company or a voluntary/charitable organization. Services can be provided by paid workers or volunteers.

Assessment – the process of identifying an individual's needs (usually taken to mean the formal process of identifying and recording these needs).

Autonomy – the ability of individuals to have their individual rights and choices respected.

Benefits – government-provided financial assistance to help in covering the costs of daily living. They can be 'means tested', i.e. based on an assessment of any other income, and/or eligibility related, i.e. dependent on being in a particular category, e.g. having a particular level of disability.

Care or case management – terms which broadly mean the process of both implementing and managing a care plan.

Care plan – a statement of how needs identified through the assessment process will be met, often involving the collaboration of more than one agency.

Carer – someone who provides substantial support to another person; can be unpaid as an informal carer, e.g. partner, child, friend, or paid as a formal carer.

Case study – a form of research which focuses on a specific individual, agency or event.

Charging – the process of paying for services (see **financial assessment**).

Choice – having the opportunity to select appropriate services, often linked to **consumerism** and the **New Right** critique of services.

Chronic illness – long-standing conditions, often associated with ageing, which cannot be 'cured'.

Commission for Social Care Inspection (CSCI) – the body with responsibility for the inspection of all adult social care services.

Common Assessment Framework – the assessment system used by all agencies working with children designed to support the implementation of 'Every Child Matters'.

Community – a group of people with clearly defined unifying characteristics, e.g. living in the same geographical area or a common culture or ethnicity.

Community care – care provided to enable someone to stay or live within the community.

Confidentiality – the principle that information about individuals is private and should not be inappropriately disclosed.

Consent – the giving of permission for something to happen, e.g. a particular treatment or sharing of information.

Consultation – the active seeking of information or opinion.

Consumerism – the belief that service users in health and social care services should be treated in the same way as customers of other goods and services.

Culture – a shared 'way of life' which might include language, customs, values and patterns of behaviour.

Data – systematically collected information. There are two broad forms: quantitative is the collation of 'factual', often numerical material; qualitative is concerned with perception or opinion.

Demography – the study of the changing characteristics of populations over time in relation to age structure, gender balance, etc.

Direct payments – the system whereby money is given to individuals to enable them to purchase their own care (or care for their children in the case of parents of children with a disability).

Disability – defined by the Disability Discrimination Act 1995 as 'a physical or mental impairment that has a substantial and long-term adverse effect on a person's ability to carry out normal day-to-day activities' (see **medical model** and **social model**).

Discrimination – treating someone less well on the basis of a particular characteristic, e.g. disability or gender.

Diversity – the recognition of the complexity of modern societies and in particular the need to be aware of the importance of culture, religion or language.

Domiciliary care – care within one's own home, also called home care.

Eligibility criteria – criteria defining who is entitled to access to services.

Empowerment – encouraging service users to take as much control as possible over their own lives.

Enabling – working with service users in ways which promote independence.

Ethics – codes giving a moral framework for practice.

Ethnicity – membership of a particular socio-cultural group. Everyone has an ethnicity, as part of either a majority or minority group.

Evaluation – the process of judging whether or not something has been effective.

Evidence-based practice – practice based on the use of research or other evidence.

Fair Access to Care Services – the current government framework of **eligibility criteria** for social care services.

Financial assessment – the process of means testing someone in order to assess their ability to pay for care services.

Formal carer (see **carer**).

General Social Care Council (GSCC) – the body which regulates the social care workforce.

Healthcare Commission – the body with responsibility for regulating health care in both the NHS and private and voluntary sectors.

Home care – an alternative term for **domiciliary care**.

Identity – sense of self; links to a range of other social and cultural factors.

Independence – the ability to control one's own lifestyle.

Independent sector – private and voluntary providers of health and social care services.

Informal carer (see **carer**).

Integrated services – services where workers from different agencies work collaboratively, a form of **multi-agency working**.

Joint working – services where workers from more than one agency work together, again a form of **multi-agency working**.

Key worker – an individual with responsibility for co-ordinating aspects of someone's care.

Learning disabilities/difficulties – an umbrella term for people who have difficulty with some aspect of learning or communication; it covers people with a very wide range of support needs.

Legislation – laws introduced by government which create the legal framework for practice.

Local authority – the elected local level of government which plays a lead role in social care and other related (e.g. education) services.

Medical model – the view that health and disability have a biological or physiological basis and are located within the individual. Intervention should be based on expert assessment and is likely to use intervention through medication or specialist (and sometimes segregated) services.

Mental health – the sense of inner well-being likened to feelings and emotions. In some circumstances difficulties with mental health can be severe requiring short- or longer-term support from a range of services.

Mixed economy – describes the fact that welfare services can or should be provided by a range of public, private and voluntary organisations and funded from a variety of sources such as taxation, charging, etc.

Multi-agency working – an umbrella term for a range of arrangements in which workers work with colleagues from other agencies in a variety of ways (see also integrated services, joint working).

Needs – what a person requires in order to maintain an acceptable quality of life.
Neglect (see **abuse**).

New Labour – the post-1997 Labour Party with its commitment to 'Third Way' politics.

New Right – political approach which emerged in the 1980s with a commitment to reducing the role of government and promoting the role of markets and market-like approaches in health and social care.

NHS – the government-run universal health care system.

Participation – the ability to influence the nature and type of services provided.

Performance indicator – criteria for monitoring the effectiveness of health and social care services.

Primary care – the 'front-line' care provided by GPs, dentists, etc.

Primary care trust – the part of the NHS responsible for local services.

Privacy – the right of service users to have individual private space or private conversations.

Private sector – individuals, organizations and companies that provide health and social care services on a 'for-profit' basis.

Protocol – formal rules or guidelines for practice in a particular area.

Provider – an individual or organization which provides services.

Purchaser – a body which buys health and social care services for either individuals or local populations.

Referral – the process of requesting action or intervention from another agency.

Risk – the possibility that an action or inaction will lead to harm.

Risk assessment – identifying the risks that apply in a particular situation and the likelihood of any of them actually occurring.

Secondary care – care provided in hospital or other referral-based services.

Service user – a person who receives support from health and social care services.

Social model – the view that health and disability are a result of the interplay between individuals and the environment (physical, social and psychological) and that services need to tackle factors such as poverty and social exclusion and public attitudes.

Social policy – the study of welfare-related issues and social and government responses to them.

Social services – social care and related services (e.g. care management and assessment, fostering and adoption) either provided directly or funded through the public sector.

Social Services Department – the local authority department with statutory responsibility for providing or commissioning social care services.

Stakeholder – someone with a direct interest in services, e.g. service users, carers, care staff.

Strategic health authority – the tier of the NHS responsible for strategic planning and co-ordination of services.

Tendering – the process of competitive bidding for contracts to provide services.

Third sector – an umbrella term for non-profit-making organizations, also called the voluntary sector.

User involvement – the process of involving service users in the planning or development of services.

Voluntary sector (see **third sector**).

Volunteer – someone who contributes to the work of organizations without being paid.

Vulnerability – the extent to which someone is 'at risk' (see **risk**).

Welfare services – an umbrella term for the range of services provided for the 'public good', namely health and social care, financial benefits and sometimes education.

Well-being – the sense of being generally healthy, incorporating physical, emotional and spiritual elements as well as adequate command of the resources for living.

Whistleblowing – the decision to disclose poor practice, negligence or illegal acts where these have been covered up by managers within an organization.

Bibliography

Abel-Smith, B. (1996) 'The escalation of health care costs: how did we get there?', in *Health Care Reform: The Will to Change*. Paris: OECD, pp. 17–30.

Adams, P. (2009) 'Ethics with character: virtues and the ethical social worker', *Journal of Sociology & Social Welfare*, 36 (3): 83–105.

Adams, R. (2003) *Social Work and Empowerment*, 3rd edn. Basingstoke: Palgrave Macmillan.

Adams, R. (2008) *Empowerment, Participation and Social Work*, 4th edn. Basingstoke: Palgrave Macmillan.

Adams, R., Dominelli, L. and Payne, M. (2005) 'Transformational social work', in R. Adams, L. Dominelli and M. Payne (eds), *Social Work Futures*. Basingstoke: Palgrave Macmillan.

Ainsworth, M.D.S., Bell, S.M. and Stayton, D.J. (1971) 'Individual differences in strange situation behaviour of one-year olds', in H.R. Schaffer (ed.), *The Origins of Human Social Relations*. London: Academic Press.

Allen, J. (2000) 'Power: its institutional guises (and disguises)', in G. Hughes and R. Fergusson (eds), *Ordering Lives: Family, Work and Welfare*. London: Routledge.

Allott, M. and Robb, M. (eds) (1998) *Understanding Health and Social Care: An Introductory Reader*. London: Sage.

Anning, A., Cottrell, D., Frost, N., Green, J. and Robinson, M. (2006) *Developing Multiprofessional Teamwork for Integrated Children's Services*. Maidenhead: Open University.

Arber, S. and Cooper, H. (2000) 'Gender inequalities in health across the life course', in E. Annandale and K. Hunt (eds), *Gender Inequalities in Health*. Buckingham: Open University.

Arber, S. and Thomas, H. (2001) 'From women's health to a gender analysis of health', in W. Cockerham (ed.), *The Blackwell Companion to Medical Sociology*. Oxford: Blackwell. pp. 94–113.

Aristotle (1929) 'Of happiness. Nicomachean ethics' (trans. Browne), in F.H. Pritchard (ed.), *Great Essays of All Nations*. London: George G. Harrap & Co.

Aspis, S. (1997) 'Self-advocacy for people with learning difficulties: does it have a future?', *Disability and Society*, 12: 647–54. (Also in Bytheway, B., Bacigalupo, V., Bornat, J., Johnson, J. and Spurr, S. (eds) (2002) *Understanding Care, Welfare and Community*. London: Open University/Routledge.)

Aspis, S. (1999) 'What they don't tell disabled people with learning difficulties', in M. Corker and S. French (eds), *Disability Discourse*. Buckingham: Open University.

Aujoulat, I., d'Hoore, W. and Deccache, A (2007) 'Patient empowerment in theory and practice: Polysemy or cacophony?', *Patient Education and Counseling*, 66 (1): 13–20.

Baggott, R. (2004) *Health and Health Care in Britain*, 3rd edn. Basingstoke: Palgrave Macmillan.

Bagihole, B. (1997) *Equal Opportunities and Social Policy*. London: Longman.

Bandura, A., Ross, D. and Ross, S.A. (1961) 'Transmission of aggression through observation of aggressive models', *Journal of Abnormal and Social Psychology*, 63: 575–82.

Banks, S. (2000) *Ethics and Values in Social Work*, 2nd edn. Basingstoke: Palgrave.

Banks, S. (2006) *Ethics and Values in Social Work*, 3rd edn. Basingstoke: Palgrave.

Banks, S. (2011) 'Ethics in an age of austerity: social work and the evolving new public management', *Journal of Social Intervention: Theory and Practice*, 20 (2): 5–23.

Banyard, P. (2012) 'Just following orders?', in N. Brace and J. Byford (ed.), *Investigating Psychology*. Milton Keynes/Oxford: Open University/Oxford University Press.

Barnes, M. (2011) 'Abandoning care? A critical perspective on personalization from an ethic of care', *Ethics and Social Welfare*, 5 (2): 153–67.

Bartley, M. (2003) *Health Inequality: An Introduction to Concepts, Theories and Methods*. Bristol: The Policy Press.

Beauchamp, T.L. and Childress, J. (2009) *Principles of Biomedical Ethics*, 6th edn. Oxford: Oxford University Press.

Becker, M.H. and Rosenstock, I.M. (1984) 'Compliance with medical advice', in A. Steptoe and A. Mathews (eds), *Health Care and Human Behaviour*. London: Academic Press.

Beckett, C. and Maynard, A. (2005) *Values and Ethics in Social Work: An Introduction*. London: Sage.

Bell, J. (2005) *Doing Your Research Project: A Guide for First-time Researchers in Education*, 4th edn. Buckingham: Open University.

Beresford, P. and Croft, S. (2003) 'Involving service users in management: citizenship, access and support', in J. Reynolds et al. (eds), *The Managing Care Reader*. London: Routledge/Open University.

Blaxter, M. (2004) *Health*. Cambridge: Polity Press.

Bogg, J., Sartain, S., Wain, M., Pontin, E. and Gibbons, C. (2005) *Allied Health Professionals: Equality and Diversity in the NHS*. Available at www.liv.ac.uk/breakingbarriers (accessed 23 March 2008).

Boud, D., Keogh, R. and Walker, D. (1985) 'Promoting reflection in learning', in R. Edwards, A. Hanson and P. Raggatt (eds) (1996) *Boundaries of Adult Learning*. London: Routledge/Open University.

Bourdieu, P. and Passeron, J-C. (1990) *Reproduction in Education, Society and Culture*. London: Sage.

Bowlby, J. (1969) *Attachment and Loss, Vol. 1*. New York: Basic Books.

Brace, N. and Byford, J. (2010) *Discovering Psychology*. Milton Keynes: Open University.

Bradby, H. (2009) *Medical Sociology: An Introduction*. London: Sage.

Brechin, A. (2000) 'Introducing critical practice', in A. Brechin, H. Brown and M. Eby (eds), *Critical Practice in Health and Social Care*. London: Sage/Open University.

Bronfenbrenner, U. (1979) 'Contexts of child rearing: problems and prospects', *American Psychologist*, 34: 844–50.

Brooker, L. (2002) *Starting School*. Buckingham: Open University.

Brown, G. and Harris, T. (1978) *The Social Origins of Depression*. London: Tavistock.

Brown, H. and Walmsley, J. (1997) 'When "Ordinary" isn't enough', in J. Bornat et al. (eds), *Community Care: A Reader*, 2nd edn. London: Sage/Open University.

Bryant, L. (2012) 'Shared decision-making: what's new, and why is it so important?', *Practice Nurse*, 42 (6): 38–43.

Burton, G. and Dimbleby, R. (1988) *Between Ourselves: An Introduction to Interpersonal Communication*. London: Edward Arnold.

Bury, M.R. (1982) 'Chronic illness as biographical disruption', *Sociology of Health and Illness*, 4: 167–82.

Busfield, J. (2006) 'Pills, power, people: sociological understandings of the pharmaceutical industry', *Sociology*, 40 (2): 297–314.

Carr, S. (2010) *Personalization: A Rough Guide*. London: Social Care Institute for Excellence.

Carr-Hill, R. (1987) 'The inequalities in health debate: a critical review of the issues', *Journal of Social Policy*, 16 (4): 509–42.

Carritt, E.F. (1930) *The Theory of Morals: An Introduction to Ethical Philosophy*. London: Oxford University Press.

Centre for Evidence Based Social Services (2004) www.ripfa.org.uk/archive (accessed September 2008).

Charmaz, K. (1999) 'Experiencing chronic illness', in G.L. Albrecht, R. Fitzpatrick and S.C. Scrimshaw (eds) (2003) *The Handbook of Social Studies in Health and Medicine*. Thousand Oaks, CA: Sage.

Cochrane, A.L. (1972) *Effectiveness and Efficiency: Random Reflections on Health Services*. Leeds: Nuffield Provincial Hospital Trust.

Cohn-Sherbok, D.C. (2003) *Judaism: History, Belief and Practice*. London: Routledge.

Conservative Party (2006) *Built to Last: The Aims and Values of the Conservative Party*. Available at www.conservatives.com/pdf/BuiltToLast-AimsandValues.pdf (accessed 5 September 2012).

Conze, E. (1959) *Buddhist Scriptures*. London: Penguin Classics.

Cooper, J. (2012) 'What the social care White Paper means for social workers', *Community Care*, 13 July.

Co-operative Bank (no date) *Ethics at The Co-operative Bank*. Available at www.co-operativebanking group.co.uk/servlet/Satellite?c=Page&cid=1169627027831&pagename=Corp/Page/tplCorp (accessed 3 July 2012).

Cottrell, S. (2003) *Skills for Success*. Basingstoke: Palgrave Macmillan.

Cottrell, S. (2011) *Critical Thinking Skills*, 2nd edn. Basingstoke: Palgrave Macmillan.

Coulter, A. and Collins, A. (2011) *Making Shared Decision-making a Reality: No Decision About Me, Without Me*. London: The King's Fund.

Cribb, A. and Entwistle, V.A. (2011) 'Shared decision making: trade-offs between narrower and broader conceptions', *Health Expectations*, 14: 210–19.

Criticos, C. (1993) 'Experiential learning and social transformation for a post-apartheid learning future', in D. Boud et al. (eds) *Using Experience for Learning*. Buckingham: SRHE and Open University.

CSCI (2006) *Support Brokerage: A Discussion Paper*. Available at www.csci.org.uk/about_us/publications/support_brokerage.asp.

Dahrendorf, R. (1959) *Class and Class Conflict in an Industrial Society*. London: Routledge and Kegan Paul.

Dahrendorf, R. (1968) 'On the origins of inequality among men', in A. Beteille (ed.) (1969), *Social Inequality*. Harmondsworth: Penguin.

Davies, M. (1981) *The Essential Social Worker: A Guide to Positive Practice*. London: Heinemann Educational Books.

Dawson, A. and Butler, I. (2003) 'The morally active manager', in J. Henderson and D. Atkinson (eds) (2004), *Managing Care in Context*. London: Open University/Routledge.

de Lange, N. (2000) *An Introduction to Judaism*. Cambridge: Cambridge University Press.

Denscombe, M. (2007) *The Good Research Guide*. Maidenhead: Open University.

Department for Education and Skills (2001) *Special Educational Needs Codes of Practice*. London: TSO.

Department for Education and Skills (2005) *The Common Core*. London: DfES.

Department for Education (2011) *The Munro Review of Child Protection: Final Report: A Child-Centred System*. Available at www.education.gov.uk/publications/standard/publicationDetail/Page1/CM%208062 (accessed 11 October 2012).

Department of Health (2000) *No Secrets: Guidance on Developing and Implementing Multi-agency Policies and Procedures to Protect Vulnerable Adults from Abuse*. London: HMSO.

Department of Health (2001) *Valuing People: A New Strategy for Learning Disability for the 21st Century*. London: TSO.

Department of Health (2003) *The Victoria Climbié Inquiry: A Report by Lord Laming*. London: HMSO.

Department of Health (2010) *A Vision for Adult Social Care: Capable Communities and Active Citizens*. Available at http://webarchive.nationalarchives.gov.uk/+/www.dh.gov.uk/en/Publicationsandstatistics/Publications/PublicationsPolicyAndGuidance/DH_121508 (accessed 11 October 2012).

Department of Health (2011) *Transparency in Outcomes: A Framework for Quality in Adult Social Care*. Available at www.dh.gov.uk/enPublicationsandstatistics/Publications/PublicationsPolicyAndGuidance/DH_133334.

Department of Health (2012a) *Adult Social Care Outcomes Framework*. London: TSO.

Department of Health (2012b) *Caring for Our Future: Reforming Care and Support*. London: TSO.

Dewey, J. (2007) *Experience and Education*. New York: Simon and Schuster.

Dickens, C. (1896) *Dombey and Son*. London: Chapman and Hall.

Doyall, L. (2005) *Integrating Gender Considerations into Health Policy Development*. Available at www.bris.ac.uk/sps/downloads/homepage/doyal (accessed 23 March 2008).

Dreyfus H.L. and Dreyfus S.E. (1986) *Mind over Machine, the Power of Human Intuition and Expertise in the Era of the Computer*. Oxford: Basil Blackwell.

Eby, M. (1994) 'Competing values', in V. Tschudin (ed.), *Ethics: Conflicts of Interest*. London: Scutari Press.

Eby, M. (2000a) 'Understanding professional development', in A. Brechin, H. Brown and M. Eby (eds), *Critical Practice in Health and Social Care*. London: Sage/Open University.

Eby, M. (2000b) 'The challenge of values and ethics in practice', in A. Brechin, H. Brown and M. Eby (eds), *Critical Practice in Health and Social Care*. London: Sage/Open University.

Eby, M. and Gallagher, A. (2008) 'Values and ethics in practice', in S. Fraser and S. Mathews (eds) *The Critical Practitioner in Social Work and Health Care*. London: Sage.

Eraut, M. (1994) *Developing Professional Knowledge and Competence*. London: Routledge Falmer.

Erikson, E.H. (1963) *Childhood and Society*, 2nd edn. New York: Norton Penguin Books, Hogarth Press.

Esposito, J.L. (1988) *Islam: The Straight Path*. Oxford: Oxford University Press.

Fealy, G.M. (2004) '"The good nurse": visions and values in images of the nurse', *Journal of Advanced Nursing*, 46 (6): 649–56.

Flood G., F., (2009) *The BBC Religion and Ethics: Hindu Concepts*. Available at www.bbc.co.uk/religion/religions/hinduism/concepts/concepts_1.shtml#h4 (accessed 2 February 2013).

Follet, M.P. (1924) *Creative Experience*. New York: Longmans, Green and Co. Digitized by the Internet Archive (2011) http://archive.org/details/creativeexperien00foll (accessed 8 October 2012).

Ford, D.F. (1999) *Theology: A Very Short Introduction*. Oxford: Oxford University Press.

Foucault, M. (1972) *The Archaeology of Knowledge*. London: Routledge.

Frost, N. (2005) *Professionalism, Partnership and Joined-up Thinking: A Research Review of Frontline Working with Children and Families*. Available at www.rip.org.uk (accessed 1 November 2007).

Gallie, D., White, M., Cheng, Y. and Tomlinson, M. (2001) 'The restructuring of work since the 1980s', in N. Abercrombie and A. Warde (eds), *The Contemporary British Society Reader*. Cambridge: Polity Press.

Giddens, A. (1991) *Modernity and Self-identity: Self and Society in the Late Modern Age*. Cambridge: Polity Press.

Giddens, A. (2000) *The Third Way and Its Critics*. London: Polity Press.

Gillis, J. (1981) *Youth and History*. London: Academic Press.

Gimlin, D. (2002) *Body Work: Beauty and Self-image in American Culture*. Berkeley, CA: University of California Press.

Goffman, E. (1963) *Stigma: Notes on the Management of Spoiled Identity*. New York: Prentice Hall.

Goffman, E. (1969) *The Presentation of Self in Everyday Life*. London: Penguin Press.

Gomersall, M. (2004) 'The humanities in education', in S. Ward (ed.) *Education Studies: A Student's Guide*. London: Routledge.

Gomm, R. (1993) 'Issues of power in health and welfare', in J. Walmsley, J. Reynolds, P. Shakespeare and R. Woolfe (eds), *Health, Welfare and Practice: Reflecting on Roles and Relationships*. London: Sage.

Gomm, R. and Davies, C. (eds) (2000) *Using Evidence in Health and Social Care*. London: Sage.

Goodley, D. (2004) 'Who is disabled? Exploring the scope of the social model of disability', in J. Swain et al. (eds), *Disabling Barriers – Enabling Environments*, 2nd edn. London: Sage/Open University.

Goodley, D. and Ramcharan, P. (2005) 'Advocacy, campaigning and people with learning difficulties', in G. Grant et al. (eds), *Learning Disability: A Life Cycle Approach to Valuing People*. Maidenhead: Open University/McGraw–Hill Education.

Green Party (2001) Policies for a Sustainable Society. Statement of Core Values. http://policy.greenparty.org.uk/core-values (accessed 28 June 2012).

Griffin, C. (1993) *Representations of Youth*. Cambridge: Polity Press.

Hall, E.T. (1966) *The Hidden Dimension*. New York: Garden City.

Hartley, P. (1993) *Interpersonal Communication*. London: Routledge.

Hill, M. (2005) *The Public Policy Process*. Harlow: Pearson.

Hirschman, A. (1970) *Exit, Voice, and Loyalty: Responses to Decline in Firms, Organizations, and States*. Boston, MA: Harvard University Press.

HM Treasury (2006) *Budget Details 2006–2008*. London: HMSO.

HM Treasury (2012) *Autumn Statement*. Available at www.hm-treasury.gov.uk/as 2012_documents.htm (accessed 21 January 2013).

Hochschild, A.R. (1983) *The Managed Heart: Commercialization of Human Feeling*. Berkeley, CA: University of California Press.

Holland, S. (2010) 'Scepticism about the virtue ethics approach to nursing ethics', *Nursing Philosophy*, 11, 151–58.

Home Office (1999) *The Stephen Lawrence Inquiry: Report of an Inquiry by Sir William Macpherson of Cluny*. London: The Stationery Office.

Hudson, B. (2002) 'Interprofessionality in health and social care: the Achilles heel of partnership', *Journal of Interprofessional Care*, 16 (1): 7–17.

Hugman, R. (2003) 'Professional values and ethics in social work: reconsidering postmodernism', *British Journal of Social Work*, 33: 1025–41.

Hurd, G. (ed.) (1974) *Human Societies*. London: Routledge.

Husband, C. (1995) 'The morally active practitioner and the ethics of anti-racist social work', in R. Hugman and D. Smith (eds), *Ethical Issues in Social Work*. London: Routledge.

Illich, I. (1976) *Limits to Medicine*. London: Marion Boyars.

Information Centre (2005) *NHS Hospital and Community Health Services: Non Medical Staff in England 1995–2005*. Available at www.ic.nhs.uk/webfiles/publications/nhsstaff/NHSStaffNonMedResults240406 (accessed 23 March 2008).

Inge, W.R. (1940) *The Fall of the Idols*. London: Putman & Co.

Inskipp F. (1996) *Skills Training for Counselling*. London: Sage.

Johnson, D. and Johnson, F. (1998) *Joining Together: Group Theory and Group Skills*. London: Prentice Hall.

Jones-Devitt, S. and Smith, L. (2007) *Critical Thinking in Health and Social Care*. London: Sage.

Kelly G.A. (1963) *A Theory of Personality*. New York: Norton.

Keown, D. (1996) *Buddhism: A Very Short Introduction*. Oxford: Oxford University Press.

Kings Fund (2010) *Securing Good Care for More People: Options for Reform*. London: Kings Fund.

Knott, K. (1998) *Hindusism: A Very Short Introduction*. Oxford: Oxford University Press.

Kobasa, S.C. (1979) 'Stressful life events, personality and health: an inquiry into hardiness', *Journal of Personality and Social Psychology*, 65: 207.

Kobus, K. (2003) 'Peers and adolescent smoking', *Addiction*, 98: 37–55.

Kübler-Ross, E. (1969) *On Death and Dying*. London: Tavistock.

Labour Party (no date a) *A New Generation*. Available at www.labour.org.uk/a-new-generation (accessed 22 June 2012).

Labour Party (no date b) *What is the Labour Party?* Available at www.labour.org.uk/what_is_the_labour_party (accessed 22 June 2012).

Lave, J. and Wenger, E. (1991) *Situated Learning – Legitimate Peripheral Participation*. Cambridge: Cambridge University Press.

Lawrence, T.E. (1940) *Seven Pillars of Wisdom*. London: Jonathan Cape.

Lawton, A. (2009) *Personalization and Learning Disabilities: A Review of Evidence on Advocacy and its Practice for People with Learning Disabilities and High Support Needs*. Adult Services Report 24. London: Social Care Institute for Excellence.

Lazarus, R.S. and Folkman, S. (1984) *Stress: Appraisal and Coping*. New York: Springer.

Leece, J. and Leece, D. (2011) 'Personalization: perceptions of the role of social work in a world of brokers and budgets', *British Journal of Social Work*, 41 (2): 204–23.

Lennon, J. and McCartney, P. (1967) 'All You Need is Love'. Northern Songs.

Lewis, S., Saulnier, M. and Renaud, M. (2000) 'Reconfiguring health policy: simple truths, complex solutions', in G.L. Albrecht, R. Fitzpatrick and S.C. Scrimshaw (eds), *The Handbook of Social Studies in Health and Medicine*. London: Sage.

Liberal Democrats (no date) *Our Constitution*. Available at www.libdems.org.uk/constitution.aspx (accessed 28 June 2012).

Lipsky, M. (1980) *Street-level Bureaucracy: Dilemmas of the Individual in Public Services*. New York: Russell Sage Foundation.

Lloyd, L. (2010) 'The individual in social care: the ethics of care and the personalisation agenda in services for older people in England', *Ethics and Social Welfare*, 4 (2): 188–200.

Low Pay Commission (2011) *The National Minimum Wage Report 2011 Cm8023*. Available at www.lowpay.gov.uk/lowpay/report/pdf/Revised_Report_PDF_with_April_date.pdf (accessed 10 October 2012).

Luke, S. (2005) *Power: A Radical View*, 2nd edn. Basingstoke: Palgrave Macmillan.

Magnani, L.E. (1990) 'Hardiness, self-perceived health, and activity among independently functioning older adults', *Scholarly Enquiry for Nursing Practice*, 4 (3): 171–84.

Marks and Spencer (2012) *How We Do Business Report, 2012*. Available at http://corporate.marksandspencer.com/howwedobusiness/hwdb_reports (accessed 5 September 2012).

Marmot Review (2010) *Fair Society Healthy Lives*. Available at www.instituteofhealthequity. org/projects/fair-society-healthy-lives-the-marmot-review (accessed 5 September 2012).

Martin, V. and Henderson, E. (2001) *Managing in Health and Social Care*. London: Open University/Routledge.

Maslow, A. (1970) *Motivation and Personality*. New York: Harper and Row.

McBeath, G. and Webb, S.A. (2002) 'Virtue ethics and social work: being lucky, realistic, and not doing one's duty', *British Journal of Social Work*, 32: 1015–36.

McKeown, T. (1976) *The Modern Rise of Population*. London: Edward Arnold.

Mears, R. (1992) 'Debating health inequalities', in M. O'Donnell (ed.), *Introductory Readings in Sociology*. Walton-on-Thames: Nelson.

Monsoon (no date) *Heritage and Ethics*. Available at http://uk.monsoon.co.uk/view/category/ uk_catalog/mon_7,mon_7.5 (accessed 28 June 2012).

Moon, J. (2006) *Learning Journals: A Handbook for Reflective Practice and Professional Development*. Abingdon: Routledge.

Mouzelis, N. (2007) 'Habitus and reflexivity: restructuring Bourdieu's theory of practice', *Sociological Research Online* 12 (6). Available at www.socresonline.org.uk/12/6/9.html (accessed 6 July 2008).

National Institute for Mental Health (2006) *Count Me In: Results of the 2006 National Census of Inpatients in Mental Health and Learning Disability Services in England and Wales*. Available at http://psychminded.co.uk/news2007/march07/Count_Me_In.pdf

Needham, C. (2011) 'Personalization: From storyline to practice', *Social Policy and Administration*, 45 (1): 54–68.

Nelson-Jones, R. (1997) *Practical Counselling and Helping Skills*, 4th edn. London: Continuum.

Nettleton, S. (2006) *The Sociology of Health and Illness*, 2nd edn. Cambridge: Polity Press.

NHS Information Centre (2010) *Survey of Carers in Households – 2009/10 England. Main Report*. Available at www.ic.nhs.uk/pubs/carersurvey0910 (accessed 21 January 2013).

Neusner, J. (2002) *Judaism: An Introduction*. London: Penguin.

O'Donnell, M. (1987) *A New Introduction to Sociology*. Walton-on-Thames: Nelson.

Office for National Statistics (2012) *Religion in England and Wales 2011*. UK: ONS.

Oliver, M. (1981) 'The individual model of disability', in V. Finkelstein (ed.) (1983) *Rehabilitation: Supplementary Readings. P556 Rehabilitation: A Collaborative Approach to Work with Disabled People*. Milton Keynes: Open University.

Open University (1996) *Speaking Out for Equal Rights*. Workbook 2, *K503 Working as Equal People*. Milton Keynes: Open University.

Open University (2006a) *A 217: Christianity Study Guide*. Milton Keynes: Open University.

Open University (2006b) *A 217: Sikhism Study Guide*. Milton Keynes: Open University.

Open University (2009) *A181 Ethics in Real Life*. Milton Keynes. The Open University.

Open University (2010) *K217 Adult Health, Social Care and Wellbeing*. Milton Keynes: Open University.

Open University (2012) *A 217: Islam Study Guide*, 2nd edn. Milton Keynes: Open University.

Orford, J. (2008) *Community Psychology: Challenges, Controversies and Emerging Consensus*. Chichester: John Wiley & Sons.

Pahl, J. (1990) 'Household spending, personal spending and the control of money in marriage', *Sociology*, 24 (1): 119–38.

Parrott, L. (2010) *Values and Ethics in Social Work Practice: Transforming Social Work Practice*, 2nd edn. Exeter: Learning Matters.

Payne, M. (1997) *Modern Social Work Theory*, 2nd edn. Basingstoke: Macmillan.

Payne, S. (2006) *The Health of Men and Women*. Cambridge: Polity Press.

Pearce, S. and Reynolds, J. (2003) 'Managing environments', in J. Henderson and D. Atkinson (eds), *Managing Care in Context*. London: Routledge/Open University.

Pearson, M. and Smith, D. (1985) 'Debriefing in experience based learning', in D. Boud, R. Keogh and D. Walker (eds) *Reflection: Turning Experience into Learning*. London: Kogan Page.

Petrie, P., Boddy, J., Cameron, C., Wigfall, V. and Simon, A. (2006) *Working with Children in Care*. Maidenhead: Open University.

Pietroni, P. (1994) 'Inter-professional teamwork: its history and development in hospitals, general practice and community care (UK)', in A. Leathard (ed.), *Going Inter-professional: Working Together for Health and Welfare*. London: Routledge.

Pilgrim, D. and Rogers, A. (2005) *A Sociology of Mental Health and Illness*. Maidenhead: Open University.

Piper, S. (2010) 'Patient empowerment: emancipatory or technological practice?', *Patient Education and Counseling*, 79 (2): 173–7.

Plato (1935) *Republic* (trans. and ed. A.D. Lindsay). London: J.M. Dent and Son.

Price, B. and Harrington, A. (2010) *Critical Thinking and Writing for Nursing Students: Transforming Nursing Practice*. Exeter: Learning Matters.

Putnam, D. (2012) 'A reply to "Scepticism about the virtue ethics approach to nursing ethics" by Stephen Holland: the relevance of virtue in nursing ethics', *Nursing Philosophy*, 13 (2): 142–5.

Putnam, R. (2000) *Bowling Alone: The Collapse and Revival of American community*. New York: Simon and Schuster.

QAA (2008) *The Framework for Higher Education Qualifications in England, Wales and Northern Ireland*. Available at www.qaa.ac.uk (accessed October 2009).

QAA (2010) *Foundation Degree Qualification Benchmark*. The Quality Assurance Agency for Higher Education.

Quinn, F.M. (1988) 'Reflection and reflective practice', in C. Davies, L. Finlay and A. Bullman (eds), *Changing Practice in Health and Social Care*, London: Sage/Open University.

Rabbani, F. (2009) *The BBC Religion and Ethics: The Philosophy of Sharia*. Available at www.bbc.co.uk/religion/religions/islam/beliefs/sharia_1.shtml (accessed 1 February 2013).

Raphael, D.D. (1994) *Moral Philosophy*, 2nd edn. Oxford: Oxford University Press.

Rappaport, J. (1981) 'In praise of paradox: a social policy of empowerment over prevention', *American Journal of Community Psychology*, 9: 1.

Rawls, J. (1972) *A Theory of Justice*. Oxford: Oxford University Press.

Riger, S. (1993) 'What's wrong with empowerment?', *American Journal of Community Psychology*, 21: 3.

Robson, C. (2011) *Real World Research*, 3rd edn. Oxford: Blackwell.

Rodd, J. (2006) *Leadership in Early Childhood*. Milton Keynes: Open University.

Rogers, C.R. (1951) *Client Centred Therapy*. London: Constable.

Rummery, K. (2011) 'A comparative analysis of personalization: balancing an ethic of care with user empowerment', *Ethics and Social Welfare*, 5 (2): 138–52.

Russell, G. (2000) *Essential Psychology for Nurses and Other Health Professionals*. London: Routledge.

Rutter, M. (1972) *Maternal Deprivation Reassessed*. Harmondsworth: Penguin Education.

Scambler, G. (2003) *Sociology as Applied to Medicine*. Oxford: Elsevier.

Schön, D.A. (1983) *The Reflective Practitioner: How Professionals Think in Action*. London: Basic Books.

SCIE (2009) *At a Glance: 12 Personalisation Briefing Implications for Advocacy Workers* London: Social Care Institute for Excellence.

Scott, R.A. (1969) *The Making of Blind Men*. New York: Sage Foundation.

Scott, R.A. (1970) 'The construction of conceptions of stigma by professional experts', in D. Boswell and J. Wingrove (eds) (1974) *The Handicapped Person in the Community*. London: Tavistock/Open University.

Seedhouse, D. (2009) *Ethics: The Heart of Healthcare*, 3rd edn. Chichester: John Wiley and Sons.

SEHB (South Eastern Health Board) (2003) *Clinical Nurse/Midwife Specialist Role Resource Pack*. SEHB. Available at www.sehb.ie/search/publications/cns_cms_resource_pack/cns_cms_resource.pdf (accessed 19 February 2008).

Seligman, P. (1975) *Helplessness: On Depression, Development and Death*. San Francisco: Freeman.

Shah, A., Pell, A. and Brooke, P. (2004) 'Beyond first destinations graduate employability survey', *Active Learning in Higher Education*, 5(1): 9–26.

Shakespeare, T. and Watson, N. (2001) 'The social model of disability: an outdated ideology', in S.N. Barnartt and B.M. Altman (eds) *Exploring Theories and Expanding Methodologies: Where We Are and Where We Need to Go* (Research in Social Science and Disability, Volume 2) Emerald, pp. 9–28.

Shannon, C.E. and Weaver, W. (1949) *The Mathematical Theory of Communication*. Urbana, IL: University of Illinois Press.

Shardlow, S. (2002) 'Values, ethics and social work', in R. Adams, L. Dominelli and M. Payne (eds), *Social Work Theories, Issues and Critical Debates*, 2nd edn. Basingstoke: Palgrave/ Open University.

Smith, M.K. (1996/2001) 'Action research', *The Encyclopedia of Informal Education*, www. infed.org/research/b-actres.htm (accessed January 2005).

Smith, M.K. (2003) 'Communities of practice', *The Encyclopedia of Informal Education*, www.infed.org/biblio/communities_of_practice.htm (accessed on 6 July 2008).

Stewart, W. (1992) *An A–Z of Counselling Theory and Practice*. London: Chapman and Hall.

Stroobants, J., Chambers, P. and Clarke, B. (2008) *Reflective Journeys*. Rome: Leonardo da Vinci Reflect Project.

Stutchbury, K. and Fox, A. (2009) 'Ethics in educational research: introducing a methodological tool for effective ethical analysis', *Cambridge Journal of Education*, 39 (4): 489–504.

Swain, J., Finkelstein, V., French, S. and Oliver, M. (eds) (1993) *Disabling Barriers – Enabling Environments*. London: Sage/Open University.

Swain, J., French, S., Barnes, C. and Thomas, C. (2004) *Disabling Barriers – Enabling Environments*, 2nd edn. London: Sage/Open University.

Swain, J., Gillman, M. and French, S. (1998) *Confronting Disabling Barriers: Towards Making Organizations Accessible*. Birmingham: Venture Press.

Tajfel, H. and Fraser, C. (eds) (1978) *Introducing Social Psychology*. Harmondsworth: Penguin.

Terrisse, B. (2000) 'The resilient child: theoretical perspectives and a review of the literature', in R. Croker (ed.), *PCERA 2000 Children and Youth at Risk: The Symposium Report*. Ottawa: Canadian Education Statistics Council.

Thomas, C. (1993) 'Deconstructing concepts of care', *Sociology*, 27 (4): 649–69.

Thompson, N. (2003) *Promoting Equality: Challenging Discrimination and Oppression in the Human Services*, 2nd edn. London: Macmillan.

Thompson, N. (2006) *Anti-Discriminatory Practice*, 4th edn. Basingstoke: Palgrave.

Tripp, D. (1993) *Critical Incidents in Teaching: Developing Professional Judgement*. London: Routledge.

Tritter, J.Q. and McCallum, A. (2006) 'The snakes and ladders of user participation: moving beyond Arnstein', *Health Policy*, 76: 156–68.

Tronto, J.C. (2010) 'Creating caring institutions: politics, plurality, and purpose', *Ethics and Social Welfare*, 4 (2): 158–71.

Tucker, S. (2004) 'Youth working: professional identities given, received or contested?', in J. Roche, S. Tucker, R. Thomson and R. Flynn (eds), *Youth in Society*, 2nd edn. London: Sage.

Turner, B. (1995) *Medical Power and Social Knowledge*. London: Sage.

University of Cambridge (2006) What are transferable skills? Available at www.caret.cam.ac.uk/transkills:what_are_ts.htm (accessed 28 December 2007).

Yuill, C., Crison, I. and Duncan, E. (2010) *Key Concepts in Health Studies*. London: Sage.

Weber, S. and Mitchell, C. (1995) *'That's Funny, You Don't Look Like a Teacher.'* London: The Falmer Press.

Wenger, E. (1998) *Communities of Practice – Learning, Meaning and Identity*. Cambridge: Cambridge University Press.

Wolfensberger, W. (1998) *A Brief Introduction to Social Role Valorization: A High-order Concept for Addressing the Plight of Societally Devalued People, and for Structuring Human Services*, 3rd edn. Syracuse, NY: Training Institute for Human Service Planning, Leadership & Change Agentry.

Wolfensberger, W. and Tullman, S. (1982) 'The principle of normalization', in B. Bytheway, V. Bacigalupo, J. Bornat, J. Johnson and S. Spurr (eds) (2002) *Understanding Care, Welfare and Community*. London: Open University/Routledge.

Yerkes, R. M. and Dodson, J. D. (1908) 'The relation of strength of stimulus to rapidity of habit-formation', *Journal of Comparative Neurology and Psychology*, 18: 459–82.

Zimmerman, M. (2000) 'Empowerment theory: psychological, organizational and community levels of analysis', in J. Rappaport and E. Seidman (eds), *Handbook of Community Psychology*. New York: Kluwer Academic/Plenum Publishers.

Index

NOTE: Page numbers in *italic type* refer to figures, page numbers in **bold type** refer to glossary entries.

choice, 196, 263, **268**
Christianity, 140–1
chronic illness, 107–9, **268**
  see also disability
citizen advocacy, *176*
citizenship, 182–3
clarification, 244
classical conditioning, 206–7
classification, 260
Clinical Commissioning Groups, 197
closed questions, 243–4
codes of conduct, 89, 128, 165–7
codification, 128
cognition, 203, 221
Collins, A., 179
Commission for Social Care Inspection
  (CSCI), **268**
Common Assessment Framework, **268**
Common Core, 43, 122
communication *see* interpersonal communication
communities of practice, 128–30
community, 145, 155, 173, **268**
community care, 155, 198, **268**
comparative research, 88
competences, 41–2
  see also skills
conclusions, 30, 245–6
confidentiality, 49, 89, **268**
conflict management, 251–3
consent, 88, **268**
consequentialism, 147
consultation, 178, 189, **268**
consumerism, 184, 263–4, **268**
content of essays, 29–32
contents pages, 34
Coulter, A., 179
Cribb, A., 179
critical awareness, 4
critical incident analysis, 60
critical reading, 21, 78, 81–2
cultural awareness, 186
cultural explanations of inequality, 103
cultural stereotypes, 111, 262
culture, **268**
curiosity, 47

Dahrendorf, R., 159
data, **268**
data gathering, 82–3, 85–8
databases, 78–9
debriefing, 89
defensive practice, 261
delegated control, 178–9
demography, 98, 256, **269**

denial, 212
deontological approaches, 147–8
dependency ratio, 98
deprofessionalization, 260, 265
detailed reading, 18
development, 204–5, 210–11, 212, 214–22
developmental cognitive theory, 210–11
devolution, 189
diagrammatical notes, 23, *24*
direct payments, 198, **269**
disability, 70, 110–11, 180–2,
  259–60, **269**
  see also chronic illness
discourse, 119, 120, 167–8, 169
discretion, 126, 260–1
  see also autonomy
discrimination, 70, 110, 173, 180–1,
  262–3, **269**
distributive justice, 157–8
diversity, 262, **269**
doctor–patient relationship, 108, 112, 125
documentary analysis, 88
domiciliary care *see* home care
dominant ideology, 181
Dreyfus model of skills acquisition, 41–3

ecological theory, 213–14
educational technology, 15–16, 76
ego, 211–12
eligibility criteria, 158, **269**
email updates, 75–6
emotion work, 106–7
emotion/feelings, 56, 57–8, 61, 202
empathy, 234
employability skills, 46–7, 53
employment, 258–9, 262
  and gender, 105, 107, 121
  workplaces, 50–1, 74–6
  see also work-based learning
empowerment, 167–9, 261,
  266, **269**
  advocacy, 175–8
  normalization, 173–4
  participation, 178–80
  personalization, 182–5
  and power, 169–73, 185
  and reflective practice, 69–71
  shared decision making, 179–80
  social model of disability, 180–2
  social role valorization, 174
enabling, 167, 175, 177, 182, **269**
Entwistle, V.A., 179
environmental influences, 205, 213–14
  see also behaviourist approaches